Community Work Skills M

Edited by Val Harris

ACKNOWLEDGEMENTS

This work was commissioned by the Community Work Training Resource Library and has been made possible by funding from the National Lotteries Charities Board.

This manual has been published by:

THE ASSOCIATION OF COMMUNITY WORKERS
and

COMMUNITY WORK TRAINING CO.

ACW is an association for community workers in the United Kingdom. It is run *by* community workers *for* community workers. It is open to all people who are community workers, whether paid or unpaid, activists or trainers, or people who have an interest in community work.

ACW is a membership organisation which is independent, and able to contribute to the development of community work theory and practice in a challenging and supportive way.

Community Work Training Co. aims to deliver quality training in Community Work across West Yorkshire and works in partnership with similar organisations in the region. It is a member of the National Federation of Community Work Training Groups.

To order more copies of this publication, please contact:

ACW, Balliol Youth and Community Centre, Longbenton Methodist Church, Chesters Avenue, NEWCASTLE UPON TYNE NE12 8QP
Tel: 0191 215 1880 e-mail: lesleyleach@acw1.fsbusiness.co.uk

or

Community Work Training Co., 128 Sunbridge Road, BRADFORD BD1 2AT
Tel: 01274 745551 e-mail: info@cwtco.org.uk

ISBN 1-903925-01-0

Previous edition published by ACW, ISBN 0-907413-22-6

Community Work Skills Manual © ACW / CWTCo. 2001

FOREWORD

Welcome to another skills manual packed with ideas and techniques for people seeking to involve others in their communities and groups in bringing about changes. I hope that you will all find something useful within this manual to help you with your community work.

This manual, like the two earlier ones, has been mainly written by practitioners, people who are working in their communities and know what might work and what doesn't! They were also willing and able to find the time to write it down to share with you. It isn't a comprehensive guide to everything you need to know to work effectively in the community, and inevitably there are gaps. There were promises of other articles, but people have real lives, and this has meant that some of the hoped-for sections didn't arrive in time; still there will be another edition I'm sure! We have updated some of the sections from the last manual where they were still relevant and important, but much of this manual is brand new, and covers different topics from the previous ones.

We have tried to take on board some of the comments made about the last manual, so we have page-numbered the whole book, changed the layout, and tried to incorporate case studies from community work practice. I hope you think it is an improvement; as always your thoughts on how to improve and develop this manual are welcomed.

This manual has been made possible by the contributions from all the writers, with the funding coming from the National Charities Lottery Board through the West Yorkshire Community Work Training Group resources project.

Thanks are due to everyone who became involved in this manual, but especial thanks should go to the intrepid band of those who helped with the editing and rewriting – Barbara, Joy and Ros; to Judy whose organisational abilities and skills with the computer ensured that this manual actually happened, to Bill who assiduously read every word of it and corrected all the typos and improved the grammar, and to Laura who spent months in the attic inputting the changes and sifting through the photographs for the cover.

Val Harris
Editor

COMMUNITY WORK SKILLS MANUAL

CONTENTS

CONTENTS

Section 7   People Management ctd.   Page

Section 8   Campaigning and Lobbying

Section 9   Funding

Section 10 Monitoring and Evaluation

CONTENTS

Section 1

Introduction

DEFINITION OF COMMUNITY WORK

INTRODUCTION

Community work is a very varied and diverse occupation, but in order to write the occupational standards a **definition** of community work had to be agreed upon which stated what the main purpose, aims and objectives of community work are.

The definition below was produced by the **England Standards Board for Community Work Training and Qualifications**.

DEFINITION

Community Work is about the active involvement of people in the issues which affect their lives and focuses on the relationship between individuals and groups and the institutions which shape their everyday experience.

It is a developmental process, which is both a collective and individual experience. It is based on a commitment to equal partnership between all those involved to enable a sharing of skills, awareness, knowledge and experience in order to bring about change.

It takes place in both neighbourhoods and communities of interest, whenever people come together to identify what is relevant to them, and act on issues of common concern.

THE KEY PURPOSE

The key purpose of community work is to work with communities experiencing disadvantage, enabling them collectively to identify needs and rights, clarify objectives and take action to meet them within a democratic framework which respects the needs and rights of others.

Community work recognises the need to celebrate diversity and differences and actively confront oppression however it is manifested.

VALUES AND PRINCIPLES OF COMMUNITY WORK

Federation of CW
Training Groups

INTRODUCTION

Regardless of where community work is carried out, or the issue being tackled, or even the style of those involved and their approach, there are a number of key principles which have to be adhered to in order for the work to be accurately described as community work.

It is often this emphasis on values, principles and processes that mark community work out from other occupations.

COMMUNITY WORK AIMS TO . . .

Promote co-operation and encourage the process of participatory democracy by:

- supporting new and existing community groups to work on issues of common interest and concern

- enabling links and liaisons between groups and individuals to take place, around issues of common concern on a basis of mutual respect, whilst recognising diversity and differences

- acknowledging the specific experience and contribution of all individuals in communities to enable them to play a greater role in shaping and determining the society of which they are part

- assisting people to reflect and act together to achieve common goals and to influence decision makers where appropriate

- assisting groups to use a variety of methods to achieve their objectives e.g. through self-help groups, pressure groups, community action, alliances and partnerships.

Encourage self-determination by:

- helping individuals and community groups to define their own objectives

- supporting individuals and groups to run autonomous and collectively managed projects

- developing appropriate organisational forms to ensure self-determination.

Ensure the sharing and development of knowledge by:

- developing awareness and understanding of issues and perspectives through working towards social, economic and political change

- enabling people to develop the expertise and skills necessary to further their own objectives

- enabling people to recognise the values which influence the ways in which they work.

Change the balance of power and power structure in ways which will facilitate local democracy, challenge inequalities and promote social justice by:

- recognising that the unequal distribution of power is both a personal and political issue, and that community work has a responsibility for linking the personal learning which empowers individuals, through to the collective learning and action for change which empowers communities

- recognising oppression within society and the necessity to confront all forms of oppression, both within ourselves and within society.

- taking the lead in confronting the attitudes and behaviour of individuals, groups and institutions which discriminate against and disempower people, both as individuals and groups

- pursuing the above through the adoption and promotion of explicit anti-discriminatory practices.

COMMUNITY WORK – IT'S POLITICAL CONTEXT Ros Chiosso

INTRODUCTION

Community Work is one of those catch-all terms – often used indiscriminately by politicians and policy makers alike. It covers a multitude of complex issues, different work approaches, and disparate areas of work. Both as a professional area of work and as a voluntary activity, it has changed significantly over the past 5 – 10 years, and it continues to diversify. This is partly in response to changing and competing community-defined needs (i.e. the result of what are sometimes called 'bottom up' community-led approaches, such as campaigning for affordable transport or to save a local school), and partly as an outcome of centrally and locally driven government initiatives (i.e. what are sometimes referred to as 'top down' initiatives such as New Deal for Communities or Health Action Zones).

THE POLITICAL CONTEXT

The context in which contemporary community work operates is something of a political minefield, and is one in which there are both positive and negative forces at play. There are certainly many more initiatives currently being funded by central and local government with a community work 'tag' attached than in the last decade. Funding for these initiatives, however, has tended to relate to specific rather than generic "joined-up" "problems" (e.g. drugs issues, employment initiatives or health action), and to particular geographic regions. However, this is slowly changing – for example, community regeneration initiatives are attempting to work more holistically, and to involve local people in decisions that will affect their lives and neighbourhoods. The degree to which this participation is meaningful, however, is a hotly contested issue.

An additional factor is that projects are invariably output driven (i.e. certain targets have to be met), with clearly defined criteria and tangible objectives expected within a short time frame. The agenda is also by and large government, or funder, rather than community determined.

Another defining characteristic of contemporary community work is the range of agencies that can be involved – this is the era of partnership working – often across a range of sectors, e.g. business, independent and statutory sectors. Inter-sector and inter-agency working is the key for projects to attract funding and sponsorship. However, partnerships are not always on an equal footing, and this again can work against the interests of local communities. For many small community groups, establishing viable 'partnerships' and finding 'matched' funding is a daunting and unrealisable task. This is a critical issue for policy makers and politicians to address.

Community work is inevitably a highly politicised area of activity because it brings into question issues of power, ownership of resources and is intent on social change (see 'Values and Principles of Community Work'). It is a dynamic and valuable activity that can lead to a radical transformation for individuals, groups and communities.

WHERE DO WE FIND COMMUNITY WORK ? — Val Harris

INTRODUCTION

There is a danger that nearly everyone can say they do community work, they work in the community, they help people in the community . . .

Community work is an occupation in its own right; there are national standards which spell out what skills and knowledge people need to be able to undertake community work. These occupational standards are underpinned by the principles and values previously outlined.

We recognise that there are two basic types of community — there is one based on locality, neighbourhoods, where people tend to live, and another which recognises that people may have common interests no matter where they live, and we talk about them being communities of interests (for example, allotment holders, cyclists in a city or the Hindu community).

COMMUNITY WORK IN ACTION

We would say that community work is about

- working with others in a community around issues/ problems that are clearly defined

- tackling these issues collectively, and in a way that is agreed by the group

- perhaps involving people from outside, as long as their views are not imposed on the group.

This is why we can find people in all sorts of jobs and in unpaid positions (who are not called community workers) who are undertaking community work, and why some people who have titles which would imply that they are community development workers may not be actually undertaking community work — maybe they are coming in from outside with their employers agenda which is not the same as the residents; maybe they live in an area and have a particular concern but this is not shared by others and they try and 'represent' the community to other organisations when they have no mandate to do this.

At a time when the national government is saying that we need communities to be involved in their own renewal, that we need more people to be volunteering and looking after each other, we find that many community workers no longer have jobs because of local government cut backs, or they spend so much time trying to get their posts refunded that they don't have too much time for doing what they are good at.

Yet community work is alive and well in all sorts of other places when we start to look around, so here are some examples . . .

In community based learning, community education, adult education - we can see groups of Asian Women, Disabled People, Women in Northern Ireland, all coming together to learn and share their experiences and to help each other learn. They are able to take back ideas and skills to other groups they are part of, as well as developing themselves as a group to take the actions they need to improve their situation and their communities.

In community health initiatives – from Health Action Zones where local projects are getting involved, to the development of Healthy Living Centres; sports activities for young people which they run themselves; walking groups for Asian women; tackling poverty through local advice centres; and many other innovative approaches to improve peoples health.

In community regeneration and neighbourhood renewal initiatives – but only where local people are actively involved and not just token partners! – so we have examples of New Deal for Communities, local SRB programmes, community safety initiatives, housing developments and local community enterprises and businesses.

In campaigns – of which there are many to choose from as they range from actions around local traffic problems through to attempts to prevent deportations; tackling racists attacks; working with asylum seekers to change the voucher system; preventing the destruction of habitats for wildlife; and promoting safe walking and cycling routes to schools.

In developing local facilities - such as millennium greens; community allotments; changing empty shops into local learning centres; using the mosques, temples and churches to provide food and socialising for older people; opening community cafes etc. All of these are aimed at providing places for people to come together to pursue a particular interest which helps to build the networks and links within communities.

There are many other places where we can see community work in action, where people (paid or not) are trying to build stronger and more inclusive communities.

Where we can see

- communities defining their concerns and issues
- issues being tackled collectively
- use being made of everyone's experiences and knowledge
- issues of power and inequality being tackled
- people actively being involved and encouraged to develop
- the process and the outcome are equally important
- that learning comes through evaluating and reflecting on what has happened so far

   . . . then we are seeing community work in action.

THE PROCESS OF COMMUNITY WORK   Val Harris

INTRODUCTION

The skills needed by a community worker will vary over time and with the different stages of the community work process that they are engaged with. Regardless of the setting or issues involved, there is a similar process for any piece of development work that is undertaken. Workers may be involved in the whole cycle, but will frequently find themselves taking over from someone else's work. For example, a student on placement may have gathered background information on an issue which has highlighted a need for a particular group which you are expected to follow up; or your post may be the result of an application to attract new resources to an area or a centre; or you may be replacing an established community development worker, and need to review your role with the existing groups.

POINTS TO NOTE

The completion of any stage may lead to the cycle starting again – for instance, a group may decide that there is a particular issue that needs tackling but that it is inappropriate for them to do it, so the workers may be asked to gather information and bring together another group to tackle the 'new' problem.

A simplified view of the process is shown overleaf:

A SIMPLIFIED VIEW OF THE STEPS INVOLVED IN COMMUNITY WORK

Gathering information from
many different sources

↓

Assessing the situation /
analysing the information

↓

Encouraging people to come together and decide what
they want to tackle

↓

Developing and supporting the group, project or campaign

↓

Assisting the group, project or campaign to plan its
strategies and tactics, and to prioritise its activities

↓

Strengthening and maintaining the group, project or
campaign as it begins to take action

↓

Supporting their activities through acquiring and sharing
relevant knowledge, skills and access to resources and
decision-makers

↓

Reviewing/evaluating the progress and
activities of the group, project or campaign

↓

Assisting the group, project or campaign to wind up, or to
decide on its next set of activities

↓

. . . and the process starts all over again . . .

SKILLS OF A COMMUNITY WORKER   Val Harris

INTRODUCTION

Community work has been recognised as an occupation in it's own right and has had occupational standards for several years now. These national standards set out the skills and knowledge that people need to undertake community work activities.

NATIONAL OCCUPATIONAL STANDARDS

National Occupational Standards can be seen as quality benchmarks for people at work: they set out the quality of performance required in the workplace. They specify the knowledge, understanding, practical and thinking skills that underpin the outcomes people are expected to achieve in the work environment. They describe not only the routine and technical aspects, but also the ways in which tasks have to be managed, the necessary interpersonal relationships and the values which the organisation wishes to be expressed into action.

All National Occupational Standards are structured into units of competence. The NVQs in community work give all the details of these standards. They are currently structured in three levels:

Level II
This describes the knowledge and skills needed by people who have recently entered community work. They will often have been active in their own community, whether it be a community of interest or a geographical area. They will be working with a number of groups in a variety of settings. Many of the jobs at this level will be unpaid or on a seasonal / part-time basis.

Level III
This describes the knowledge and skills needed by people who have a fairly wide experience of community work in a paid or unpaid capacity. They will be working at neighbourhood level, engaging in multi-group support and development. Many of the jobs at this level will have a wide variety of titles including the words support, development, action or area based.

Level IV
This describes the knowledge and skills required of people with several years experience of working in the community. They will often be involved in managing a team, or project, involving groups of unpaid workers or volunteers. The role requires management and development skills used in a variety of settings (i.e. organisational, neighbourhood, district, city, region and national) to make links within and across communities and institutions.

As well as being the basis for the NVQ awards, the occupational standards are used for other purposes – such as:-

➢ Preparing job descriptions and person specifications for community work posts

> Forming the basis of appraisals and personal development plans

> Setting the content of courses being written for community workers and people involved with community development

> Forming the cornerstone of the professional endorsement process carried out by the Standards Board for Training and Qualifications in Community Work in England, and in the pilot Endorsement Projects of Northern Ireland and Wales.

The Community Work Training Company in West Yorkshire has developed introductory workshop packs for people interested in the NVQs in Community Work. As part of the process of determining which award level people could undertake, we developed a skills scan questionnaire which would give an indication of the level at which people are working. It is based on the occupational standards.

CONTACT ADDRESS

The Community Work Training Company (CWTCo) can be contacted at: 128 Sunbridge Rd, Bradford BD1 2AT. Tel: 01274 745551.
e-mail: training@communitrain1.demon.co.uk

SKILLS SCAN – LEVEL 2

The key tasks of a Community Worker	How you feel about carrying them out		
Please tick which applies to you	Yes, I do/ have done this	No, I don't do this but willing to try	I would not do this at the moment
Getting to know a community and how you will work with it Includes:			
▪ Identifying & contacting key people and resources in the community.	❑	❑	❑
Enable communities to work and learn together effectively Includes:			
▪ Working with members of the community to identify needs and how to meet them.	❑	❑	❑
▪ Supporting groups to ensure everyone can participate fully and not discriminate against others.	❑	❑	❑
Enable people in communities to identify their needs and rights, and plan action to meet them Includes:			
▪ Working with groups to agree aims & objectives and prioritise what needs to be done.	❑	❑	❑
▪ Assisting groups to work together and plan how to take action.	❑	❑	❑
Enable communities and groups to take action and review it Includes:			
▪ Supporting & encouraging groups to carry out activities and review their progress.	❑	❑	❑
Provide organisational support to collective action Includes:			
▪ Managing your work load effectively and efficiently.	❑	❑	❑
▪ Working with community groups to arrange events	❑	❑	❑

SKILLS SCAN – LEVEL 3

The key tasks of a Community Worker	How you feel about carrying them out		
Please tick which applies to you	Yes, I do/ have done this	No, I don't do this but willing to try	I would not do this at the moment
Getting to know a community and how you will work with it Includes:			
• Making communities aware of the value of working together to meet community needs and encouraging relationships between groups.	❏	❏	❏
Enable communities to work and learn together effectively Includes:			
• Working with members of the community to identify needs and how to meet them.	❏	❏	❏
• Working with groups to promote anti-discriminatory practice and ensure everyone has the opportunity to participate fully.	❏	❏	❏
• Enabling groups and communities to deal with conflict and work together.	❏	❏	❏
• Enabling groups to identify learning needs and ways of meeting them.	❏	❏	❏
Enable people in communities to identify their needs and rights and plan action to meet them Includes:			
• Working with groups to agree aims & objectives, prioritise what needs to be done, and plan ways of taking action.	❏	❏	❏
Enable communities and groups to take action and review it Includes:			
• Monitoring & evaluating group action and support groups in carrying out their activities and reviewing & evaluating their progress.	❏	❏	❏

Please tick which applies to you	Yes, I do/ have done this	No, I don't do this but willing to try	I would not do this at the moment
Develop your own and your organisation's work			
Includes:			
▪ Managing your work to meet agreed objectives and working effectively in teams.	❑	❑	❑
▪ Evaluating your work, identifying areas for development, and ways of meeting the criteria.	❑	❑	❑
Are you doing any of the following?:			
▪ Identifying and collecting information on key people and resources in the community and agreeing areas of need.	❑	❑	❑
▪ Helping to plan, monitor and control resources	❑	❑	❑
▪ Researching, preparing and supplying information appropriately.	❑	❑	❑
▪ Organising and recording meetings.	❑	❑	❑
▪ Drafting and preparing documents.	❑	❑	❑
▪ Helping organisations to establish and monitor policies, plans and procedures.	❑	❑	❑

SKILLS SCAN – LEVEL 4

The key tasks of a Community Worker	How you feel about carrying them out		
Please tick which applies to you	Yes, I do/ have done this	No, I don't do this but willing to try	I would not do this at the moment
Getting to know a community and how you will work with it Includes:			
▪ Identifying and collecting information on key people and resources in the community and agreeing areas of need.	❑	❑	❑
▪ Building relationships with key people and groups both within and across different communities.	❑	❑	❑
Enable communities to work and learn together effectively Includes:			
▪ Working with groups to promote anti-discriminatory practice, ensuring everyone has the opportunity to participate fully.	❑	❑	❑
▪ Enabling groups and communities to deal with conflict and work together.	❑	❑	❑
▪ Enabling groups to identify learning needs and ways of meeting them.	❑	❑	❑
▪ Understanding how groups work and facilitating them to work and learn effectively	❑	❑	❑
Enable people in communities to identify their needs and rights and plan action to meet them Includes:			
▪ Working with communities in co-ordinating the planning and reviewing of action.	❑	❑	❑
Enable communities and groups to take action and review it Includes:			
▪ Working with communities to enable them to identify and advocate their rights and needs.	❑	❑	❑

Please tick which applies to you	Yes, I do/ have done this	No, I don't do this but willing to try	I would not do this at the moment
Provide organisational support to collective action			
Includes:			
▪ Recommending, monitoring and controlling the use of resources.	❑	❑	❑
Develop your own and your organisation's work			
Includes:			
▪ Contributing to the formulation of organisational policies.	❑	❑	❑
▪ Evaluating your work, identifying areas for development and ways of meeting the criteria.	❑	❑	❑
Are you doing any of the following?			
▪ Designing learning programmes.	❑	❑	❑
▪ Working with groups to agree aims & objectives, prioritise what needs to be done and plan ways of taking action.	❑	❑	❑
▪ Contribute to the recruitment and selection of people.	❑	❑	❑
▪ Developing yourself, and the people you work with, to improve performance.	❑	❑	❑
▪ Planning, allocating and evaluating your own work within your team, and giving feedback.	❑	❑	❑

Section 2

Key Themes Around Equality

ISSUES AROUND EQUALITY   Val Harris

INTRODUCTION

One of the fundamental principles of community work is that we are here to change the world so as to make it a more equal and less unjust place for its citizens. If we are serious about promoting social justice, and about the empowerment of the less powerful groups within our societies, then we need to think very carefully about the way we currently work with, and relate to, communities, and how we may be leaving out some people and groups who should be included.

We need to understand what it means to be marginalised, ignored, oppressed and discriminated against, not to be treated as equal, not to be accepted as having anything worth contributing. We need to listen to our own stories, and those of other people, and try to understand their reality, even if its hard to do, especially when we are all so busy and the problems seem so huge.

In this manual we shall try and give some tips and techniques for tackling some of the barriers that stop people from fully participating. In this sheet I shall give an overview of some of the main points for you and your group to consider.

BARRIERS TO INVOLVEMENT

The first one we tend to think of is access – the physical barriers which stop people getting to meetings and into buildings. Ruth Malkin has provided a detailed access checklist (see Appendix) and here are a few items from that list

➢ Steps which prevent or hinder entry for wheelchair users or people with buggies

➢ Long corridors and ramps which are hard for people who walk with sticks/ long arm crutches

➢ Large echoing halls so it's hard for people to hear - even in small venues check if there is a hearing loop fitted

➢ Provision of translators and signers for people working with a different first language than spoken English ?

But there are many other more invisible barriers to people being able to join in and these can be as much about people's attitudes as anything else, so think about

♦ how you handle the vexed problem of jargon and abbreviation – do you ban it? Is that possible? Do you put up a sheet so people can put up the jargon words they want explaining? Do you have ground rules asking people to explain words and abbreviations as you go along?

♦ how you stop people feeling intimidated. Do you break up large meetings and allow people to talk to their neighbours? How do you get people to feel it's okay and safe to ask questions, and convince them that they won't be seen as stupid?

- how you prepare visiting speakers, officers etc. to tailor their input to the audience

- how you stop the more powerful people dominating the group/ meeting, or running it as they would a board meeting

- how you make sure people have information in a way that they can use - not everyone likes reading sheets of closely written text. People tend to prefer straightforward information, with key points which will affect them.

- how you try and counter people's prejudices, e.g. 'they only live here so what do they know – we are the experts'; or assumptions about who makes the tea (women), who will chair meetings (men) or who may or may not be interested ('Asian and Black young men won't get involved')

- how you get beyond those who are identified, or identify themselves, as the community leaders. How do you meet other people in the community and hear their stories?

- how you encourage those who have never been listened to that you really do want to hear their voices. Do you start by using venues where people feel comfortable? Do you get the timing right, or hold consultation events at all different times so that everyone who wants to can get along at some point?

- whether you've developed your listening skills, and helped others in power to really listen, and not just to hear what they want to hear.

- how you make sure that the communities get their items on the agenda to ensure that that their concerns are not just ignored and never even talked about.

- whether you know the range of interests and communities within a locality? Do you act as a bridge between different communities initially, as you try and see how they want to work together?

- what you do when you are being pressured to meet crazy deadlines, which means there is no time for consultation, let alone for ensuring that people have a real chance to participate

- how well developed your networking skills are; are you a conduit for information or a gatekeeper?

Hopefully, the different ideas and techniques in this manual will help you to find ways to address these issues.

ANTI-RACIST WORK

Ros Chiosso &
Yvette Smalle

INTRODUCTION

What does it mean to be an active anti-racist at work? We all accept that racism and other forms of oppression need to be challenged, but how can we do this in a meaningful way – i.e. not just talk the talk, but walk the walk! The following points are intended to raise awareness / act as a guide / prompt discussion around 'race' and other forms of oppression.

BEING PRO-ACTIVE AROUND RACE ISSUES IN THE WORKPLACE

What does it mean to be pro-active around 'race' issues in the workplace?

- draw up a clear policy statement on anti-oppressive practice, and establish a monitoring policy that scrutinises its effective application

- campaign for the recruitment of more Black (and other under-represented) workers

- do not expect Black colleagues to take on 'race' issues - it is your responsibility too!

- do not assume your Black colleagues are 'race' experts / counsellors / trainers / campaigners

- if appropriate, support the establishment of a Black workers' support group

- support access to appropriate and supportive supervision mentoring - (avoid the colour blind approach)

- insist on anti-racist / anti-oppressive training for all workers - employ experienced trainers/consultants to work with you.

- validate and support work with Black individuals / community groups - not just verbally, but in terms of access to resources; create initiatives that address these issues

- support requests for skill development and training for all colleagues around equality related issues

- be aware of the work environment ethos - is it inclusive or exclusive? does it promote positive images of minorities / oppressed groups?

- establish close links with other like-minded community groups and agencies; share experiences

- be aware of the power differentials that operate in the workplace - not just in terms of roles and responsibilities, e.g. white male worker / Black female manager.

- try to understand the life experience of Black workers - do not assume that these are the same for all Black people.

WORKING WITH REFUGEE COMMUNITIES   Refugee Action

INTRODUCTION

Britain is, or it should be, having signed the Human Rights Declaration, providing asylum for refugees. At the same time there is a state-encouraged fortress attitude which is increasingly hostile to 'asylum seekers'.

The majority of refugees are completely disadvantaged by their situation, with Black and Asian refugees, women, children, and the elderly carrying the additional burden of discrimination. Community development is essential, as state provision is minimal, and individual isolation and powerlessness is the norm.

Recent developments, such as the voucher system, as well as the increase in attacks on people, means that the most vulnerable people need more help from their community than ever.

ISSUES THAT ARISE

In considering work with refugee communities some, or all, of the following will have to be confronted:

♦ Since 3rd April 2000, refugees are being dispersed on a no-choice basis away from the southeast, often to areas unused to multi-cultural populations and the very special needs of refugees.

♦ Refugees' experiences are beyond the experience, and probably the imagination, of indigenous workers.

♦ Cultures are different, and knowledge of them is limited.

♦ Workers often don't know any language other than English.

♦ Racism and other factors can block development opportunities, access to resources and funds, as well as the help of community workers.

A STEP-BY-STEP APPROACH

The following is a step-by-step approach to working with refugee communities:

1. Find out if there are any refugees in your area, or if your area is a 'cluster area' where asylum seekers will be dispersed, by contacting:
   - Your local council
   - The Refugee Council
   - Refugee Action
   - Local voluntary organisations, e.g. CABs

   If there aren't any, ask why.

2. Find out where the refugees are from, and inform yourself about their country of origin, its history, and the current situation there.

   Sources include:
   - The Refugee Council
   - Refugee Action

- The Minority Rights Group
- Newspaper articles and periodicals, e.g. the Guardian, Amnesty, New Internationalist, etc.
- TV documentaries
- Your local library.

3. Offer help, e.g. a meeting place, photocopying, mailing.

4. Provide information on how the system works locally.

5. Campaign for an interpretation and translation service, and for publicity to be produced in appropriate languages.

6. Raise awareness of issues, e.g. Immigration and Asylum Act 2000. Experts can be invited from the Asylum Rights Campaign (ARC) and refugee organisations.

7. Include refugee communities in community events, and add them to mailing lists for meetings and conferences.

8. Find out about national infrastructural support development, e.g. Refugee Action is a national charity that has worked throughout the UK for 20 years. Refugee Action, the Refugee Council and other refugee agencies are now directly funded by the Home Office to provide reception services and some on-going support to asylum seekers dispersed to their areas.

9. Encourage local voluntary and statutory organisations to put refugees on their agendas and develop relevant policies

10. Assist and encourage communities in holding cultural / social events.

11. Develop joint work with host communities e.g. shared premises, playschemes and youth clubs.

12. Make a profile of the services in an area and monitor use by refugees.

13. Encourage links between different refugee communities.

USEFUL CONTACTS

The Refugee Council 3/9 Bondway House, LONDON SW8 1SJ Tel. 020 7582 6922

The Refugee Support Centre 47 South Lambeth Road, London SW8 1RH 020 7820 3606

Minority Rights Group 379 Brixton Road, London SW9 7DE Tel. 020 7978 9498

Refugee Action The Old Fire Station, 150 Waterloo Road, LONDON SE1 8SB Tel: 0207 654 7700
Plus offices in Birmingham, Bristol, Exeter, Leeds, Leicester, Liverpool, Manchester, Northampton, Nottingham, Oxford and Southampton

DISABILITY ISSUES   Barbara Booton

INTRODUCTION

The past two decades has seen a dramatic increase in awareness of the Disabled Persons movement, both nationally and internationally. Disabled People have forced disability issues onto public and governmental agendas, by utilising the benefits of collective action, and recognising the importance of sharing and learning from each other's experience. Some of the key issues raised have been:

- re-defining the term 'disability'
- identifying the needs of Disabled People
- taking direct action on issues of transport, access and benefits
- campaigning for full civil rights legislation and direct payments
- promoting and supporting grass-roots groups.

THE KEY ISSUES

Defining Disability

The established definition of disability is

A person is disabled because of their impairments

This places the cause of disability firmly on the individual. Any difficulties that arise are the individual's own problem, and they must learn to 'cope' and adapt to any restrictions their disability places on their life. The logical conclusion to this view is that Disabled People need to be 'cured' if they are to become 'normal' people. This medical definition of disability forms the basis for all services, legislation and attitudes towards Disabled People.

Disabled People have challenged this view. It is the social, economic and political barriers to Disabled People's independence and integration that 'disables' people. This view empowers Disabled People, because it recognises that their oppression is caused by society, and not by their individual impairments. The Disabled Persons movement states that:

***Disabled People* are people with *impairments* who are disabled by society.**

Many non-disabled people, and professionals in 'disability' services, while accepting the social model in principle, do not understand a definition that says 'impairment is impairment' and this contributes to their confusion as to the difference. In most situations professionals still control the definition of 'impairment' and this threatens the development of the social model.

Language

Debates on what is considered acceptable/unacceptable language with regard to disability are often emotive and confusing. Words can create powerful images and, in the media particularly, are used to great effect. Brave, sufferer, crippled, special, handicapped, people with disabilities, are all terms still commonly used and yet are all founded on a medical definition of disability, focusing on the individual's personal tragedy.

The Needs of Disabled People

Defining the needs of Disabled People is also largely controlled by 'professionals', i.e. social workers, doctors etc. The experiences of large numbers of Disabled People, however, have shown that there is nothing 'special' about their needs; but unless these needs are satisfied, they are prevented from leading an independent life. (Being independent means being in <u>control</u> of what happens - it is about self-determination rather than self-reliance.)

Seven fundamental needs are:

- **INFORMATION** – needed to make decisions; it must be provided in accessible formats (tape, Braille, large print, signed), and in accessible places.
- **HOUSING** - houses in which Disabled People can get about, in locations of their choice.
- **TECHNICAL AIDS** - equipment that helps them to do things in the home e.g. bath hoist, minicom.
- **PERSONAL ASSISTANCE** - help from other people when it is needed, not when it is convenient for someone else to provide it.
- **TRANSPORT** - that Disabled People can use as required, and which enables them to go anywhere.
- **ACCESS** - the whole environment must be accessible to everyone so that they can move about freely and use all the services.
- **PEER SUPPORT** - talking to others who have been in the same situation.

Thought for the day!

"Once social barriers to re-integration of people with physical impairments are removed, the disability itself is eliminated. The requirements are for changes to society, material changes to the environment, changes in the environmental control systems, changes in social roles, and changes in attitudes by people in the community as a whole. The focus is decisively shifted on to the source of the problem - the society in which disability is created". Finkelstein, V., **Attitudes and Disabled People.**

CASE STUDY

As a community worker in a rural area I was contacted by a Disabled man unable to make the short trip to his village centre in his wheelchair due to a lack of dropped kerbs. A public meeting was arranged, at which people identified the need for a local Access Group. The support of local councillors helped secure local authority funding to enable the formation of an Access Group. With support and training the group was soon undertaking access surveys, campaigning for a dropped kerb scheme and networking with other Access Groups .

USEFUL ADDRESS

British Council of Disabled People Litchurch Plaza, Litchurch Lane, Derby, DE24 8AA.   Tel:01332 295551 Fax: 01332 295580
E mail: bcodp@bcodp.org.uk. Web: www.bcodp.org.uk

WORKING WITH PEOPLE WITH MENTAL HEALTH PROBLEMS AS VOLUNTEERS

Sue
Dodsworth

INTRODUCTION

Mental health related issues are becoming increasingly prevalent in society, yet there remains relatively little awareness about them. Many people with mental health problems have lost confidence and self-esteem through periods of illness, experiences within the mental health system, and often the rejection of family members, friends or neighbourhood communities.

It is important to remember that people with mental health problems have skills and abilities; they need to be able to make positive contributions to society, and can often be very creative, constructive, responsible and valuable members of a group or organisation. For many people this is denied in a paid capacity, but it is possible as a volunteer. The development of confidence, practical skills and ability which this gives is vital in developing self-esteem, as well as providing positive role models for others.

TACKLING DISCRIMINATION

An active approach needs to be taken to tackle discrimination on the basis of a person's mental health. Community Workers need to be aware of issues and needs in the area of mental health (as in any other disability) in order not to add to the discrimination against people with mental health problems. These are some points to bear in mind:

➢ Having mental health problems is **not** the same as having a learning difficulty, although some people with learning difficulties may also have a mental health problem.

➢ There is still a lot of prejudice, fear and stigma attached to having a psychiatric diagnosis, spending periods in the mental health system, or just suffering from mental distress.

➢ Be aware of language - common terms such as 'psycho', 'nutter', 'maniac', etc need challenging. They are part of the culture that oppresses, disempowers and ultimately dismisses people struggling with mental health problems.

➢ People with mental health problems wishing to be volunteers need support, value, understanding and treatment as an individual (rather than a label or a diagnosis) - as do any other volunteers.

PRACTICAL ISSUES TO BE AWARE OF

➢ A person's mental health (ie. stress levels, concentration, ability, decision-making skills) can vary from week to week, day to day, and sometimes from hour to hour, but they can still be a committed and capable volunteer.

➢ People may need to take more regular breaks. Many medications cause a dry mouth all the time. Consideration needs to be made for people who smoke, so they are not made to feel ostracised because of their habit.

➢ Mornings are not a good time for many people to attend meetings or undertake voluntary work eg. because medication can leave people feeling drowsy or because of disturbed sleep patterns.

> Be a bit wary if people are taking on too much too soon, or too much at once. Encourage people to build up gradually, rather than find themselves unable to do the work, and then leave, feeling a sense of failure.

> People need to feel that there is a sympathetic and welcoming attitude towards them. A relationship of trust needs to be built up. Many people have had bad experiences of people who work in health, social services or other professional capacities and been on the receiving end of negative stereotypes.

> Periods of illness and negative experiences from the public, professionals, and other services can leave people with low self-confidence and low self-esteem. Volunteers with mental health problems need support and feedback in their role. It is helpful to have someone to talk to, particularly if the volunteer is feeling unwell, unsure of their worth to the organisation, being discriminated against, etc.

> There needs to be a greater flexibility in working with people with mental health problems (eg. in time out or time off sick) in order to get the best out of them as volunteers. Knowing that time out is possible without them losing their role can help the individual sustain work for longer periods.

> Volunteers with mental health problems will have training needs, as do any other volunteers. The organisation, and its workers and volunteers, may also need training in mental health issues and awareness.

> If it is unclear what is going on for a volunteer with mental health problems, then ask them (rather than assume 'it's their illness' or 'they can't do the job').

> Try and explain tasks clearly and simply, and if necessary go over them a number of times. People experiencing anxiety often find their minds just go blank, or they panic at too much new information. On the other hand, don't assume this means low intelligence or that they need patronising.

> People with mental health problems often cannot access community based courses and activities because they find the pace and structure of them intimidating, which leads to further anxiety, loss of confidence and feelings of low self-esteem.

USEFUL ADDRESSES

Mind in Bradford Ground Floor, Tradeforce Building, Cornwall Place, Bradford BD8 7JT Tel. 01274 730815 Runs Guideline - a telephone help-line. Open 7 days a week from 12.00 to 9.00pm. Tel. 01274 734735

Bradford & Airedale Mental Health Advocacy Group 2nd Floor, Tradeforce Building, Cornwall Place, Bradford BD8 7JT Tel. 01274 770118

MIND Granta House, 15-19 Broadway, Stratford, London E15 4BQ Tel. 020 8519 2122 Fax: 020 8522 1725 website : www.mind.org.uk

Mind*info*line : 0845 766 0163 (outside London) or 020 8522 1728 (in London)

Mind Mail Order Service 15-19 Broadway, London E15 4BQ Tel. 020 8221 9666   Fax: 020 8534 6399 e-mail : publications@mind.org.uk

UKAN   (UK Advocacy Network), Volserve House, 14-18 West Bar Green, Sheffield S1 2DA Tel 0114 272 8171

WORKING WITH OLDER PEOPLE

Updated by
Ros Chiosso

INTRODUCTION

Working with older people raises two important matters that must be borne in mind. The first is ageism, and the second, which may seem contradictory, concerns physical factors that often accompany old age.

Ageism is a poorly recognised form of oppression. It is just as insidious and patronising as sexism and racism. We tend to talk about old people behaving in a certain manner, or having "funny little ways". We tend to talk about them in the third person plural, although it's quite likely that we will all be there one day. One phrase that is particularly indicative of ageism is "they get like that, don't they?"

THINGS TO THINK ABOUT

The "over-60s" are not a homogenous group. There will be different generations within that group, different races, cultures, genders, levels of educational attainment, levels of mobility and physical ability. A liking for bingo and world war songs doesn't come with the first pension book. It's also worth remembering that old people, like the rest of us, still make mistakes, and making allowances for them can be very patronising.

It needs to be borne in mind that certain physical characteristics are statistically more common in older people, and these need catering for if older people are to be made welcome in your organisation. Think about:

- the accessibility of your premises and your toilet facilities
- induction loops
- information provided in larger print
- holding meetings and events on bus routes: there are fewer car owners in the older age groups, and most Councils provide bus passes
- checking bus times to ensure people can arrive at the start
- the timing of your events: media scares about pensioners being attacked have caused some people to be nervous about being out after dark.

Attitudes can also be a problem; older people may feel excluded if their views are never listened to, or they are patronised, or always expected to make the tea. There has been some really exciting intergenerational work, e.g. with older people going into schools to work with younger people, which has begun to challenge such attitudes.

Pensioners and those who have retired early are a valuable resource to any voluntary organisation in terms of time, experience and energy. If you have an age limit for volunteers and paid workers in your organisation, maybe you should think about whether it is really relevant.

There are still substantial levels of poverty experienced by many older people, and the fact that this group of people has the lowest take-up for welfare benefits. Involving older people in community based activities needs to recognise this factor – which is why luncheon clubs in warm convivial surroundings, preferably with transport laid on, is always a winner.

Ideas for attracting older people to events include –

- posters in Post Offices, doctors' surgeries, halls and buildings where older people meet
- asking to speak at a pensioners' Action Group meeting or at a pensioners' group. See if the local Age Concern has a newsletter or mailing in which you may be able to insert an item
- check which of the national pensioners' organisations have newspapers – they may be worth advertising in.

WORKING WITH LESBIAN, GAY AND BISEXUAL GROUPS

Alice Wallace

INTRODUCTION

Despite the fact that social attitudes towards lesbian and gay sexuality has been changing for the better, this does not mean that it is necessarily safe for every lesbian, gay man or bisexual person to disclose their sexuality. Intolerance, exclusion, rejection and discrimination still happen on a daily basis. Furthermore fear of such reactions is pervasive and limits where people feel able to be 'out'. It is these reactions, together with poor experiences of mainstream agencies and support, which have led to the development of separate lesbian, gay and bisexual (LGB) voluntary organisations and community groups.

The LGB voluntary and community sectors are diverse. In the first instance, in the range of initiatives (which vary from large housing and health service providers, to help-lines, self-help campaigning groups and a wide range of socially-focussed groups) and secondly, while the sector as a whole is marginalised, there are also disparities in the resources and development of projects reflecting inequalities in race, gender, disability and other discrimination. For example, the number of Black and Minority Ethnic lesbian, gay and bisexual projects is limited, and this often results in many demands being put on these organisations.

FUNDING

Like many voluntary and community groups, the majority of LGB groups exist with little or no funding. Whilst health funders have provided resources for gay men's health projects in response to HIV and AIDS, there is little evidence to suggest that awareness of the wider needs of the LGB communities has changed greatly. This is exacerbated by the lack of background facts and figures to support funding bids. Research which has been undertaken is often local rather than national, and until now there has been no centralised library of research information available. In addition many local authorities have been reluctant to fund LGB initiatives, fearing political reaction and (mis-guidedly) that this might contravene Section 28.

MYTHS

- **The pervading myth of the 'Pink Pound'** has resulted in people believing that all LGB people have money enough to spend (and to contribute to their groups).

   In reality, being lesbian or gay increases the risk of poverty, since discriminatory employment practices are still lawful on the grounds of sexuality. Additionally, the effects of gender disadvantage in the workplace may amplify discrimination for lesbian couples.

- **LGB people have no childcare/carer responsibilities** – some people believe that most LGB people are single and without any parental responsibilities and so have time and energy to run their own groups, and that they do not have responsibility for dependants.

The reality is that children do not only come from women/men relationships. Lesbians and gay men may choose to have children, or foster/adopt, together or separately. Additionally, LGB people may have care responsibilities within their own families, or within their own relationships. The latter may need particular support if relationships with extended family or community are difficult.

- **The LGB community is heterogeneous** and that the needs of lesbians, gay men and bi-sexuals are all the same.

  The needs and situations of these three groups are often quite distinct, and are affected by other power relationships within society; within each community there will be a range of preferred lifestyles. There may also be histories of less successful collaboration between these communities in some areas. Any work with 'LGB communities' as a whole should recognise that this involves working across many differences. It is often important to allow scope for separate organisation.

- **Being lesbian, gay or bisexual is about what one does in bed** (or elsewhere!), and therefore an essentially private matter

  Whilst sexuality is undoubtedly complex, 'lesbian', 'gay' and 'bisexual' are sexual identities adopted by many people attracted to or in relationships with the same sex. These identities reflect a common experience of marginalisation and discrimination, which should be matters of more public concern. It is also true that some people are uncomfortable with these identities, and may use other or no specific term

- **LGB communities are an urban phenomenon**
  Lesbians, Gay men and Bisexuals are everywhere! There is some history of migration towards some urban centres and other neighbourhoods known as having larger LGB populations, but if anything this makes the isolation of those living in other areas – and the need for community development - more pronounced.

- **Raising issues around sexuality in some religious or cultural communities is a taboo and even disrespectful**
  While many religions do either object to, or struggle with diverse sexualities, ignoring LGB needs does an enormous dis-service to lesbians, gay men and bisexuals from those communities.

ISSUES OF COMMUNITY DEVELOPMENT WITHIN THE LGB COMMUNITIES

- The sector as a whole is underdeveloped. Like many other oppressed groups, the LGB sector lacks an effective infrastructure / cohesion; how can more mainstream infrastructure organisations provide support to emerging LGB networks and groups?

- Some LGB communities are beginning to develop 'alliances' or 'networks'; if they approached you how would you respond? Would you make contact with LGB communities to look at areas of joint working or mutual support? For example would you remember to include lesbian mothers groups within a child care campaign?

- Many community groups are unfunded and often have few if any staff; they therefore do not always have the time or resources to network. Is there anything you can do to assist with this?

- Issues of personal safety are really important:
  - what can you do to ensure that any meetings/ events LGB groups are invited to are safe for them?
  - what might you need to do to prepare your own organisation to enter into a partnership or supportive relationship with LGB groups?

- LGB communities are a community of interest rather than a geographical community. The issues of safety may well be that organising at the neighbourhood or 'patch' level is inappropriate. Who will take responsibility to support the development of work at district, borough or broader level? This may be especially true for work with particular groups such as disabled or Black lesbians and gay men.

- If you are a LGB community development worker working with LGB groups does this compromise your own safety?

- If you are a heterosexual community development worker are you aware of the issues of confidentiality that affect LGB groups and individuals?

WORKING WITH LESBIAN, GAY AND BISEXUAL PEOPLE WITHIN MAINSTREAM COMMUNITY ORGANISATIONS

Many mainstream organisations do not acknowledge lesbians, gay men or bisexual people as workers or service users. This has led to the development of separate organisations but does not mean that organisations should continue to fail to meet the needs of a group of people who account for up to 10% of the population.

There are various ways that organisations can become more LGB friendly:

- Ensure that lesbians, gay men and bisexual people are explicitly included in any equal opportunities policy.

- Include lesbians, gay men and bisexuals in any monitoring procedures relating to your work or internal organisation (see below)

- Promote the organisations services within the LGB communities – e.g. by using LGB media and venues, and having a stall at events

- Promote positive images of lesbians and gay men – the NAZ Project in London produce a range of positive image posters.

- Encourage members of the management committees to undertake training around equality of opportunity and hetero-sexism awareness.

- Challenge negative comments / 'jokes' based on sexuality

Monitoring of work raises a complex range of issues in many areas, but especially around sexuality and sexual identity. Issues of terminology, privacy, safety, and the use to which data is put need to be considered, but monitoring is likely to be important in any evaluation of success in addressing these issues. Some organisations have found that the introduction of such monitoring is a useful catalyst for discussion and debate.

Bear in mind that you probably do not know whether any of the users of a particular service are lesbian, gay or bisexual. An organisation needs to 'come out' as being LGB friendly before individuals will 'come out' as being lesbian or gay. The main point to remember is to make community activity as inclusive as possible.

CONTACTS (also see Contacts list in the Appendix)

The Consortium of Lesbian, Gay and Bisexual Voluntary and Community Organisations
322 Upper Street London N1 2XQ
Tel: 020 7354 8848   **Fax:** 020 7345 8002   **E-mail:** lgbvsc@talk21.com
The Consortium works with LGB organisations to develop their capacity, to promote good practice, and to promote volunteering within the lgb communities. It also works with other volunteer support agencies to promote awareness of lesbian , gay and bisexual issues.

National Friend
216 The Custard Factory, Gibb Street, Digbeth, Birmingham, B9 4AA
Tel: 0121 684 1261   **Fax**: 0121 684 1262   **E-mail**: friend@dircon.co.uk
The umbrella body for the UK network of help-lines in LGB communities. Encourages minimum standards of service, and generally supports groups in their work through publicity, training, publications, a bi-monthly newsletter 'Between the Lines', and national conferences.

Black Lesbian and Gay Resource Centre
Room 113, 5a Westminster Bridge Road, London, SE1 7XW
Tel: 020 7620 3885 **E-mail:** blgc@btinternet.com
Advice, support, referrals or information about what is going on for the Black lesbian & gay community, within limited current resources.

NACVS: Sexuality Issues Network Group (SING)
3rd Floor, Arundel Court, 177 Arundel Street, Sheffield, S1 2NU
Tel: 0114 278 6636   **Fax**: 0114 278 7004
NACVS administers an email network to support individuals and circulate information about sexuality issues and events. The group meets twice a year and is currently working in partnership, developing ideas to promote and support LGB issues within the CVS network.

Freedom Youth
8-10 West Street, Old Market, Bristol, BS2 0BH
Tel: 0117 955 3355   **Fax:** 0117 954 1200 **e-mail:** freedomy@dircon.co.uk
Provides a safe space for lesbian, gay and bisexual youth, 25 yrs and younger. Offers a variety of groups and an alternative to the commercial gay scene. Has produced a series of 'positive images' posters

NAZ Project London
Palingswick House, 241 Kings Street, Hammersmith, W6 9LP
Tel: 020 8741 1879 **Fax:** 020 8741 9609 **e-mail:** naz@naz.org.uk
HIV/AIDS and sexual health agency providing education, prevention and support services to South Asian, Middle Eastern, North African and Latin American communities: Dost group is a gay/bi/msm social & support group; Dost Youth is a G-B-msm youth group for under 25's; Kiss is a L-B-whsww social support group. Also produce a range of resources.

WORKING ON WOMEN'S ISSUES   Ros Chiosso

INTRODUCTION

In recent years there has been something of a backlash against issue-based work with women - unless it is targeted work that conforms to a particular funding initiative (e.g. parenting skills, employment and training opportunities or health issues). Whilst these initiatives are important, and can offer much needed space, resources and support, there is still a significant place for work with women, on issues **they** determine. For example, I was asked by a group of unwaged women - brought together to look at employment and training opportunities - to work with them on challenging the way a local Benefits Agency made decisions on Social Fund applications.

Women are still disadvantaged in many spheres of economic and social life, and are currently over-represented in all the statistics on poverty. In 2000 women comprise approximately 62% of the adult population dependent on Income Support; and for many in paid work, it is in low-waged / low-status jobs in the service sector of the economy.

ISSUES WHICH AFFECT WOMEN

Working with women living in disadvantaged communities on the wide range of issues that both directly and disproportionately affect them is a huge task. In discussions you might come up with some / all of the following (plus others):

- poverty
- health
- violence / abuse / personal safety
- childcare / caring responsibilities
- immigration
- policing
- racial / sexual harassment
- disabled access
- access to income rights
- employment
- education / training
- transport
- community care
- housing
- schools play / leisure facilities

How to decide which ones are the most relevant, and which ones to prioritise, needs to be the subject of careful discussion, and other sections of the Skills Manual can offer guidance in terms of group process, negotiation etc. What is less commonly discussed / acknowledged is the issue of diversity, and the extent to which women experience oppression. Key to effective working on the above issues is the need to identify women's different experiences of them.

Some examples of difference are:

◆ a visible increase in policing may be welcome in one area but opposed in another – or, indeed, there may be a variance of opinion within the same area

◆ dealing with the local Benefits Agency can be a frustrating and time consuming experience for many claimants, but this may be further compounded for refugees and second language speakers

◆ gaining access to appropriate mental health services can be particularly difficult for minority ethnic women.

It is important to recognise the interconnections between different forms of oppression, as these can qualitatively change the nature of oppression experienced. Some women may experience multiple forms of oppression, perhaps because of their class **and** sexuality **and** disability, e.g. the particular needs of Black disabled women, lesbian parents and Black elders are all too frequently either overlooked or not recognised. Cultural stereotypes, which preclude some women from accessing much needed services, can operate.

We need to recognise women's heterogeneity, and not simply see them as a single category - women's lives are complex, full of contradictions and often conflicting loyalties.

ANTI-OPPRESSIVE PRINCIPLES

Working with women might include the following anti-oppressive principles:

◆ start by identifying women's different experiences

  - clarify needs, expectations, priorities

  - acknowledge difference

  - do not assume or expect 'sisterhood'!

◆ recognise that gender oppression interacts with other forms of oppression, and can qualitatively change the nature and experience of oppression - we need to make connections, e.g. between race and sexuality and perhaps disability.

◆ promote solidarity against other forms of oppression, not only at a local level but also in a wider global context - it is divisive to operate a hierarchy of oppression

◆ recognise that some women can hold power (and be oppressive) in certain contexts - perhaps at work, at home, in their community - and be disempowered in another

◆ integral to the above is the need to self-reflect, evaluate, and accept constructive criticism.

N.B. This is not intended to be a comprehensive 'list' but ideas to generate discussion.

DEVELOPING A BLACK AND MINORITY ETHNIC NETWORK

Gersh Subhra

INTRODUCTION

The Derby Millennium Network (DMN) was established in April 1999 to bring together Black and Minority Ethnic (B.M.E) community groups within Derby. One of the first pieces of work they agreed was to commission a mapping exercise to provide an accurate picture of the situation facing the B.M.E sector in the city. The project was undertaken as a partnership between Derby University and DMN. This section outlines the process they adopted, and may encourage other organisations to undertake a similar project.

THE AIMS OF THE PROJECT

The specific aims of the research project were negotiated with the Steering Group right at the beginning of the process:

1. To gain a more accurate picture of the size and scope of activities being undertaken by the B.M.E voluntary sector in Derby

2. To research and collate the issues and difficulties that are hindering/enhancing the growth and development of this sector

3. To identify a range of strategies that will enhance the development and growth of this sector in Derby

THE PROCESS USED

1. Literature Review.
There is very little written about the B.M.E sector in its own right, although there are quite a lot of implied references to the B.M.E sector. The literature that does exist mainly comprises of two types:

- Strategy and policy intention statements by bodies such as Government and national B.M.E organisations

- Research, consultative or policy reports issued by bodies such as local B.M.E sector consortiums and individual B.M.E organisations.

From the review we were able to outline the historical development of the B.M.E sector, and gain an appreciation of the diversity of the groups existing around the country. The extent of the exclusion of the black voluntary sector from policy development and implementation became apparent.

The review revealed the lack of resources available to the B.M.E sector and the lack of effective infrastructure.

2. Action Research.
The research was undertaken using the principles of community development (see Section 1 in the manual), and based on those which underlie quality action research. These include:

- a practical, problem-solving approach which aims to carry out research alongside, and integrated with, the development of projects and community initiatives. This places the researcher in the role of an active participant of the issue(s)

- ◆ Research is de-mystified and offered as a tool that can be owned and practised by, and empowering for, the community and its organisations
- ◆ Skills that are held by both the researcher and the community organisations are shared, and built upon, rather than expertise being seen to lie exclusively with the researcher
- ◆ Gathering `data` is undertaken by both the researcher and the community representatives. Iindeed it is argued that the latter may gather better quality information because they are known to, and have greater credibility within, the community
- ◆ The information, clarification and solutions that emerge from the research are `looped` back into the community organisation throughout the process, rather than waiting until the end
- ◆ The relationship between the researcher and community isn't finished when the project is completed - ongoing links usually emerge.

These principles were discussed between the University and the steering group and built into the research project.

3. The Research Process.

The research process can be presented in broadly five phases:

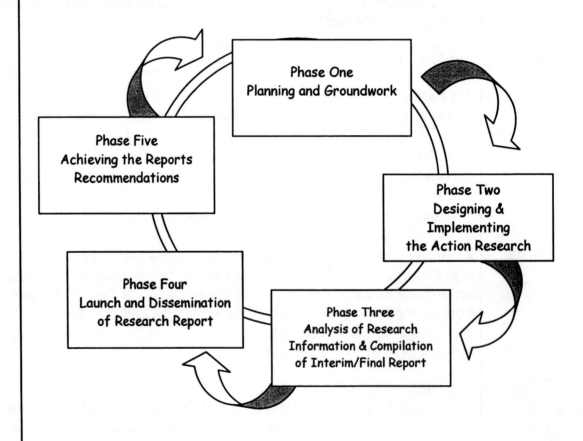

This research was undertaken by a university research student with the support of a university lecturer who assisted the steering group as well as the student. The co-ordinator of DMN was actively involved in this work.

In phase 2

- questionnaires were designed, mailing lists drawn up, and the questionnaires posted.
- funding bids were made
- people willing to act as researchers were trained in their roles and matched to community groups and individuals - using factors such as gender, language and prior knowledge of the group
- visits were made, and follow up telephone calls to those who had not responded to the questionnaires
- seminars were used to enable people to make contributions to the research, particularly those who didn't want to fill in a questionnaire. Two seminars were organised, one aimed at B.M.E communities/workers, and the other open to all.

The research team gathered all the information together and an interim report was produced. This was circulated for comment and discussed at a conference where workshops were held to allow people to continue contributing to the research findings. These views will be incorporated into the final report. The decision to have an interim report was deliberate; it allows a process of consultation and feedback (sometimes critical!) about the findings.

KEY FINDINGS

These are fully detailed in the report which links the outcomes to the original aims.

Size and scope of the sector
In the map of Derby which emerges there are social/ informal groups that have grown in response to the demands of B.M.E communities, service providers in housing, welfare and training, a few advocacy and campaigning organisations, and the limited umbrella organisations.
Details are provided of the size and scale of the sector and the organisations within it based – the latter based on the length of time organisations had existed and the number of staff.

The main issues for the sector included

- The lack of time to undertake research and needs analysis
- Lack of experience, and interest in, undertaking research and needs analysis
- Separate B.M.E services, or integration with generic voluntary organisations
- The relevance of mainstreaming for the sector
- The professionalisation of management committees
- Raising the quality and capacity of B.M.E management committees
- Finding the next generation of volunteers and pioneers to take the sector forward
- The isolation and needs of B.M.E workers
- The skills needed by the sector
- Appropriate training strategies and delivery
- Low/ rent-free premises for new organisations

- Being strategic as well as doing the work
- Forming partnerships with white organisations, and between B.M.E organisations
- Recognising the diversity of the sector
- Funding!
- The relationship between Derby's capacity builders and the B.M.E sector.

From the analysis of these issues the research concludes with proposing a strategic way forward for the sector which includes the roles that a new B.M.E led organisation could take on.

This is extracted from the full report of the project, entitled **Black and Minority Ethnic (B.M.E) Voluntary Sector Research project**, available from

Hallmark Housing Association
93 Friar Gate
DERBY DE1 1FL

Tel: 01332 614700

PLANNING SUSTAINABLE SERVICES WITH BLACK COMMUNITIES

Vipin Chauhan and Gersh Subhra

INTRODUCTION

The aim of this section is to help community, voluntary and public sector organisations improve the quality, range and type of services they offer to Black communities - by which we mean African, Caribbean and Asian communities, who are systematically discriminated against on the basis of skin colour.

Organisations should recognise and acknowledge that British society is now multifaith, multilingual, multiethnic and multiracial, and develop their services to reflect this. Organisations must respond to the challenges of such a diverse society and not continue to provide services and provisions largely tried and tested on white Eurocentric models.

Acquiring the knowledge to do something about the diversity of people who use your services, or join your organisation, is not a natural process. It will not happen unless a commitment to resources, research, networking and access is made. The organisational culture and collective attitude of those involved has to evolve and develop. It is not so much about how many Black staff or clients an organisation has, as about its approach to including Black communities.

EFFECTIVE PREPARATION AND PLANNING

Organisations need to carry out research and groundwork (both internal and external) before starting to deliver services to Black communities. They can start with a self-assessment in order to deliver effective anti-racist working practices in the long term. Such forward thinking will also enable agencies to be seen by many potential Black staff as `good` organisations for which to work, and thus help with recruitment, selection and retention.

Effective Internal groundwork needs to include:
- an assessment of how Black services fit in with, and complement, existing priorities
- familiarisation of all staff and volunteers with the purpose, aims and delivery of the proposed Black services
- management and resolution of any resistance to the development of Black services
- sufficient preparatory lead-in time to ensure a good start
- strategies for the recruitment, support, management, development and retention of new Black staff
- self-preparation by managers and management committees who have never previously managed Black employees
- the creation of an organisational culture open and receptive to critical, but constructive, feedback from Black staff.

Effective external groundwork needs to include:
- the evolution of closer and more interactive relationships by organisations within their area, communities, key bodies and

community organisations
- community development strategies to assess needs and inform the design and delivery of services
- outreach strategies which enable Black communities and clients to become involved in shaping and delivering services
- formal mechanisms, such as reference or advisory groups, through which consultation, participation and **ongoing** partnerships with local communities can be developed
- the piloting of services, or aspects of them, before a formal launch
- the development of networks from which potential Black job applicants, volunteers and management committee members can be recruited
- the use of external Black expertise, consultants and mentors to help develop and improve services.

THE PIVOTAL ROLE OF THE MANAGER

The manager as the "controller" of resources, a "leader" and "director" of policies and practices is central to the development of appropriate services to the Black communities. He/she can play a key role in:
- designing and implementing a project effectively and strategically
- thinking beyond the inevitable short-term funding cycles and consolidating the experiences gained by all staff
- driving staff to higher quality standards, and ensuring that the services delivered are appropriate and anti-racist
- ensuring that Black staff are effectively supported to develop their work with clients, be they Black or white;
- enhancing the overall quality and range of services delivered to Black communities
- liaising with local Black communities and people using the services.

These types of skills are learned, not inherited. The training and support needs of existing or incoming managers should be taken into early consideration when planning the delivery of services to Black communities.

RECRUITMENT AND SUPPORT OF BLACK STAFF

Agencies should not assume that in order to develop Black services all they need to do is to employ Black staff.

It has been a common experience that Black workers (sometimes as the sole Black employee) have had to take on compensatory multiple roles internal and external to the agency - including helping white organisations to develop their anti-racist policies and practices. The term 'Super Black workers' is an apt description of the versatility workers have had to demonstrate in response to such excessive expectations.

Managers play an important role in ensuring that Black staff are effectively supported in developing their work - including the facility of a good staff development set-up which incorporates:
- induction, on-going training and personal/professional development

opportunities
- pay parity with other workers undertaking similar duties within the organisation
- realistic job descriptions, and manageable professional responsibilities
- effective and appropriate managerial and non-managerial support
- access to, and collaborative work with, external consultants, volunteers and reference groups
- clarity and openness about the lines of accountability, roles and responsibilities in relation to funders.

Where organisations fail to provide such support and clarity, many Black staff have experienced a high degree of isolation, overload and professional undermining.

MONITORING AND EVALUATION SYSTEMS

Whether new services are being established as an expansion of existing ones, or as a new project, there are a number of issues relating to monitoring and evaluation which need to be sorted out:, viz:

- A substantial amount of the early work by Black staff and the agency may relate to setting up the infrastructure (e.g. buying office furniture, writing equal opportunities policies, making applications for further funding) rather than actually delivering services, because of deficits within the original proposal, etc. Clearly, such use of the Black workers' time will affect the targets that they and the project can be realistically expected to achieve in the first, and even subsequent, years

- In organisations which may not have previously employed Black staff, or seen only a small number of Black service users, the Black worker may be expected to act as an internal consultant/advisor for colleagues on equal opportunities and, in some instances, the `surrogate` manager. Such internal compensatory activities can occupy a significant amount of the Black worker's time; time which is not always measurable in terms of service outputs and targets.

- The emphasis on quantitative outcomes (number crunching) risks ignoring many of the qualitative impacts a Black worker may make on internal aspects of the organisation, or in terms of external community relations and service delivery.

- The evaluation data gathered on the impact of new or re-designed services to Black communities from short-term initiatives, needs to be strategically and creatively shared in order to ensure long-term financial sustainability. This is particularly important in ensuring that services are further developed, and longer-term funding is secured through local funders (such as Health Authorities).

DESIGNING CULTURALLY APPROPRIATE SERVICES

Black clients and communities are not always able to access provision appropriate to their needs or circumstances. Organisations need to step outside their traditional ways of doing things, and find more innovative ways of providing their services or developing their membership Such innovation and change can result in an improvement of services for **everybody**. A variety of methods can be used to make services more relevant and appropriate to Black clients, including:

- anti-racist, and inclusive, services;
- multi-lingual facilities, and access to interpreters and translators;
- multi-lingual promotional materials and images;
- the inclusion of religious and spiritual dimensions in service delivery and management;
- dual strategies of promoting Black specific services and anti-racist practices;
- the use of more outreach and community development approaches - including home visits and befriending schemes;
- the employment of more Black staff with the appropriate cultural, linguistic and technical skills;
- the provision of satellite services in culturally acceptable venues.

These can be evaluated by looking at an organisation's effectiveness, service appropriateness and user satisfaction.

INVESTING IN SUSTAINABLE SERVICES

Working towards the delivery of sustainable services requires a systematic and strategic approach consisting some of the following:

- the introduction and development of income generating strategies;
- a real commitment to ongoing dialogue with the Black communities;
- the development of services accessible, appropriate and effective for all;
- networking and partnerships with local, regional and national capacity building organisations;
- an active and ongoing relationship with funding bodies;
- the use of external consultants and advisors to assist with issues such as preparation for anti-racist change, provision of non-managerial supervision, and development of exit strategies;
- the adoption of an explicit community development approach at the core of an organisation's values and methods of service delivery.

In order to develop and deliver sustainable services, agencies should consider any changes necessary to meet the needs of the Black communities. It is no longer acceptable to just wait for the next round of funding before another short-term project is implemented. Agencies embarking on such changes to develop more culturally appropriate anti-racist services need to be guided and steered by the Black communities. Otherwise opportunism, motivated largely by financial gains, will continue to prevail and the Black communities will continue to lose out.

This paper draws from our evaluation report *'Developing Black Services',* published in April 1999 by Alcohol Concern

Section 3

Gathering Information

RESEARCH METHODS: AN INTRODUCTION   Angus McCabe

INTRODUCTION

Research is often seen as some strange, almost alien, activity which only takes place in universities. It involves a complex, and exclusive, language. Nevertheless, in our daily lives we all carry out research; whether it is following a particular story in the press or finding out where to buy items at an affordable price. Equally, research is often viewed as something 'done unto' people – without their active consent or participation. Indeed, poverty research has been described as the study of the 'have nots' by the 'haves'. Research, however, can be participation; it can involve the 'subjects of research', whether this is a geographical community or interest groups such as hospital patients, in actually undertaking the work themselves; developing their own questions, skills, knowledge and solutions.

In short, research is neither more, nor less, than enquiry which is systematic. Where it encourages participation beyond the narrow field of 'experts' it can be a powerful tool for community development and change.

AN INTRODUCTION TO RESEARCH METHODS

"There are no answers, only cross references" is the cynical view of research. In avoiding this pitfall, the crucial stage in developing a research project is in the planning. Ask some basic questions:

Is the research
- Quantitative? – It is important to 'quantify' the results in terms of numbers e.g. "for 360 patients treatment X in hospital resulted in no call back appointments in 6 months, as opposed to treatment Y, where monthly call back appointments were required for 272 patients"
- Qualitative? - more interested in gathering information on people's thoughts, feelings, ideas and suggestions than 'quantifying' results in numerical terms.
- A combination of qualitative and quantitative methods? - e.g. "....for 360 patients treatment resulted in..... Their views on this treatment, however, were......".

Why   is the research needed (to change services; to review the impact of policies; to assess community priorities) ?

What   is the research question?
methods will be used – and why?
needs to be in place to support participation (e.g. participant care costs etc) ?
will happen with the research findings ?

Who   needs to be involved (e.g. agencies, communities, particular interest or cultural groups) ?
will undertake the research ?
is the 'audience' for the research (e.g. local people, policy makers, professionals) ?

How	will the research be funded/resourced ?
	many people will be involved ?
	will information be gathered?
	will information be analysed?
	will feedback on progress be given?
	will the findings of the research be acted upon?
When	will the research start/finish?
	will progress (or difficulties) be reviewed?
	will findings be available?

These are very basic, but important and sometimes overlooked, questions. Asking them right at the beginning of a research project can save time and energy as the work evolves. For example, particular research methods may be adopted, but if there is no clear idea at the outset of how the information will be analysed the data gathered is likely to be of limited use. Who should be involved? The desirable answer may be 'everyone in the community' – but this is unlikely to happen, has major resource implications and would generate too much information to analyse effectively.

In short, research is the art of the feasible.It is, therefore, critically important to
- Set realistic goals
- Allocate adequate resources (money and time)
- Set achievable timescales (rushed research will lack quality but long timescales for research may risk people losing interest)
- Decide on a realistic level of participation.

The key to realising this is agreeing on the 'sample size' for the research -
- How many people need to be involved to give meaningful information about a community?
- How will the sample be selected; will it be purely random e.g. selecting 10 houses in each street)? will it be self selecting (only those people who volunteer)? or will it be structured (e.g. to reflect the age, gender and cultural mix of a particular area)?

The decision may well have major implications for how the findings of the research are received and their credibility. Interviewing 10% of people living on an estate may seem a strong basis for making research recommendations – but what if none of those involved are women, or from Black communities?

The issue of credibility of research findings will also influence the methods used – and the decision on who should undertake the work. External (professional/ academic) researchers may be seen as objective by external agencies, but may be expensive and lack a detailed understanding of local contexts and circumstances. Conversely, local people/service users undertaking research may lack external credibility, but already be familiar with the area or subject for research.

No one research method is perfect. All have their strengths and weaknesses. Where possible, use more than one approach, e.g. using focus groups and individual interviews to 'check out' questionnaire findings. Using a mixed 'methodology' is likely to strengthen both the research process and outcomes – but may not be feasible in terms of the time or resources available.

RESEARCH METHODS   Angus McCabe

INTRODUCTION

This section briefly outlines key research methods and identifies their relative strengths and weaknesses.

1. DESK RESEARCH / LITERATURE REVIEWS

Desk research/ literature reviews can offer a strong basis from which research projects can develop. Who has written about this issue before? What are the strengths and weaknesses of their approach? How can their findings inform our research? It may also provide baseline information from which the research project design can develop – for example, in terms of population profiles from census data.

The main strengths of desk research / literature reviews are:
- Providing baseline information
- Offering a means of 'checking out' research findings in terms of other people's research i.e. are there findings which support/challenge your own research
- Providing additional context information for the research –e.g. on cultural issues, local organisations etc.
- Enabling researchers to identify key participants/agencies in advance of more action research approaches.

The main weaknesses are:
- Time consuming
- Not participatory
- Data may be out of date (e.g. using the 1991 census)
- Findings may be out of date – the lapse in time from research to (academic) publication can be 18 months to 3 years
- Some literature may be difficult to access. In terms of community development, much of the information needed for research is in the, so called, 'grey' literature – namely, it has never been published and exists in annual reports, internal agency documents etc.

CASE STUDY

Local Health Visitors on an inner city estate identified, from service statistics, childhood asthma as a major health issue in the community. For fellow health professionals the reasons for this were clear: people smoked, houses were in a state of disrepair. In discussions with local groups, and by analysing their caseload, workers found that:
- Asthma was also a problem in households where adults did not smoke and where housing conditions were good
- Local residents identified high levels of pollution as a root cause of asthma.

Working with local groups, Health Visitors gathered information on the density of road traffic in the locality, levels of car pollution and transport use. Although this approach relied on 'desk research', rather than interviews or questionnaires, the locality was found to have the highest pollution levels in the city – pollution levels linked to the incidence of asthma.

The research then formed the basis for a community campaign on local traffic and transport policy.

RESEARCH METHODS   Angus McCabe

2. QUESTIONNAIRES

A standard approach to research is the use of questionnaires – either conducted 'in person' or via the post.

Questionnaires may include either, or both -

- Open questions; "What changes do you feel would improve your area?"
- Closed questions; where participants are asked to select from an agreed set of options e.g. This area could be best improved by
  - ✓ Traffic calming
  - ✓ A community centre
  - ✓ A play area
  - ✓ More buses.

Analysing the former can be difficult; responses may be so varied that identifying any patterns or trends in the replies becomes problematic. The latter approach may limit people's options or suggest that there are no alternatives to the statements provided.

The strengths of questionnaires are -

- Relatively easy to design
- Low cost
- Can, potentially, involve gathering information from a large number of people
- Are time limited (please respond by ………….).

The weaknesses are -

- Low response rates, particularly to postal questionnaires
- Respondents are self-selecting and may not be 'representative' of a particular community – in terms of age, gender, cultural background etc. This can 'skew' findings
- Can be difficult to analyse, particularly where 'open' questions are asked.

RESEARCH METHODS   Angus McCabe

3. INDIVIDUAL INTERVIEWS

Individual interviews are perhaps the most common research method. These can be

- Structured – where participants are asked a standard set of questions
- Semi-structured - where participants may be asked 'unscripted' questions, or given prompts, to explore particular views or answers in greater depth.

Individual interviews are an extremely useful method in gathering the views of different stakeholders and allow for a greater depth of information than may be possible in (postal) questionnaires.

The main strengths of individual interviews are -

- Confidentiality
- Exploring research topics in depth
- Allowing for a range of views to surface
- Drawing out participant's particular areas of expertise
- Allowing potential for follow up interviews as the research progresses.

The main weaknesses of individual interviews are -

- Fewer responses than focus groups/questionnaires
- Cost
- Time, especially if interviews are taped for accuracy and then transcribed
- Key people may not want to participate
- Lacking in focus/clarity, unless well conducted
- Difficulty in analysing information gathered.

Individual interviews can raise difficult or painful issues (e.g. research into domestic violence) after which the participants and researcher may need further support.

RESEARCH METHODS   Angus McCabe

4. FOCUS GROUPS

Focus group interviews are, as the title suggests, group sessions (usually of between 8 and 16 people) with a clear focus for discussion. Focus groups, ideally, involve people who may have diverse backgrounds but have something in common and some knowledge of the research topic; for example, they all use a particular service or are involved in a regeneration project.

The usual structure for a focus group is to start with an open question, e.g. For example; "How can we improve our services for the community?"

Then using a 'topic guide' of questions and prompts, exploring particular aspects of the general question: this might include, for example – improving transport services or education provision. Discussion is then led to a concluding, or summary point, which can be used as a priority setting exercise i.e. the top three service changes. It is important in arranging and designing focus group sessions to work towards an end point which builds consensus – whilst being able to record majority/minority views. As such they are a means of capturing more than the personal views expressed in individual interviews.

Focus group interviews usually require a facilitator – to keep the group's focus and co-facilitator – to taken notes, add prompts and reflect on the group dynamic. Ideally, sessions should be recorded – but this does require high quality equipment. Even then quieter voices may be lost and additional notes can be helpful.

The main strengths of focus group interviews are -

- They provide an opportunity to increase participation in the research process
- Generation of new/original ideas through group discussion
- Consensus building.

The weaknesses of focus group interviews can be -

- They become dominated by one or two participants
- People feeling uncomfortable talking in a group setting
- Cliques form; without clear ground rules, dissent and disagreement are generated rather than consensus
- Keeping a detailed record of the conversation can be difficult
- Substantial time is required to transcribe focus group sessions, if recorded.

CASE STUDY

A local GP Commissioning Group funded research into local views on primary care service plans. A priority area was mental health services provided by primary care staff. The research team adopted an action/participatory research approach which involved:

- Training local mental health service users and survivors in research techniques
- Developing focus group interview sessions with users and survivors
- Running peer-led focus groups with 84 service users
- Analysing the findings of group interviews, with appropriate support
- Preparing a report and presenting findings to the GP Commissioning Group.

This resulted in GPs revising their service plans to take full account of service user and survivor views. In short, whilst the professionals initially expected conflict and confrontation, consensus was built on the recognition that "service users are the other experts".

RESEARCH METHODS   Angus McCabe

5. OBSERVATION

Observational research is often used in exploring issues of how groups work – both in terms of inter-personal relationships and effectiveness, e.g. observing a playscheme session, a tenants group meeting or management session.

Care needs to be taken in recording observation sessions – both in terms of yielding useable research information and avoiding purely subjective commentaries. Various methods (see useful reading) have been developed for recording observational research sessions – including "logs" of how often people speak, to whom people do/do not speak and the overall group dynamic.

Whilst some researchers advocate recording sessions for accuracy, for others this technique of recording risks 'skewing' or altering participants 'natural' or usual behaviours.

The main strengths of observational research techniques are -

- They do not involve a 'research intervention' or agenda, unlike individual/ focus group sessions. 'Natural' behaviour is recorded
- They provide an opportunity to gather information not only on what happens (in groups) but how it happens
- They increase the potential numbers involved in the research process
- They may be appropriate in research with particular groups where other written-based methods could be inappropriate – e.g. working with young children.

The main weaknesses are -

- Just by being there, the researcher changes the group dynamic
- Methods of recording (e.g. video) may be seen as invasive
- Participants may be unclear about "what is being observed" – and why
- The validity of observational research can be questioned as "too subjective"

RESEARCH METHODS　　　　Angus McCabe

6. ALTERNATIVE APPROACHES

In recent years a range of alternative research techniques have been developed – as least, in part, to address issues of 'hard to reach' groups and in working with people with literacy problems.

Arts based research: using drawings, paintings and new media to enable people to express their views. Examples -

> Videos with young people on 'How I feel about my community',

> paintings of 'What I like/dislike about the area I live in',

> 'Happy/sad faces', used in evaluating services for children with learning difficulties

> 'My difficult mountain', diagrams used to identify factors which hinder (the 'up side' of the mountain and the 'down slope' suggesting ways in which such difficulties might be overcome)

Personal or community development

> mapping; simple maps – either of a geographical area or of a series of relationships - have been used to

- research patterns of service use: where people come from, and at what times

- analyse local networks: who/which agency is connected with who? How strong are the relationships – and how frequent are the connections?

> Diaries; providing research participants with a diary to record changing relationships, policy contexts and outcomes. For ease of analysis, these need to be structured around the research information required. For example, diary keepers may be asked to record

- What happened (e.g. meeting, phone conversation etc.)

- Why it happened

- Outcomes

- Feelings and observations.

The strengths of alternative approaches to research are -

> They may enable research projects to work with individuals and groups who could be alienated by more traditional/literacy based methods

> May promote engagement and participation

> Age appropriate and 'user friendly'.

The weaknesses of such approaches include -

> Credibility with external bodies

> A lack of consistency in the data collected (very few people draw or produce maps in a standard format – even when provided)

> Analysis may be difficult

> Reproducing maps, drawings etc. may be problematic in a final report.

RESEARCH METHODS: NOTES OF WARNING   Angus McCabe

INTRODUCTION

Participatory research can be a powerful tool for community workers. It can be a means of building movements and promoting personal and group development. It can, even, be fun. But – some notes of caution.

SOME NOTES OF CAUTION

- Allow adequate time for research planning and write up. This almost always takes longer than expected
- Make sure participants in the research process receive appropriate feedback: otherwise their future involvement is unlikely
- Ensure that the research methods are appropriate for the groups involved
- Allow time to pilot, or test, research methods (e.g. questionnaires) before using them for a full sample; this takes time, but saves it in the long run
- Do not rely on any one method to supply all the information required
- Review progress; is the research engaging with a range of communities, or just reaching 'the usual suspects'?
- Think through the reliability of sources of information. Whether using websites or individual interviews, agencies will bring their own agendas to the research process
- Do not falsify results, just to meet deadlines, personal or agency agendas
- Avoid gathering too much data. If there isn't the time, or resource, to analyse information, its collection is pointless
- Don't assume that the findings of small scale research can be generalised to wider communities. "Our survey of 10 people shows that this community wants….." is not a wise approach
- Ensure that the research findings will be acted upon. Or, if this is not possible, inform participants about the reasons why their views and thoughts have not brought about change.

And finally use community work values and principles in the research process. They are tools for development and change in which, despite the initially off-putting language, communities can participate, and through which people learn.

Do research with communities – not unto them!

FURTHER READING

There is a vast range of material available on research methods. For an accessible introduction to both research methods and issues, the following publications are helpful:

Bell, J (1987) **Doing Your Research Project**; Milton Keynes, Open University Press.

Hawkins, M, Hughes, G and Percy Smith, J. (1994) **Community Profiling; auditing social needs**.

RESEARCH: WRITING THE REPORT   Angus McCabe

INTRODUCTION

Writing the report is often seen as the final stage – in a research project, community audit or evaluation work. Thinking about writing it is, therefore, often left until the last moment. Report writing needs to be built into the initial stages of any project, when you need to decide:

- who the audience for the report is - the local community, practitioners or policy makers?
- how you can effectively reach that audience - does the report need to be produced in different ways or formats?
- how the data will be presented - statistical charts, case studies?
- whether the information gathered needs to be produced in different media – e.g. video, audio-tape, as well as a written report
- if you have allocated sufficient resources to the design, printing and production of the report
- if adequate time has been allowed for the actual process of writing
- whether the deadlines for production are realistic.

Nor, in reality, is the written report the 'final stage' of a project. How will the findings of the report be disseminated, promoted and publicised - simply by circulating the report or via the internet, in workshop sessions, at conferences or through other activities? Without an effective dissemination strategy, the results of even excellent reports may be lost – or may not have the requisite impact (at either a policy or practice level) you want to achieve.

THE REPORT STRUCTURE

There is no one standard format for report writing. Indeed, the content, style, design and layout will vary – depending on the intended audience. However, most include:

- A cover sheet; with a title, author's name, and credits to the funding agency (if appropriate)
- A contents page
- Acknowledgements; key people, or organisations which have assisted the work
- A summary of key findings and recommendations for action
- Background to the report; what it is about, why it is needed and its target audience
- Methods; a summary of how the research, evaluation or community audit was undertaken, who was involved and why.
- Findings; drawing on existing data (such as the census, or other written materials) and original research – e.g. surveys, questionnaires, interviews etc.
- Discussion; what are the implications of the findings? What are the strengths and weaknesses of the information gathered? Are there any gaps?

- Conclusions; outlining key themes and recommendations for action. How the recommendations for action have been arrived at and their implications – for local people, agencies and/or policymakers
- Appendices; depending on the audience, these may include references to the materials used (e.g. census, published books, web pages etc.), a list of those interviewed/contacted as part of the project, details of the organisation and authors who have produced the report, and additional materials (such as useful contact addresses etc.).

Some reports will include a foreword by some expert, local dignitary or politician, endorsing the findings and recommendations of the research/ evaluation.

The key, however, is the summary. If the report is aimed at 'busy people', it is likely that this is the only section they will read. It is <u>the</u> opportunity to get key messages across - if the full report is read, that's a bonus. This is an approach taken by, for example, the Rowntree Foundation, who produce relatively small quantities of the full text of the report commissioned, but circulate short 'findings' papers to a much wider audience.

PRESENTING INFORMATION

Perhaps the most difficult part of report writing is presenting the information gathered, the raw data, in ways which are both interesting and support the reports findings and recommendations. 200 local people may have been interviewed as part of a project evaluation or community audit – but were they 'representative' of the wider population?

This data can be presented in a number of ways:

➢ as bullet points In the main text

    200 local residents were interviewed during the research, of these
- 96 (48%) were men
- 36 (18%) were of African Caribbean origin
- 40 (20%) were of Bangladeshi origin
- 29 (14.5%) were of Pakistani origin

➢ as a pie chart

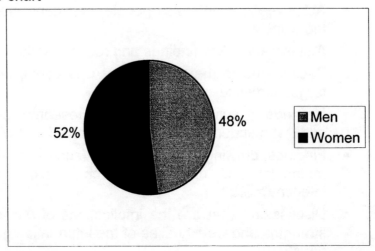

➤ as Bar Charts

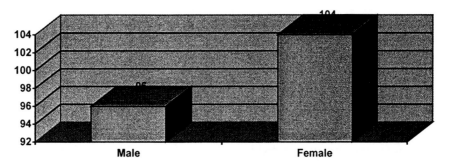

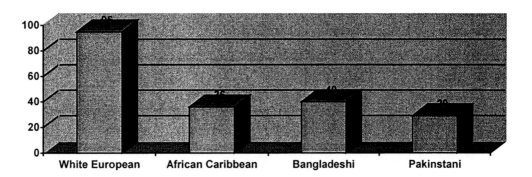

REFERENCING

Most reports will include references to, or use direct quotations from, other published works. These can be signposted in the text by citing the author and year of publication – for example:

> To quote from Smith's (1999) work on community regeneration . . . .
>   Or
> It has been argued (Smith, 1999) that community regeneration . . . .

Ideally, the page number for direct quotations should be provided.

Full references will then need to be identified in a reference section in the appendices. Again, there is no one set layout for referencing, although the information required is the same: namely

- authors (or editors) of the publication
- title of book
- edition (unless first edition)
- place of publication
- publisher.

The title of the book should be clearly identifiable, either by presenting it in a bold or italic typeface, or by underlining for example:

Smith, J. (1999) <u>Communities and Regeneration</u>; London, Oblivion Press.

Alternatively,

Smith, J. (1999); *Communities and Regeneration*; London, Oblivion Press.

When referring to articles from journals, additional information is required, although presented in a similar way, to include the title of the journal (as well as the article), the volume number and page numbers:

Smith, J. (1999) Communities and Regeneration; <u>Regeneration Studies</u>, Vol. 10, No. 3, pp115 -124.

SUMMARY

Writing takes time. Writing well takes practice. The key is to ensure that the information and messages contained in a report are conveyed

- clearly
- concisely
- in ways which are appropriate for the audience.

A real danger, especially when writing on a topic where you have expertise, is to slip back into jargon and assume that the audience will understand. If this is a concern, asking a 'lay person', with no (or limited) knowledge of the topic to review a draft of the final report can be helpful – as a check on both language and clarity.

Writing can be a lonely occupation. But for communities and community work it is an important task. How much good practice has been lost because it wasn't written up? How often have the voices of the oppressed been silenced – or kept in silence – because their narratives were never told?

Take up your pens! Switch on the computer! Whatever it takes.

COMMUNITY PROFILES Murray Hawtin

INTRODUCTION

Needs assessments, social audits and community profiles are terms that are often used interchangeably for a similar process. The broadest of these terms is community profiling. Community profiling has been defined as

> A comprehensive description of the needs of a population that is defined, or defines itself, as a community, and the resources that exist within that community, carried out with the active involvement of the community itself, for the purpose of developing an action plan or other means of improving the quality of life of the community.
>
> Hawtin et al. 1994

The concept of need is complex - who defines it? The residents themselves? politicians who allocate scarce resources? managers who ration them? or professionals trained to identify need? Also, some groups may well have needs that others do not; such as those with religious or disability needs. (See Percy-Smith 1996)

The notion of 'community' also means different things to different people. Here we may refer to a community either as

- a geographic area, such as a ward, an estate, a neighbourhood, or administrative area e.g. a school catchment area; or

- a group of people with a collective identity, shared interests or needs. This may be based on demographic factors, such as women, ethnic minority groups, children, elderly people, or those with other common bonds such as miners or members of a religious or political organisation.

HOW DO YOU UNDERTAKE A COMMUNITY PROFILE?

For the profile to be effective it is necessary to be clear about the reasons for undertaking it. These may include;

- to assess local needs, or to consider people's views and aspirations, in order to contribute to policy making, resource allocation, monitoring and evaluation, or improve service delivery (e.g. SRB and other renewal areas);

- to initiate a campaign in an area where the existence of unmet need or inadequate resources needs to be demonstrated (e.g. for a community action campaign);

- to make a funding bid requiring information on a community (e.g. to the local authority, lottery or European funding);

- to establish baseline information against which future developments can be measured (e.g. where monitoring is a criterion of funding);

- to pursue a community profile project as part of a broader community development strategy, i.e. "getting to know the area", in which case the process will be as important as the outcome. (Community development workers have used this technique for decades).

Community profiles give individuals, or a group of people, the opportunity to express their needs; they seek out the voice of people who are not normally listened to, and who may be excluded. They should aim to avoid assumptions made by traditional decision-making based more on conjecture and stereotypes. They achieve this through their content, the way they are undertaken and how people are involved in the process.

The Content
This may either cover the whole range of relevant policy areas i.e. health, housing, education, employment, transport, the environment etc. or focus on just one or two key issues. The source of the information that goes into the profile may rely solely on **existing data** (e.g. culled from the Census, health statistics, labour market statistics and reports compiled for other purposes by statutory or voluntary agencies), or **new data** collected specifically for this purpose (e.g. through surveys, interviews, group work, public meetings).

The Process
A community profile may be undertaken in a number of ways. To be effective and influential, however, the methods used need to be thorough and well thought out. An ideal process for undertaking a profile may involve all the following steps, (although in practice the procedure will change somewhat according to funding and other circumstances):

- **Preparing the ground:** Establish a steering group with local residents; initial planning; make contacts; learn from others' experiences; identify resources; develop a management structure. (Professional researchers or consultants may be engaged for all or part of the process).
- **Setting aims and objectives:** Stated clearly and based on overall purpose of the profile.
- **Deciding on methods:** Chosen to suit the objectives, they are flexible and include gathering primary as well as secondary data. Postal or door-to-door surveys are usually used as the main methods, often supplemented by in-depth interviews of key people and possibly resident focus groups.
- **Fieldwork:** Produce information-gathering tools, e.g. questionnaires; train those involved in data collection; collect existing and 'new' information; record and analyse information.
- **Reporting:** Write up fieldwork, produce, consult and amend draft profile; produce final community profile; disseminate research findings. It might be presented as a written report, an exhibition, a video, an oral presentation etc..
- **Action:** Consult over key issues, priorities, action to be taken; draft community action plan.

Community Involvement
The nature and level of resident involvement will be determined by the type of project. Although a community profile may be undertaken with minimal community involvement, the results will be better grounded and accurate, and subsequent decisions more relevant, the greater the level of involvement. Residents should, therefore, be involved in every stage and level from managing to undertaking the work. There is, potentially, no limit to the number of residents who can become involved, other than the practicalities of group decision making.

It is also useful to include people from different agencies and organisations as well as members of the community. Such representatives may include the statutory services (such as housing, social services, police, library, schools etc.); community and voluntary organisations (such as community development workers, tenants' or residents' group and other local special interest groups); and community representatives e.g. ward councillors, MPs, as religious leaders.

Resources Needed

Community profiling projects require certain resources - depending on the objectives, scale of the project and methods chosen. Although not all are essential, those needed may include:

- person power (including local volunteers and staff from agencies); in addition to managing and producing the profile, skills needed may include research design, computing, interviewing skills.
- Money
- Computer
- Photocopier
- Access to information
- Maps
- local contacts and good will.

Each profiling project needs to consider whether the resources are already available; if not, are they vital to the project; and, if so, where can they be obtained.

FURTHER READING, USEFUL ADDRESSES

Burton, P. (1993) *Community Profiling: A guide to identifying local needs*. University of Bristol.

Hawtin, M., Hughes, G., Percy-Smith, J. (1994) *Community Profiling: auditing social needs*, Open University Press, Buckingham.

Economic Foundation *21 ways to Engage people*

Economic Foundation *Participation Works*

Henderson and Thomas (1980) *Skills in Neighbourhood Work*

Percy-Smith, J. (ed.) (1996) *Needs Assessments in Public Policy*, Open University Press, Buckingham.

Save the Children (1996) *Community Profile Resource Pack Guide,* Glasgow Caledonian University and Save the Children, Glasgow.

COMPASS for Windows is a software package for community profiling designed by The Policy Research Institute. It brings together the main elements of primary research to form an integrated, user-friendly, affordable software package enabling community and voluntary organisations and other agencies to conduct social audits or community profiles in their local areas. It covers questionnaire design, data processing and data analysis:

For further information, demo version, or order form please contact: COMPASS. Enquiries on 0113 283 1747 or email compass@lmu.ac.uk

WORKING IN RURAL COMMUNITIES   Helen Bovey

INTRODUCTION

Community workers clearly need to understand the communities with which they work, and those working in rural areas are no exception.

DIFFERENT TYPES OF COMMUNITY

There are, clearly, striking contrasts between rural communities ~ we could describe them as post-industrial villages, commuter villages, remote upland villages and 'chocolate box' villages. Yet such superficial categorisations are deceptive and indeed misleading. They are stereotypes the rural community worker should avoid.

The nature of poverty in rural areas, for example, is slowly becoming better understood. We know that such poverty is commonly hidden, that about 25% households live in poverty, and that their poverty is linked to multiple forms of deprivation.

This serves to remind us that rural communities cannot be categorised in any simple fashion; rather, rural communities are complex and changing social systems. While there are differences across the United Kingdom and between communities in close proximity to each other, there are also marked differences within each community.

Every rural community is therefore unique, and community workers must attempt to identify what constitutes this uniqueness in each individual situation.

Each community will inevitably include a wide mix of people; it will be inhabited by a mixture of newcomers and indigenous people, of rich and poor, of all ages, and all dispositions towards community involvement. Community workers are faced with a spectrum of needs, relationships and contrasting abilities.

Rural community workers have a number of issues to take into account in their work, such as -

♦ Identifying of the unique features of each community.

♦ Working from a knowledge of some of the more common characteristics of rural communities:

- **Conservatism** ~ including low expectations, slow adjustment to change and limited experience of collective action

- **self help** ~ has a strong tradition but has been intertwined with issues about social relationships and leadership in villages

- **community based action** ~ is often not linked to the 'political' activity it commonly is.

♦ Understanding where power lies in a village. Power relationships are often complex.

- ◆ Being aware of the multi faceted nature of rural deprivation.
- ◆ Being prepared to work with individuals rather than groups ~ both where no groups exist or where they are dominated by powerful and repressive elites.

ISSUES FOR RURAL COMMUNITY WORKERS

Rural community workers are employed by a number of different agencies, from both the voluntary and statutory sectors. They will have all sorts of different job titles, but will also have many aspects of their work in common.

Big 'patches'.... rural community workers commonly cover large geographical areas, often a whole county.

Dispersed communities .... The communities with which they work may well be spread widely across their area, with little or no networking between them.

Road atlases.... good navigation is a skill of the rural community worker; travelling at night to villages for the first time is often 'exciting'.

Travelling...... there is inevitably a considerable amount of travelling involved. Many miles can be covered every day and good planning becomes part and parcel of the job so as to minimise the number of times the area is criss-crossed.

Poor support/voluntary sector infrastructure.......many rural community workers operate in areas where there are few, if any, other workers, and where the voluntary sector infrastructure is underdeveloped. This leads to multi-skilled workers, but the dangers of isolation and over-work are very real.

A mixed bag of work.......working with rural community groups can also mean having to advocate on their behalf at a strategic level. The workload is therefore varied, with workers operating at a wide range of levels.

The Archers.......so much time is spent travelling you have to occupy yourself somehow!

FURTHER READING

This section has been based on the work of Francis and Henderson. Interested readers should consult: Francis, D. & Henderson, P. (1992) *Working with Rural Communities*, London: Macmillan Press.

GROUPS DOING THEIR OWN CONSULTATION   Helen Bovey

INTRODUCTION

Consultation is an important activity for any group. It can have a number of purposes.

- To gather information about what is wanted from the group.
- To help the group select its priorities.
- To check progress of the group to ensure it is 'going in the right direction'.

Consultation is just one way in which groups will engage with their funders, beneficiaries, members and the wider community. It is therefore important to be clear what we mean by the term.

> Consultation is where a group asks appropriate stakeholders their views on a specific issue or question. They can ask this as an open question or offer a set of pre-determined options and seek views on all of them.

ISSUES TO CONSIDER

Good consultation needs careful planning, and there are a number of issues every group considering consultation should think about.

What is the question we are consulting on?

It might well sound obvious, but many consultation exercises do not have a clear focus. Always start by asking the question

> What do we want to know as a result of this consultation?

- ✓ Ensure the question is as simple as possible.
- ✓ Be clear that the people being consulted will have enough knowledge or information to respond adequately.
- ✓ Only consult when it is necessary to do so.

- ✗ Don't consult on too many issues at any one time.
- ✗ Don't ask unrelated questions.
- ✗ Don't consult too often.

Who are the stakeholders?

> Stakeholders are defined as " those who can affect . . . and those who are affected by . . ."

Each consultation exercise should start with an analysis of the stakeholders. A simple way of doing this involves using post-it notes, as follows:

- Each person in the group writes down who they think their stakeholders are. Each stakeholder is written on a separate post-it and the activity is done in silence.

- All the post-its are stuck on to large sheets of paper and the group starts discussing them.
- Similar and duplicate stakeholders are then grouped together in clusters.
- Each cluster is named.

The group uses this information to decide
- their priority groups for consultation
- the different methods they will use for each grouping.

How should we consult?

A whole range of consultation methods exist. For example:
- Questionnaires
- Informal interviews
- Interviews using a questionnaire format
- Face to face interviews
- Telephone interviews
- Videoed interviews
- Focus groups
- Village appraisals
- Planning for Real.

The method selected will depend upon a number of factors, such as the skills of the group members, funding and other resources, the nature of the stakeholders to be consulted, whether it is a 'one off' issue or ongoing, and the confidence of group members. It is also vital that they consider how the information will be analysed and the results collated.

Other considerations

Groups undertaking consultation need to consider the following additional points in order to make the exercise fully inclusive:
- Do materials need to be produced in other languages or other formats?
- What methods can be used that get round the need for a high level of literacy?
- How can the stakeholders be encouraged to respond?

THE SECRETS OF SUCCESS

✓ The people consulted need to see that the consultation results feed into the work of the group, policies etc.

✓ Groups should only adopt consultation methods that are appropriate for the stakeholder in question, and those they feel comfortable in managing.

✓ Acknowledge that consultation is not always easy; it is often fraught with difficulties and 'politics'.

✓ Consultation exercises should be evaluated ~ "did we learn what we wanted from this exercise" ~ in order for lessons to be learnt for the future.

MAKING A WIDE RANGE OF CONTACTS

Tom Taylor &
Nick Waterfield

INTRODUCTION

Most of us find it easier to be with people like us - or people who we are used to being with. Communication is generally smoother as there are shared understandings, we feel accepted and we know where we fit in.

However, making a wide range of contacts means getting out of our 'comfort zone', and building up relationships with people who, perhaps, we don't easily 'fit' with. So, why bother? It sounds like hard work, and it can be, but the benefits are huge in terms of information, support and developing your work.

GETTING STARTED

Who are you in contact with already?
Mapping out your existing contacts is the first step. Get a big piece of paper and start writing names of individuals, groups and organisations on it. Draw lines to show strong connections between them, and use different colour pens to add other details – e.g. where, when & why you have contact with them, or their links to wider networks. Then you need to think about these contacts – what do they have in common? Who are you not in contact with?

Create a clear record system
This could be your address book, a database or a card index. Whichever, it will quickly be out of date, so you need an easy and effective way of storing and updating your contact list.

Collect contacts
Get into the habit of writing down names and numbers, dates and venues as you go. Posters, leaflets, reports, minutes of meetings, stalls at events, local newspaper articles, 'For Sale' notice boards, bingo venues, Council consultation meetings, lists of community groups, internet groups and web pages etc. Once you have a diverse list of potential contacts, you need to meet them and build relationships.

BE THERE OR ELSE BE SOMEWHERE ELSE

Personal contact is vital to building relationships with a wide range of people. You should attend meetings, open days, events, parties, launches and Annual General Meetings – anywhere local people, activists, workers, volunteers might be - so that you can meet, in person, those you are trying to reach. The time before and after the meeting/event can be the most useful in terms of building relationships, sharing information and making contact with people who perhaps you hadn't planned to. Arrive early, and don't rush off at the end, if you can help it.

You can arrange to visit Community centres, offices, youth clubs, mosques etc – just to say hello. If you want to structure this, perhaps you could do some community profiling work. Each place tends to develop a culture, and networks, of its own, and so can be a way of making contact with new (to you) people and groups.

Accidentally on purpose

Create space for accidental meetings – just bumping into people. Conversations about what's going on with someone on the street/in the shop etc. can lead to new contacts, in a totally random way. So, try to use local or cultural facilities (cafes, libraries, shops), walk or cycle instead of using the car, and catch local buses. These conversations are so different from those in 'meetings' - they are more natural and can spark off new ideas for action.

> "If you always do what you've always done, you'll always get what you've always got."

If you've got a clear routine, take some time to vary it – and create the possibility of new accidental meetings, and new perspectives.

USE 'EM OR LOSE 'EM

Developing relationships

Meeting people, sharing information, and getting them in your address book is only the start! Developing relationships with a wide range of people is the really important bit.

Make sure you invite people to your events and meetings, where it is useful to both you and them – and let them know about it even if it's not really aimed at them. How you contact different people will be different – there are cultural, professional and personal factors to take into account. You may be able to phone one person up for a general chat, whereas another person may find that an irritating waste of time, and would prefer a type-written letter or memo.

Generally, though, it's good to talk. Ask your contacts for help with your work or projects, and return the favour when you can. Send out your publicity to them, and respond to their publicity material. Give generously of your time and support when you can.

Good relationships with a range of people – different ages, sexes, roles, cultures, backgrounds, abilities and experience – is a resource. It requires maintenance, but provides advice and feedback from a whole range of perspectives, so that you can develop yourself and your work. This might not be comfortable all the time, but it's worth it.

GUIDELINES FOR COMPILING A DIRECTORY

Updated by
Ros Chiosso

INTRODUCTION

Directories of information are invaluable to community workers and activists: for instance, you may choose to compile a directory of what is happening in your neighbourhood to advertise the range of groups and services available.

The purpose of this paper is to provide some guidelines on the gathering and handling of information when compiling a directory of organisations.

You might also want to consider designing your own website – this is not only an opportunity to publicise your organisation / project / agency / group, but also to network with many other groups. The disability movement, for example, has produced some stunning material on the Internet on rights networks, etc. Help in designing a website is often available - contact your local community computing project.

PRELIMINARIES

1. Clarify your purpose in preparing a directory. Traditionally a directory is a reference document, providing a limited amount of detailed information on a large number of organisations. The prime purpose is often the same as a telephone directory, namely to enable people and organisations to contact each other. Recently directories have tended to include reference information about the geographical area or subject covered as well.

You need to answer these questions:
   - Why do we want/need to produce the directory?
   - Who are we seeking to inform?

2. Define the information you wish to include in the directory .
   - What range of organisations do you wish to include? - all voluntary organisations or more limited categories (e.g. local political organisations, sports, cultural, education, leisure, youth, religious, community, campaigns, branches of national organisations, advice, the local authority, local industry etc.)
   - What geographical area is the directory going to cover? – neighbourhood, town/city, borough, county etc.

3. Check that a directory does not already exist, or that someone else is not already compiling the same directory. Try to obtain a copy of any relevant directory/list, whether current or out of date - this will provide a starting point when collecting information later. It is also useful to study some examples of directories for different areas or subjects. These may provide some useful ideas for designing the directory - particularly on the question of layout.

DESIGNING THE DIRECTORY

Designing the directory should be done before any attempt is made to collect the information, except for that in step 3 above. Failure to design and plan adequately will inevitably lead to considerable waste of time and effort.

1. Review steps 1 and 2 above, and redefine or expand as necessary.

2. Decide the form of presentation of the directory. It will then be possible to store the information in the required form. Three variables are usually used, namely, alphabetical order, subject order, and geographical area. In the case of the last two, these are usually combined with alphabetical order within the subject or geographical division. If alphabetical order is adopted, a subject index ought to be included. A geographical index could be optional, depending on the purpose and size of the area covered by the directory.

3. Decide the organisational details to be included in each entry . The following details might be included:
   - Title of organisation
   - Objectives of organisation
   - Activities
   - Number of members
   - Types of membership
   - Regular meeting (times and place)
   - Address and telephone number of office/contact
   - Name of contact
   - Means of financial support
   - Status of organisation - charity , friendly society etc.

Avoid personal names, addresses and telephone numbers wherever possible, as these will be the details which will change most frequently; or make it clear that they are personal telephone numbers, and give the date they were last updated.

4. Decide on the form of publication and layout you wish to use. When collecting information on the organisations, it will save a considerable amount of time if you use a form or database based on the chosen layout. It will enable you to check easily if you have all the required information, and be far easier to transcribe.

5. Decide on any additional reference information you wish to include. It is advisable to collect and prepare any reference information ready for printing before the information on organisations is collected.

6. Because information goes out of date so quickly, you must consider the problem of updating even before you collect the information. Basically you have two choices:
   - Produce a cheap booklet which will serve your purpose for the time being, and can be replaced every two or three years. This option is preferable for directories which cover a narrow band of information or those which are aimed at the general public.

   Produce a directory in loose leaf format for which updating sheets will be provided. This option is preferable for limited circulation directories mainly used by key people.

PLANNING

Compiling a directory involves a considerable amount of work and, wherever possible should be undertaken by a group rather than an individual.

1. Identify those likely to have the information required, and those who are in contact with the types of organisations you wish to include in the directory. Likely sources of information on organisations include:

   - Local Authority Sources: The Local Authority is required by law to maintain a register of local charities. The information is supplied by the Registrar of Charities. The register is open to the public and is likely to be kept in either the Chief Executive Department or Legal and Administration Department.

   - Libraries usually maintain various indices/lists of organisations, and frequently produce forthcoming events sheets.

   - Education Departments: Youth and Community service sections will usually know of most, if not all, local youth organisations.

   - Parent/Teacher Associations.

   - Leisure/Community Divisions of Councils.

   - Social Services (Under 8's Sections) are required to maintain registers of childminders, playgroups and nurseries. They are also likely to have a reasonable knowledge of groups of users.

   - Public Relations Departments may also be helpful.

   - Co-ordinating bodies usually know about organisations within their own subject area - Councils of Voluntary Service, Trades Councils, Community Relations Councils, Play Councils, Age Concern, etc.

   - Local directories: don't forget the Telephone directory and Yellow Pages - try the local reference library for both.

   - Some likely individuals include: local activists, community workers, trade union officials, newspaper reporters and religious leaders. Do not overlook the caretakers of local meeting places, and local publicans.

   - Local newspapers, both news stories and the diary column: remember, the further back you go, the more likely the organisation is to have folded.

   - Internet sources – the web has a vast range of data – local, regional, national and international. You can search for a specific subject, or follow links from one website to another.

   - Other sources: it may be necessary to trace an organisation through it's national or regional body.

   There generally is no shortage of information, it just takes a lot of hard slog.

2. Decide how information is to be stored during compilation. If it can be put on to a computer, it will make updating much easier.

3. Allocate tasks and responsibility for contacting each identified source - compiling a directory is time consuming enough without wasting effort. It will help if a central register is maintained.

4. Once all the design and planning is complete, set a time limit for collecting the information on organisations. Try and ensure that the directory is printed and distributed as soon as possible after the time limit. If you need to raise money, raise it before you collect your information. Directories inevitably include inaccuracies as soon as they are printed, but compilers should make every effort to keep them to a minimum.

5. Pay attention to physical appearance. Something attractive and easy to read is more likely to be used.

Check all plans and designs very carefully; mistakes and omissions not rectified at the planning stage can lead to a lot of wasted time, effort and paper.

SOME FINAL POINTS

1. When collecting information on organisations, you should always check the it with the organisation concerned. You should also check that they don't object to being included in the directory.

2. Proof read the directory carefully to check for any mistakes or inaccuracies before sending it to the printer. If you notice any mistakes after printing, issue an 'erratum', or 'stop press', if necessary. Wrong telephone numbers can be very frustrating.

3. Few directories can be fully comprehensive. Don't try to achieve the impossible – omissions can always be included in a supplement or new edition.

4. If you intend to update the directory, ask organisations to inform you of any inaccuracies, changes and omissions. It is helpful to maintain an original copy on which all changes are recorded ready for the next edition.

5. State prominently when the information was collected.

6. Do not overlook the distribution of the directory – it won't get up and walk to people. As much effort should be put into distribution as into compilation.

COMPILING A RESOURCE LIST

Updated by
Val Harris

INTRODUCTION

The purpose of this technique is to provide a quick guide to resources, facilities, equipment, suppliers etc. for local groups. Lists are a straightforward way of having information to hand when it is needed.

STEPS TO TAKE

STEP 1 : Decide the subject of the resource list (or lists) you wish to compile and who the list is aimed at - i.e. who you are seeking to provide with information and whether or not they are likely to need it; if not, why bother?

Possible subjects for resource lists include:
- local information/advice services
- local meeting places
- halls for hire
- printing services
- places where equipment may be used, borrowed, or hired (e.g. video, printing, projectors, loop systems)
- resource centres where you can get access to computer
- local entertainers
- companies prepared to donate waste materials for use in playgroups/craft groups
- summer projects
- sports equipment
- groups prepared to enclose circulars in regular mailings
- local trusts, or other sources of funding etc.

STEP 2 : Identify those who have the information you want. There are likely to be two categories -
- the providers/owners of resource
- local organisations who have already used the service or resource.

Decide whether you need to approach both categories, and how you wish to collect the information (personal visiting, telephone, or postal survey).

STEP 3 : Decide on the information you require - usually:
- what is available and where it is available
- conditions upon which resource is available
- cost/charges
- who to contact to arrange use: include name, address and telephone number
- any comments (optional)
- RECORD THE DATE THE INFORMATION WAS CORRECT.

These are the minimum requirements (see example for a longer list). Draw up a checklist of the information you require for each entry on the list.

STEP 4 : Decide when you will reach a point of decreasing return, i.e. when further effort to identify further resources is not warranted. Lists don't need to be fully comprehensive to be useful; you just require enough for people to be able to sort out their needs quickly.

STEP 5 : Decide how you are going to produce and distribute the information once it has been collected.

STEP 6 : Collect and collate information.

STEP 7 : Before printing the final lists, information should be checked with the owners or providers of the resource if the information was not originally obtained from them. CHECK FINAL DRAFT AND ARTWORK FOR ANY INACCURACIES. Small details are important; wrong addresses or telephone numbers will not please anyone. Finally, ensure that the date on which the information contained in the list was correct is prominently displayed.

STEP 8: Produce and distribute lists.

Comments:
- While it is possible for a single individual to prepare a resource list, the more people involved, the less work is required from individuals - as long as it is co-ordinated!
- The experience should be shared to develop the skill in the community; if the skill is not shared, groups will be dependent on the provider. It is important that others are able to prepare resource lists when and as the need arises.

SAMPLE CHECKLIST FOR RESOURCE LIST OF LOCAL MEETING PLACES

- Name & address of meeting place
- Owner
- Person responsible for hiring/booking
- Type of premises
- No. of rooms and capacity (number of people) of each room
- Charges per hour for each room
- Can disabled people obtain easy access/are there suitable toilets ?
- Is there a crèche/playgroup ?
- Any restrictions on the use of the premises – e.g. no music, bingo, alcohol
- Hours available
- Is the meeting place already heavily booked ?
- How much notice is required for booking ?
- Facilities

- Parking	- Charges
- Cooking facilities/ refreshments	- P.A. System
- Toilets	- Number of tables and chairs
- Stage	- Black out
- Storage space	- Cleaning

NETWORKS
Alison Gilchrist

INTRODUCTION

Networks are based on informal membership. They assume that all members are equal (though this is not usually the case in practice). They do not have a hierarchical structure, and usually have no formal policies. Their main purpose is to share information, ideas and support. Participation is optional.

- Networks may have officers and regular meetings of the members, but they don't have to. They may act as a consultative body to another authority, and also elect individuals to represent their perspective to some other body.

- Networks may operate on an "ad hoc" basis, coming together to organise a particular event or activity. However this is not seen as their primary purpose, which is rather a response to a specific situation, or shared need/desire.

- Networks may develop a policy position on some issue and advise members on this, but decisions are not seen as binding.

- Usually networks simply provide space to debate and reflect on difficult, or new, areas of policy or legislation.

- Networks do not always have a common identity, nor any resources, except those contributed by members. The individual members may not be aware of each other's existence.

Networks operate as "horizontal" channels of communication within communities. Sometimes they might have a co-ordinating node, which collates and disseminates information, but this is not always the case.

USES OF NETWORKS

Working with people in informal ways and linking them into existing networks, or helping them to set up new ones, can help people to:

- develop support and solidarity amongst themselves
- acquire and promote a positive identity
- share skills, knowledge and resources
- develop a common purpose, which may not be represented by a formally agreed goal, but can provide a strategic framework
- co-ordinate their approach to problem solving or campaigning
- represent a collective and specific point of view.

HOW MIGHT THE WORKER USE OR CREATE NETWORKS ?

Looking at networks as a water system model, the worker could be seen as a conduit, pump or tap.

Conduit : The worker is simply a channel, or provides channels through which members of a network are kept in contact with each other. This might be through a Newsletter, or the worker's own brain.

Pump :   The worker organises and encourages people to stay in touch with each other; e.g. by organising meetings, or deliberately arranging channels of communication which might not otherwise exist or be constricted. This acknowledges that the flow of information may not be uniform through a network; e.g. to people on the periphery or people whose language or mode of communication differed.

Tap :   The worker actively feeds in information and ideas to the network, and injects enthusiasm and support from time to time.

Methods and skills of networking:

Mostly these involve informal gathering and passing on of information. They include structured conversation, active listening, empathising, understanding, introducing ideas and information, researching, eavesdropping, organising and facilitating.

Networking usually takes place between individuals; or in large, semi-structured groups, where roles are not clearly defined.

PROBLEMS AND ISSUES

As a result of the informality and unstructured nature of networks, confusion can arise over the status of collective decisions, especially when these are controversial. The looseness of membership can lead to undemocratic procedures and cliques forming. Inequalities of access to the network, especially when these are determined through casual, occasional and informal contacts, can lead to information not always reaching the parts of the network that might need it most. There are also issues around the confidentiality and general reliability of information.

CASE STUDY: THE BURLEY NETWORK: an example of a   Penny Bainbridge
multi-agency collaboration

About 5 years ago the Burley Network was set up to bring together all the statutory, voluntary and community organisations working in Burley, Hyde Park and South Headingley – an inner-city area in North West Leeds.
Membership is open to any agency which works and is based in the area. There are currently 70 members, and meetings are held every 6 weeks. There are a number of sub-groups where specific work can be discussed, such as young people, older people, housing, health and education.
The aims of the network are to :
- share information so as to reach potential clients
- collaborate on plans so as to avoid duplication of services and activities
- work together on joint projects and initiatives.

A core group is elected to draw up agendas and carry out other management tasks.

USING THE INTERNET   Julie Pryke

INTRODUCTION

Many communities and individuals are beginning to have access to the Internet or 'World Wide Web' (www), but not everyone is sure about how to get access to it, how to use it, how much it costs and how useful it is.

This brief chapter is designed to help you find your way around the web. It looks at how it can be used for information gathering to support campaigning or funding projects you may be involved with. The main ideas are given as a series of points to make it easier to use. They can be taken as a starting point for discussion within your group, or be used by someone on their own.

HOW DO WE GET ACCESS TO THE INTERNET?

To get access to the Internet you need a PC with a modem attached (inside, or added on), a telephone line and some money (it needn't be a large amount) to pay for the telephone bill and also sometimes for the time you are 'on-line' (i.e. using the Internet service). For communities it is often possible to use a machine belonging to a local agency or organisation, such as the community centre or youth club. Otherwise, if you haven't got your own machine you can buy time on one at a library, a Community Resource Centre or an Internet Cafe.

HOW DO WE GET STARTED?

Organisations that run the Internet are known as 'Service Providers'. Many of them give away free CDs which will allow you onto the web using their company.

A well-known example of this is 'Freeserve'. It makes no charges for the time users are on-line, so they are only paying for the cost of a local rate phone call. This is great; BUT there are one or two problems with using them and similar 'free' providers. Most of them charge at quite a high rate for advice should you have any problems - e.g. 50p per minute (in 1999) ,and you can be on their helpline for 20 minutes or more before the problem is solved. Another difficulty is that they have attracted so many users they can be very slow to connect you to the website you want - this again means extra costs on the phone bill.

Some service providers charge you according to the time you are on-line -you may choose either to limit your access to say 3 hours per month or have unlimited access at a higher cost. Some service providers are now offering a further rate - unlimited use, including the cost of phone-calls, so that you only have one fee to pay each month. Resource Centres, libraries and Internet Cafes usually have a particular service provider linked to their machines already. It may be a local provider, such as Legend in Bradford, a national one, such as Demon, or an international one, e.g. Microsoft & AOL. Hotmail is a useful service available through service providers - it means that once you have your own 'hotmail address' you can send or pick up e-mails from wherever you are world-wide and not just your usual PC - just like having a letter re-directed.

ONCE I'M ON-LINE WHAT DO I DO?

If you use a PC frequently you may not find it too difficult to get started. Others may find it takes a little longer to get used to the system (and to typing!). It is quite possible to teach yourself how to use it, and many service providers offers a tutorial or lesson to get you started.

The secret is not to be afraid of the machine. It's important that lots of you can use it, especially if the PC etc. belongs to the group. If only one person learns, it can become their 'job' and they become the 'expert' the group relies on. If they're sick, or leave, you might not know how to get the information you need. If they are in a dispute with others in the group they could use, damage or destroy precious work before they leave. If they're good at what they are doing they may not want to share the machine - but you should all have fun, shouldn't you? If people rely on one person too much that person may get fed-up with always being in demand.

♦ **How do we learn how to use the Internet?** This bit is the easy bit!
- Get the free start-up disc from a service provider
- Get on a free course with the local community centre or college
- Ask someone who already knows how to do it to show you what to do
- Use group funds to pay for training
- Visit an Internet Cafe and ask for help.

♦ **Once you have an e-mail address** you can practice your skills without worrying. It's usual (and cheaper) to write an e-mail before you go onto the Internet ('off-line') and it's possible to send it to yourself so you can see what happens and whether you've got it right.

♦ **So how do you use the 'World Wide Web' (www)?**
The web is like an encyclopedia, or information bank, with sounds, pictures and fun added.

Try using a 'search-engine' such as Yahoo, Hotbot, or Ask Jeeves and type in the word 'playschemes'. You will see that it finds you lots of sites which have information for you. Click on the address (the www. name bit) of the one that interests you and it will show you that page. Don't read all of them - there will be 2001 or more – the first couple will be enough for you to practise with. Remember - it's costing money - set an alarm clock for 15 or 30 minutes as a reminder. 'Adult' sites can be blocked so that people can't read them through your site.

♦ **Once you've practised you can use the Internet to**
- get information for your group
- establish links with others concerned with the similar issues
- get expert advice.

There are more details in 'Using the Internet for Campaigning', Section 8.

FURTHER READING

A cheap beginners guide such as one in the 'Dummies' series is very useful and easy to follow. The main secret is not to be afraid of it - and enjoy it!

Section 4

Getting Started

ACCESS ISSUES
Ruth Malkin

INTRODUCTION

Community Work is all about bringing people together. But this is sometimes the most difficult thing to do. Meeting the access needs of everyone in a diverse community seems at first to be an impossible task. When you attempt to bring people together, the first thing to ask yourself is: Do you really need to meet?

Most people think that physically meeting is the only way of going about things. Given the advances in technology over the past 20 years, this is no longer the case.

Physically getting people to buildings, and then into them, can be almost impossible. If your community has people with physical impairments, people of varying religious backgrounds, people who do not have access to cars and people with sensory impairments – i.e. if it is like any other community anywhere else in the country - then you may want to think of other non-physical ways of bringing them together.

WHAT ARE THE OPTIONS?

E-mail is the obvious way of coming together without meeting. Setting up a chat room is a good alternative to holding a meeting. Setting up a community Web sites can also be a good way of keeping people informed. However, not every member of the community has access to the technology. People without access to such technology could be encouraged to visit local E-centres to link in. Find out where the Internet cafes and the libraries with internet connection are in your area, and whether they are accessible.

Phone trees are another way people can get in touch with one another. Or telephone conferences. Or letters. Or through a community magazine that is owned by everyone, and to which everyone can contribute. Remember, though, that you will need to have large print copies of the magazine, tapes, and translations – meeting everyone's access needs through print can be very time consuming.

If you do need to meet up physically, the first thing to do is to make sure that your venue is accessible to everyone, including physically disabled people, people with children, people with sensory impairments, and people who don't read English.

A good access audit starts outside the meeting room.

- How close is the room to public transport links?

- What number are the buses do people need to take, and how frequent are they?

- Do they this coincide with the time of your meeting?

- Are the buses on the route at the time low-floor ones accessible to wheelchair users and parents with buggies?

- Are there any car park facilities?

- If so can some of the spaces be marked for the sole use of orange badge holders?

- Does the route to the building have dropped kerbs? (Lowered sections of kerb are essential for wheelchair users to get to a building, but they often have cars parked over them, or are on one side of the road, but not on the other.)

SUMMARY

Before using a meeting room for the first time, it is essential to do a thorough access audit of the area around the building and the building itself (see the Access Check List in the Appendix).

If you are really determined to bring the community together, then perhaps the best advice is to try and do a bit of everything - have physical meetings, telephone conferences and E-meetings - and make sure that housebound people without the technology are contacted regularly by phone or post.

ONE WAY TO SET UP A COMMUNITY GROUP

Updated by
Ros Chiosso

INTRODUCTION

A variety of people in a community feel strongly about an issue and they, and/or others they know in the community, want to come together to pursue their shared interest. This section suggests a way that will enable such people to form a community group.

DECIDING WHETHER TO SET A GROUP UP?

STEP 1

Identify the issue which has some importance within the community . Be clear about its potential in the development of that community .

STEP 2

Gather the names of people in the local community who might be interested. For example, you might go to key people in the community and ask them about those whom they know could be approached about the issue. Ask the people who give you lists to also ask the individuals they have listed whether you, the community worker, can pay them a visit. Ask them to explain who you are. Try to ensure you contact a broad cross-section - remember young people are part of the community too!

STEP 3

Go and knock on the door of those listed. Spend time discussing the issue, and be clear about the interest each person has in it. Notice how they express their feelings about it, which aspect they focus on and whether there are other issues they feel strongly about.

STEP 4

Evaluate all the information. Get it written down. Look at it. Go back to the people who originally provided the lists. Discuss with them how a group might come together. Discuss what role you will play and what role they will play.

STEP 5

Go back to your employer. Explain this is the direction you intend to go in, and why.

STEP 6

Make a decision whether to go ahead or not. If you decide not to go ahead, get back to all those people and explain why. If you decide to go ahead let people know.

STEP 7

Deciding to go ahead

Make a personal visit to all the potential people for the group telling them that you are calling a meeting (date, time, place). Say who else is going to be there and what it is going to be about. Make sure you have arranged a room and that refreshments are laid on. Be pretty clear that the meeting is going to be productive. Depending on the type of group, you may want to centre it around a speaker, or outsider, to take the edge off things and also ensure that the group members are not simply trying to talk amongst themselves at the first meeting. It can be valuable to have someone from an established group with similar aims who can demonstrate that it is possible to set up successful groups, and also talk about any potential pitfalls ahead. A few days before the first meeting put a note through doors, as a reminder.

STEP 8

Hold your meeting.

SETTING UP AN ASIAN YOUNG MEN'S GROUP

Emma
Manners

INTRODUCTION

As two female white youth and community workers we were approached by a group of young Asian men who wanted us to work with them. Our initial contact with the group was through running an information drop-in at a local community centre - The Cardigan Centre, based in Hyde Park, inner city Leeds that is well used by the Asian Community. The Cardigan Centre is a local charity, and we are employed as youth information and support workers.

DEVELOPING A GROUP

Through the relationship developed in these open drop-in sessions the young men wanted to take the work further, and for regular, closed sessions to be run by ourselves with activities planned between ourselves and the young men. We felt that there was a sufficient need to justify the setting up of a closed group as there was no other appropriate youth provision in the community. A number of issues (that needed addressing) were raised in the open sessions and, most importantly, the young men were stating a need.

For the group to get to this initial stage of wanting a closed group run by ourselves there were several stages that the relationship between us as workers and the young men had to go through;

- The young men initially accessing the information service. We are based in a building that is used by the Asian community.
- The young men feeling confident and comfortable in the environment to ask for information relevant to themselves.
- The workers and the young men developing a relationship of trust.
- The young men having the confidence in the workers to trust the confidentiality of the project.
- The young men having the confidence in the workers' ability to set up a closed, confidential group that was for them and the issues particular to them.

ISSUES TO CONSIDER

The above issues, and the skills used by the workers, are transferable to building relationships with any groups. However, in setting up the group, points we needed to consider were:

- Do not make any assumptions about religion or culture.
- Do not assume that all the group are of the same, or different religion or culture. In this particular case there were Muslim and Hindu young men.
- When setting the time for the group, check out the times of any mosque or temple meetings they may attend.
- The location of group meetings is very important: we were fortunate that we are based in a building that is a safe and comfortable environment for young Asian people.

- It is always important to have confidentiality policies in place, but in our experience it was particularly relevant to this group.

SUMMARY

Of the difficulties we encountered the main one was being questioned by other community workers as to the appropriateness of two female white workers working with a group of young Asian men. Our main justification here was that we were approached by the young men themselves, and they believed us to be appropriate to meet their needs. We were acting as community workers meeting a stated need from the community. We did ask the group their reasons, and these came down to confidentiality and the feeling that they were listened to by us.

The importance and validity of this group is based on the fact that it was a community group that itself identified a need. It found a way of meeting that need through The Cardigan Centre's support and the workers' group facilitation.

This group ran successfully to a natural end, but was the start of a rolling programme for several groups of young Asian men that came to us to be part of the group work process.

DEVELOPING NEIGHBOURHOOD GROUPINGS

Updated by
Ros Chiosso

INTRODUCTION

A community worker may find that a small local group represents a very large area. Or a central group in a neighbourhood may not be representing and articulating issues that affect smaller groups and minorities in that neighbourhood (e.g. a block or a street). Alternatively a central group may be swamped by many local concerns and unable to make headway on more general issues affecting the neighbourhood.

One strategy is to encourage the formation of smaller groupings representing blocks, or streets, or other natural units in the neighbourhood. The idea is that block, or street groups would get on with their own business, taking the load off the central group, and also be represented on the central group to take up shared issues.

Naturally, local situations vary and the development of 'component parts' can be done to a greater or lesser extent depending on the nature and needs of the situation. There are many ways in which a community worker can encourage people to become involved, and this section outlines a few approaches.

ENCOURAGING PEOPLE TO BECOME INVOLVED

Finding individuals

The situation may best be met by simply finding individuals who are prepared to act on behalf of a block or a street, without necessarily being elected, or formally proposed, by their neighbours. Likely people can be found, for example:

- from people who are already active in the neighbourhood
- by developing other activities or events, such as a play scheme and looking out for 'new' active people in a neighbourhood
- by ascertaining from 'professional' workers such as teachers, social workers, etc. - if there are people they know who might be willing to represent their street, or block
- by door knocking etc.

Creating a structure for individuals to work in

The new grouping of individual representatives may become a subgroup or subcommittee of the existing central group, working on specific issues. For example, on a council estate this might be taking up repair and maintenance problems affecting particular blocks.

DEVELOPMENT

- A central committee is formed from a public meeting. Once a group is well-established, or already has skilled members, it will then elect representatives to the central committee.

- The members of this committee go around the area with leaflets, doorknocking at a time when most people are in. They do this on several occasions, each time focusing on a particular natural area within the estate or neighbourhood.

- The leafletting/doorknocking announces a meeting to be held fairly soon, giving the time and place.

- Hopefully, small meetings will take place; someone from the central group or committee makes the purpose of the meeting clear; from this meeting it should be possible to form street or block committees or grouping.

- Block, or street committees are asked by the central group if they would like to send someone along to the central group as a representative.

Setting up block, or street meetings

Another option is to -

- spend time finding out who is well-liked in a block and also genuinely wants to see a block, or street group formed

- hold the first meeting in this person's house

- involve at least 2-3 residents in selecting a time and date for this meeting

- make the date sufficiently far in advance, so that you and any others willing to help organise it can contact all the residents personally

- give the people to whom you talk sufficient notice of the meeting

- don't worry if not everyone can make it

- put a simple reminder through letter boxes a day or so before the meeting

- It might be a good idea to give people a number they can call at to say that they unable to make it but would be interested in future meetings.

Note:
- Where a central grouping already exists in a neighbourhood it is crucial, in developing component parts, that this central group agree to this happening and, if possible, to actively involve themselves in helping it to happen.

- Different approaches reflect different objectives. e.g. one approach may be more to do with the 'more effective take up of issues using pressure group tactics' while another may be to do with 'developing a sense of community and the maximum use of local resources'.

THOUGHTS ON CONDUCTING A MEETING

The need to develop block, or street groupings may be to create better relations between people in the block, or street, rather than take up particular 'external' issues. Thus the meetings may need to contain informal conversations (so that people get to know each other) as well as a short business session.

People may feel a strong desire to share negative stories and feelings with each other. If this develops, the meeting could end up promoting and reinforcing a greater level of depression. The heart of the meeting should be the exchange of good information between neighbours; connecting the needs and concerns of some with the resources and suggestions of others. To build towards this it may be necessary to start meetings on a positive note - one way is to ask people to introduce themselves and say something good which has happened since the last meeting.

Where individuals are keen to follow up an interest or concern they may want to form a small group of volunteers to work on it prior to the next meeting; one of the volunteers may act as a convenor.

Meetings in the block, or street, can be held at different houses/ flats so that people get to know one another better.

MAKING THE LINKS   Val Harris

INTRODUCTION

One of the skills people using a community work approach soon develop is that of making links between individuals and between groups. This may be the beginning of something new developing – finding out that there are a few individuals concerned about the same issue, and getting them to come together to take some action. It may be a way of strengthening existing groups by feeding in potential new members who wouldn't normally come to anything but, if there was someone else on their street who would tell them more about it and then take them to the first meeting, then they might get started.

Making links between groups may be a way of sharing expertise and stopping people from re-inventing wheels; often visits to a more established group are used to find out how they started, or kept going. There may be opportunities for some joint work or involvement in a partnership deal.

In this sheet I suggest some ways to make and maintain effective links.

INDIVIDUALS

We know that we live in a time when individual privacy is all important; that people may want to find out what is going on, but they don't have family networks to help them because they are new to an area - its scary to walk into a room full of strangers; they may be very busy with their own lives, or think they have nothing to offer.

We can think of many reasons why people don't respond to posters and leaflets inviting them to events. So what can you do?

- Use all sorts of opportunities just to introduce yourself and say what you do - in queues for the Post Office, shopping, outside schools, in places of worship, attending public events

- Try to find out what interests them

- Introduce them to one other person who you are with when you see them again

- Invite them to a small event and offer to take them with you

- Make sure that in events and meetings there is some time for socialising, for people to make contact with each other, make introductions, and tell their stories

- Use different techniques to find out what skills people have, and try and use that skill for a local group

- Make sure you keep people involved by passing on information - over time they may come to join in

GROUPS

You may well know about other groups in the same locality, or have heard about other groups doing similar things but in other areas; or you may want to find another group that has had to deal with a particular problem which you have to resolve with your group.

You are likely to have access to a number of opportunities which you can use to help generate links between groups.

- Inviting group reps to some of the interagency meetings you attend; or setting up new interagency meetings and inviting local people along, like some of the chew and chat lunchtime get-togethers

- Organising specific discussions on a topical matter and sending out invites – maybe on how to respond to the council suggesting that the area could be the focus for a big regeneration funding bid

- Formally asking one group if they can provide a mentor for people in another group – such as people who are becoming partnership representatives and need to learn quickly how to handle large partnership meetings

- Organising shared training, or workshop events, for all groups in an area e.g. on how to use the media, or apply for funding

- Creating opportunities for joint working – developing a millennium project for the area, a sculpture trail in the local woods as part of a festival

- Encouraging joint or shared use of buildings

- Undertaking visioning exercises about the future of an area and how ideas can be taken forward

- Assisting groups to arrange visits to other groups/ projects

N.B. For new groups:

It's a good idea to start with small scale achievable projects - e.g. more street lighting / litter bins / football posts for the local recreation ground - than, say, a community centre.

Successes here will give groups the confidence to tackle bigger projects.

CASE STUDY: BRANDHALL COMMUNITY PROJECT   Jarvia Blake

THE VISION

Brandhall Community Building Project began in 1997 when the local volunteer youth worker visited a group of young people from the Brandhall area. The visit was motivated by a growing concern that the youth club had been closed for some time, as the building where it was held was due for demolition. Unfortunately there have been no plans to replace this facility.

The young people expressed a need for a place where they could meet get involved in activities, and generally 'hang out'. Their alternative was to meet in each other homes, or walk around the streets - the latter being the most common. Their parents expressed their concern and said that they would support anyone who would provide somewhere for their children to go. The young people said that they would like to be involved in a fund raising project for the new building. So we began talking about where the new building would be and what it would be like.

On the Church premises, adjacent to the existing building, there is a wooden hut. This is uninhabitable at present and is due to be pulled down. We decided to make inquiries as to whether there would be enough space to build a community facility. Initial investigation showed that there was enough room to build a facility that would cater for the community's needs.

WHY WE NEEDED ADDITIONAL HELP

Although the Church expressed total support for the project, and said they would be willing to have the community facility built on the church ground, they, on their own, do not have the capability to raise the amount of money necessary to build a facility of this size. Therefore, a meeting was organised with Barnardos, due to their experience and links with other organisations. They suggested that the project would fit into the criteria for funding from various trusts and funds.

The volunteers lacked the skills required to run a project of this kind. This was resolved by inviting members of other organisations with experience in these areas to be part of the project. Their help and advice has been invaluable. Also, core members of the steering group have attended training on business planning, fund raising and equal opportunities.

The Project felt that they needed a Project Manager who could support and guide them in the legal aspect of the work. His role was to provide them with information on the management structure and how it could be set up, and to negotiate with solicitors and architects: to support them in the writing of memorandum, articles, and support them with the writing of business plans and also assist in raising £600,000 needed to build the centre.

CONFLICTS

From the beginning the Project has been eager to get local people involved in the decision making process.

This was addressed by :

- meeting with various groups already established in the community

- organising community events while informing them of the Project

- setting up a tenants' and residents' federation.

However, this process has not been plain sailing - there has been much opposition. One came from a local resident, who felt that the centre would block out her light. She did not want children hanging around outside her house and was also concerned about the noise level the centre would generate. We managed to answer all these questions, and even negotiated with the residents in that road by allowing them to park their cars in the car park when the centre was not being used. We also invited the residents to come and be a part of the steering committee helping with the development of the project. This was agreed, and they are now actively supporting the venture.

Another conflict we came across was with planning permission. There was some opposition within the Planning Committee Board, which held up the process. However, in the end the Project was granted permission.

WHAT WE HAVE DONE OURSELVES

The volunteers and workers from King's Community Church have done much of the work. They have formed a Management Committee, and raised several thousand pounds. They have employed a fund raiser business manager, who has helped them with their memoranda, articles, and fund raising; and also employed an architect. They have set up various community groups and facilities, and organised consultation meetings with the local community. They have networked with various community organisations. They have attended training courses in business planning. They are in the process of writing their business plan. They have fund raised and employed three new workers. They have worked with the business manager to gain planning permission.

WHERE ARE WE NOW?

The Project is in the process of completing the foundation work and also in fundraising. We anticipate that is will take about 6 to 10 months to gather all the finances. We hope to start laying the first bricks in summer 2001 and be up and running by the autumn.

TECHNIQUES FOR INVOLVING PEOPLE   John Street

INTRODUCTION

Many people who get involved in community work are not doing it as a paid job. We get involved in our own communities to try and make a bit of a difference. Sometimes we think we have the answer to all the injustice, crime, poverty and disunity in a neighbourhood that's been crumbling for years; but we know you can't do it all on our own, and you need support and help from other local people.

So how can we go about finding these allies to talk over our ideas and to agree on what can be done?

Everyday we hear people saying that everyone is apathetic, no-one cares about their community; but we also need to hear some ongoing stories of what people have achieved.

For a few of us, getting involved in our communities becomes our way of life, but our motivation to change the world isn't always shared by others. Most people get involved in community activities because something happens which affects them, their family or friends, or they are at a point in their lives where they can see a value in getting involved – they may have just moved into the area, or have some time now that they have retired or their children have gone to school.

Many other people have some interest in what is going on around them, but some don't have much time, others don't know what to do or may feel there isn't much they can do, or they may have tried something before and it didn't come to anything.

HOW TO ENTHUSE PEOPLE

All our training and experience may lead us to begin with the traditional routes of using flyers and posters to advertise our first meeting or event. Or, if we're creative, we might try the local media; but, generally, we still get little response from local residents. As our society lives in the fast lane and people by and large don't have time to stop and read posters, or the huge amount of flyers they receive, this form of advertising does not communicate to the majority of the community. For those who do stop and read (or look at the pictures) a simple poster with plenty of colour (or coloured paper) with only a few words will be more appealing.

People need to be more than just involved, they need to be actively involved. This does not mean giving them a job that nobody else wants! Help them to work through their abilities/ qualities; and even create a new job for them to do if necessary. Help them to recognise their potential.

- Spend time with individuals, talk to them about your ideas and hopes, and see who begins to respond

- Gather together in an informal way people to whom you have spoken, and others they have invited, to talk over some of your ideas and problems

♦ Listen to what people feel is important to them – often it's the little things like the street lights not working, or the broken glass in the play areas

♦ Encourage people to think about what/why they want to achieve, and enable them to be realistic about the next steps

♦ When there are some ideas generated, look for ways to involve other people – this may work through posters or flyers, local radio announcements or interviews, and by making sure community groups know so that they can spread the word

♦ If you want people to come to a longer meeting to discuss ideas or to get reactions from Council officers, then think carefully about how you will make them feel welcome and able to take part (don't assume everyone knows how meetings work)

♦ Having a set of clear aims and objectives is crucial. Try and think of the aim as being the overall purpose of the project and how it will be of benefit to the development of the community. As for the objectives, make them achievable at different stages: - immediate, first three months, etc. Think about whether there are any other benefits during the 'setting up' of the project: - job creation, training, etc. Your aims and objectives have to be full of passion, enthusiasm and realism so that when people learn about them they will catch your excitement and want to know more

♦ Once the ideas have been discussed and actions agreed by a number of people, you need to help them to realise what their own strengths and skills are. Then when jobs need doing, people can be encouraged to work together to achieve their objective

♦ Encouragement, support, constructive challenges, and friendship are all part of valuing those you work with. If you do not actively show a person they are valued they will leave.

Although our aim should be to enthuse local people to become involved in their community, and to raise indigenous leaders, we should always remember that without correct preparation, information and personal support, we could do more harm than good.

Martin Luther King Jr. succeeded because he sold his dream as one that was necessary, achievable, and of benefit to those whom it affected. People owned his vision, and they too became passionate about it, because it affected them and they wanted to see and be a part of the change that it would bring.

PUBLICITY AND USING THE MEDIA   Rob Martin

INTRODUCTION

If you want to publicise an event, or draw attention to an issue, you first need to invest in some thinking time, and ask questions to determine exactly what it is you want to achieve. Start wide, and then focus down to the detail. Remember that, however good the idea, if you are not able to do it properly it may be better not to do it at all.

QUESTIONS TO ASK

One way of determining exactly what you want to do, and how you can do, it is to use H and the wise ones:

> **What** is happening?
> **Why** is it happening?
> **Who** is doing it and who is it for?
> **When** is it happening?
> **Where** is it happening?
> **How** is it happening?

At every stage you have to have answers to all these questions before you talk to anyone in the media. Quite likely you will generate some choices, so the next question is ... a seventh Wise-one! **Which?**

What is happening?

Is it a one-off, or an ongoing campaign, or service that you are providing? What do you want people to do, or come to? e.g. write a letter, light a candle, honk their car horn, not pay their taxes or just come to the community fair.

Why is it happening?

Why are you doing this? Is it to feed the world, increase funds, get someone out of/into jail, publicise the work of your group, fight crime, clean the environment, meet new people, get more funding?

Who is doing it and who is it for?

Your choice of spokesperson is quite crucial. In choosing WHO your spokesperson is going to be, pay particular attention to WHAT is happening. Sensitive issues often lurk in this area. It is wise to check out that anyone who is publicly promoting your event is known for work that fits your image – the Manager of Barclays Bank may not be the best person to help launch your Credit Union. Also remember that you may upset a hard-working member of your team by not asking them.

Draw up a profile of your ideal spokesperson. You don't want a shrinking violet, but neither do you want a wannabe celebrity with an ego the size of the Community Centre. A spokesperson needs to be reliable, articulate, and able to "think on their feet". Interviews, especially on radio and television, can be quite nerve-wracking. However charismatic or high profile your spokesperson may be, if they are not fully involved and enthusiastic about YOUR project, they may just publicise themselves and lose support for what you are doing.

As well as a main spokesperson, you may need someone who can act as a contact for a press release. If the reporter is unable to contact anyone the story may be dropped. Make sure everyone in your group knows who the spokespeople are, and that they refer all enquiries to them..

When is it happening?

Time(s) and date(s). Try to get as much lead-in time as possible. A rushed job can be very successful, but it may also be much more stressful.

Where is it happening?

Be specific, do you need to include a map or simple directions?

How is it happening?

Include here things like who is getting in touch with who, who is writing the press release, who is proof reading it, who is getting in touch with the celebrity. How is it being paid for, and (most important) what is the timetable to meet the deadlines?

For a "one off" event you may only need one thinking/deciding session, followed by the event itself. For an ongoing campaign then you will need to think, decide and act more often. All the seven questions should be asked at each stage. It is very tempting to cut corners, but time spent asking which, why, what, who, when, where and how will ensure nothing is overlooked.

Which Medium?

The medium you choose is directly concerned with who you want to reach. The more direct the contact with the target group the more effective you will be in whatever you want to do. Key determinants for deciding are; where your target audience lives, what they read / watch / listen. Do they all go to the same places where they would see a poster or you could talk to them?

If you only want to let a few people in one street know about "it", the best way will be to knock on their doors and tell them. Leaving some written material will help them to remember - and they may pass on the information. If they are always out when you call, leave the leaflet, or use the telephone; be ready for an answering machine. Make sure you do not leave any one out.

Local newspapers and radio are usually quite desperate for material, especially if it does not entail much work for them. So time spent on the press release (e.g. keeping to the point and in the style used by the paper) will help to limit editing of your piece. Knowledge of the most popular local newspapers and community magazines is essential; if you don't know them do some research, it will pay off. Don't forget to use the minority papers as well, so that no-one is left out. Community publications may not keep to a regular timetable, so check that they are going out in time to publicise your event. Community cable television and radio are becoming more widespread, but are unlikely to broadcast all year round, so do some research.

Your target audience may be very small and widespread. In this case, the Internet, trade or special interest magazines may be best.

Even if you have someone in your group who is used to dealing with the media it is a good idea to do practice interviews to make sure that they are well acquainted with the facts. Not everyone has your best interests at heart, so be prepared.

STARTING NEW GROUPS
Emma Manners

INTRODUCTION

The early stages of a group are really important as they set the ethos and style of the group. If we want to attract people from a diverse range of backgrounds and perspectives who bring with them all their experiences and expertise, then it is important to plan ahead on how best to achieve this goal.

The following is a checklist of many of the issues to be considered when planning or starting a new group. The list is broken down into key points.

WHY IS THE GROUP STARTING?

- Is the need coming from the community, or is it a perceived need arising from the workers or other professionals?
- Are there other similar groups already established?
- If it is a demand from the community, why does it they want the group?
- What sort of group do it want? e.g. - is it 'just somewhere to meet up and chill out', a pro-active group, or an interest group?
- If it is a pro active group, what does it wish to achieve - and why?

These are questions which need to be addressed before the planning stages begin. The following issues also arise:

- Who should be involved?
- How can they be effectively included?

SETTING OBJECTIVES

- It is important right at the beginning of the group work process to enable the group to set achievable and realistic objectives and targets.
- These need to be established by the group members and to reflect the capabilities and interests of the group members.
- It is useful when setting the objectives to consider targets, timescales
- , other commitments and funding.
- If you are acting as a group facilitator it is important to ensure that the group do not set themselves up to fail.

FUNDING

- Is funding needed to run the group?
- If so where is this funding to come from?
- How will the group obtain and handle funds?
- Identify possible funding sources; see what is available in kind and what can be obtained by working in partnership with other suitable agencies.

RUNNING THE GROUP, ITS MEETINGS & ACTIVITIES

- Where is the group to be run from?
- It is important to consider the accessibility of the venue for all participants; see the Access Checklist in the Appendix
- How regular are the sessions to be and at what times?
- These need to be based on the group needs and deadlines, with times suitable for all the participants.
- What resources are needed and where are these to come from?

GROUP DECISIONS

In the early stages of the life of a group certain decisions need to be made. These include:

- How decisions will be made
- Is the group open or closed?
- If it is to be open then:
  - how are new people to be introduced and welcomed into the group?
  - how will the group publicise itself?
- Is there to be a set life span to the group, or could it be a rolling programme?
- How will it set up and amend ground rules?
- Could the policies which may be needed be adopted or adapted from project or agency policies, or do they need writing specifically for this group?.
- How will the group organise itself?
- What is the role of any workers?

CASE STUDY

The above processes are based on the experience of Youth Points Youth and Community workers in setting up a peer education group of young people. The group in question was identified through individuals expressing an interest in taking their drugs education (delivered by Youth Point's PSHE course) further.

Starting the group was a learning process for the workers, as well as the young people. Mistakes were made, but it was through them that the learning was developed. Areas that we learnt from included not being clear about all the group members' reasons for wanting the group. Some members were more committed to the peer education process than others. This could have been resolved by running the sessions out of school hours so that only the fully committed would have attended.

Since the first peer education group was developed other groups have been set up by following the above guidelines.

Section 5

Effective Groups

DEVELOPING AUTONOMOUS GROUPS

Leeds Earth First!

INTRODUCTION

Autonomous groups are useful tools that can be used to challenge hierarchies within groups and within wider society. They are also a way of working without a leader/s. For autonomous groups to work well, everyone has to have access to and understanding of all relevant information, and be involved in decision making. This way everyone feels included, and is far more empowered and inspired to act.

Working in autonomous groups uses skills around involving and including people, without the need to compromise in the face of more powerful interests. This leads to real empowerment and inspiration as people have the ability to make a difference to their own lives. Autonomy has been experienced and developed through direct action movements, and the skills we want to share here are based on our experiences with an autonomous squatted social centre in Leeds.

FORMING

Autonomous groups are often formed by people who are frustrated that they are not being listened to by others in positions of greater power. They may take the form of women organising as a group within a male dominated resident's association, or young people on an estate who feel left out of their local community forum. For groups like these, autonomy can serve their interests better as they don't have to apologise for who they are and what they feel, but can just get on with what they want to do about it.

The first step is to get together as a group, check what unites you and decide your aims and objectives:

- Do you give yourself a name, and if so does it reflect what you are about? e.g.: Women's Working Group
- What criteria is there for joining your group, e.g.: is being a female resident enough, do you need to go further?
- Will your group constantly be open to new people, or will you benefit from being a closed collective who know and trust each other?

SUSTAINING

One of the main reasons that autonomous groups are formed is to challenge power inequalities. It is therefore important to be aware that there are power relationships *within* your group.

- Be aware that those who have the most time, energy and enthusiasm can have the most influence over a group (leading to a "hierarchy of the most committed")
- Actively use groupwork skills and give yourself time as a group to reflect and evaluate how well these skills are challenging power inequalities within your group and within your work as a group. (see diagram overleaf)

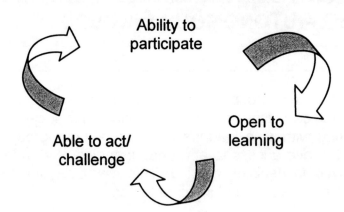

- Sustaining the group is the responsibility of everyone in the group
- Investigate making group decisions by consensus.

EXERCISE: HOW TO COPE WITH LOTS OF TASKS WITHOUT A LEADER

- When there are many tasks that the group has taken on, it may be useful to group these into similar areas.
- Write these up as headings on a blank sheet of paper e.g.: Publicity, Getting new people involved, Cooking food
- People can then write their name and contact details against the area of work that either interests them or in which they have experience.
- These smaller working groups will need to meet on their own, and report back to the main group on progress made.

NOTE
- You may want to make sure that each group has a mix of experienced people and those with little experience who want to learn and contribute.
- Smaller groups can be a better way of allowing people to participate, and can be more efficient for day to day practicalities. Smaller groups can also be easier for people to develop trust.
- Remember that responsibility for the actions of working groups lies with the whole collective. You will have to tell someone if you are unhappy with their actions, and give them praise when it is due.

SURVIVING

The majority of people are not used to working in autonomous groups, and may even have trouble working *with* autonomous groups. Your group should be constantly aware of threats to how you have decided to work, external as well as internal. For example:

- There may be attempts to co-opt you to other people's agendas. This may come from paid workers, funders, local authorities, national and membership organisations.
- Beware of alliances with official organisations which may seem useful, but are actually highly unequal and may be threats to your autonomy.
- As your autonomy helps you to be more active, vocal and perceptive, be aware of interests that may try to divide you from natural allies, who may as yet be less active.

WORKING WITH ASIAN WOMEN   Khalida Luqman

INTRODUCTION

The Tassibee Project works directly with local Asian Mirpuri-Punjabi speaking women in Rotherham. Particularly those who are isolated, not fluent in English and do not have the skills and confidence to access other services or training agencies. The Friday prayer/ luncheon group acts as a safe and culturally acceptable starting point from which women can go on to access other training, social and educational opportunities.

The project is currently in contact with 200+ local Asian women, ranging in age from 12 – 85 years. The project also provides opportunities for volunteering and for paid seasonal work as course tutors, crèche workers and outreach workers.

The project specifically targets and is responsive to the needs of the women and their children and families who experience significant health problems as well as numerous difficulties in accessing appropriate health services. The community has significantly higher than average levels of unemployment, overcrowding and poor housing, long term illness and morbidity.

KEY ISSUES

- Language barrier.
- Lack of understanding of Asian people's needs by professionals.
- Traditional life stages, e.g. getting older and feeling a loss of respect, a consequence of not being taken seriously and different attitudes to older people in the British culture.
- Isolation felt by women as a result of many not understanding English and feeling that there is nobody to help them and that they are stuck at home on their own all the time.
- Communication: use of trained interpreters. Often organisations use anyone who speaks the language – often family and friends, thus leading to unfairness to the person and situation.
- Lack of cultural awareness of people who are in a position to offer constructive help.
- Lack of services for children of any ethnic background.
- Housing: isolation when offered housing in inappropriate areas, i.e. all white, lack of support services available, untrained interpreters.

OVERCOMING THE BARRIERS

- Use trained interpreters.
- Work in single gender groups
- Don't expect Asian women to join white organisations. They need lots of time to work together as a group first (years and years).
- Ask the women what their needs are and develop strategies for meeting those needs.

- Organise transport/ crèche facilities if you are setting up a meeting and ask which venue they would feel safe in.

- It is useful to go on cultural awareness training about the specific community you are working with, but remember all Asian women are individuals – just like you are.

- To work well with Asian women you need to have a good understanding of culture, language and religious barriers, good communication skills – verbal and non verbal and be willing to learn and listen.

- The service needs to be provided by a black woman from a similar cultural and religious background as the group. Service users would then have confidence that advice, support and information was originating from a black perspective and that their cultural needs were being respected and taken into account. An appreciation for and understanding of black issues is vital and would not be adequately conveyed to vulnerable service users by a white woman. Vulnerable service users will not feel safe unless they can communicate well with the worker and feel that she understands their cultural and religious background.

- Publicity: translating into community languages is helpful, but not enough culturally sensitive images for non-literate women, word of mouth works best and also simple information on tape.

- Use bi-lingual consultants to advise you on how to work with Asian women

CASE STUDY

The Tassibee Project started as a prayer group which met in a private house because we had no other venue. It is now an education project with its own facilities and paid worker.

The project has worked because it values and works positively with the issues which are central to the lives of older Asian women:

- Prayer
- Learning about Islam
- Asian family life
- Commitment to self development

The project respects these core values in Asian women's lives and has worked to support and develop them.

Being a project which values women's Muslim Asian identity has been a positive and has strengthened the project. These things have not got in the way of Asian women doing what they want.

WORKING WITH EXISTING GROUPS
- NEGOTIATING ENTRY

Joy Leach

INTRODUCTION

We may be asked to undertake work with an existing group, with which another community worker, or in which colleagues from the same agency, but with different job descriptions, are involved. This can enable the group to develop further the needs expressed by its members. In the long term, the work can lead to effective, sustainable community benefits.

WORKING EXAMPLES

a) A Latch-key Scheme

The community worker at the newly established Rectory Area Residents' Association (R.A.R.A.) was given a programme of projects to implement at the start of a short (18 month employment) contract. As the Association had no sizeable meeting space and the funding was short term, it became evident that working with existing groups would be essential. One project identified was a Latch-key scheme (or after school club) for working parents.

The new R.A.R.A. employee approached existing local organisations to assess the scope for joint work with an organisation that had the space to offer. Common objectives were soon established and agreed with the local Community Association - a larger organisation, already considering a response to the need for after school provision. A steering group had been set up.

The worker needed to quickly establish the credibility, both of herself and the Association, as well as getting a grasp of the local politics. In addition to involvement in the steering group, she also undertook visits to schools with another steering group member. The successful outcome of an unforeseen industrial relations dispute resulted in a quick cementing of local credibility within four months of appointment.

It was agreed that the Community Association would make the funding application, whilst R.A.R.A. undertook a 6 month pilot scheme. The worker had to ensure that R.A.R.A. was given recognition for the part it played when the Latch-key scheme was successfully established 9 months later.

The Latch-key scheme continues nearly 20 years on.

It can be seen that the worker negotiated her way into membership of the group as a result of:-

> ➤ Background reading of papers
> ➤ visits to other agencies and community representatives
> ➤ clarity of remit from R.A.R.A.
> ➤ contact with individual steering group members
> ➤ a demonstration of practical commitment to the project
> ➤ the outcome of the industrial relations dispute.

b)   The Gillespie Action Group for the Elderly (GAGE)

The Group began as 'Elderly Concern', an information exchange between officers from the Local Authority Social Services Department and the Health Authority, specific to a social services 'patch' in Islington. The community worker post was newly established and the officer appointed had previously worked only in the voluntary sector. Involvement with Elderly Concern (E.C.) was part of the initial community work brief.

The post began at the end of autumn. The worker negotiated her way into E.C by background research, contributing to short term practical projects identified by the agencies, picking up administration tasks, and learning the terminology and work procedures of the Council and the Health Authority. The short-term task focus of the early months helped the worker to gain the trust of group members.

Nine months on, a significant opportunity for development arose. The newly decentralised system of council service provision required that the geographical boundaries for both the Health Authority and Social Services should be re-drawn by neighbourhood. Also, the health authority had begun reviewing its services, which led to a revision of officer job descriptions. The remit of E.C. was open for change.

The new community worker, and a colleagues from the E.C., proposed that representatives from local organisations with a concern for the elderly, including ethnic minority groups, faith groups and tenants' associations, be invited to join. The community representatives would be invited to identify issues and set the agenda for the organisation.

'Elderly Concern' was transformed into the Gillespie Action Group for the Elderly. The new emphasis brought active user involvement by the elderly and a broader programme of action and activity. Forms of action taken included: - campaigns on the discharge of elderly from hospital and unwarranted bailiff's letters from a utility company, a multi-lingual welfare benefits advice surgery on major changes to benefit provision, and social events. G.A.G.E. ran for over 10 years until another re-organisation of the Council's services. Regular exercise classes that had developed led to the formation of the Green Candle Dance Company.

KEY POINTS

> Be clear about the remit of your own organisation/ agency.
> Demonstrate reliability.
> Respect other members and their agencies.
> Gain a working knowledge of the group through short-term practical tasks.
> Research relevant background papers and local political issues at the outset.
> Encourage a community based, needs-led agenda.

ENCOURAGING WORK BETWEEN GROUPS   Joy Leach

INTRODUCTION

We may work with existing groups for a variety of purposes - for example, running a community festival, exchange of information, the formation of an umbrella organisation (e.g. a community forum), or collaborative action on a health issue such as street drinking or smoking.

It can frequently make practical sense to work with existing groups - success can lead to measurable benefits for many people, and some funders will ask for evidence of joint working. However, problems can arise between groups, and this can lead to long term difficulties and adversely affect the provision of community resources.

Fundamental to the process, as I see it, is the need to keep the best interests of the whole community uppermost, and to discourage power games. Listed below are a series of points to bear in mind, based on good and bad experiences gathered over many years.

KEY POINTS

These points assume that in many situations, the work with groups will involve meetings with the representatives (reps). Where indicated, they also refer to partnerships (also referred to as multi-agency groups) with other agencies such as the local council, the police and private sector companies.

- Ascertain the remit and resources of the other groups at the start. Use this information when arranging any meetings - it will influence aspects such as date and time, language, venues, and length of meetings. Also, it will help clarify expectations that may arise when working together.

- The agenda should be set by democratically elected representatives within the local community. Priorities may need negotiation.

- Be aware of using jargon in meetings - it can exclude people.

- Where the work concerns an activity or project, draw up an agreement of expectations and working practice which all groups can sign up to. This can be useful for future reference.

- Be clear about the mandate of reps from different groups. Some may need a committee agreement, and this can affect the speed of decision making.

- Paid workers will be assumed to have greater access to resources and time than will volunteers.

- Some lead-in experience is helpful before undertaking multi-agency work.

- For multi-agency initiatives, agree the terms of reference at the start.

- All groups should contribute on an equal footing. In partnerships, issues of resource, cultural, religious, ability and age differences may need to be pointed out to other agencies taking part.

- When agreements are made, record them either in the form of minutes or in a follow-up letter.

- Ensure that minutes or letters are sent out well before the next meeting.

◆ Include action points in minutes: they should indicate any tasks that have been agreed and the names of those who have undertaken to do them.

◆ In any publicity, acknowledge the involvement of other groups / partners.

◆ A first meeting may be well attended. Don't be discouraged if attendance later dwindles, as long as there is a quorum or a working number.

◆ Bear in mind that successful events and activities need a range of skills: some people will be happier to contribute in practical ways, rather than go to lots of meetings.

◆ Keep a list of groups initially invited. Where possible, ensure that they are kept informed of later developments (especially useful with campaigns).

◆ If the work with existing groups concerns a common client group, check the position regarding the Data Protection Act before sharing client information.

◆ Consider the agendas of outside agencies that may 'court' the favour of organisations that represent a number of groups. Ensure access to good independent advisors, either from a council for voluntary service or an appropriate national body.

◆ Be aware of power games that may surface between groups and individuals. Problems that could arise may have historical origins.

◆ Act fairly and be seen to act fairly.

CASE STUDY

The setting is an urban area in a northern city, which has secured SRB funding for a period of seven years. A key aspect of the delivery plan is that the community is directly involved. The council proposed that a community forum (CF) be established on each of 4 local estates within the benefit area. Each would act as a conduit for information and consultation for the lifetime of the SRB. The measure was proposed following the failure of an earlier model, that of the Community Association, on which each estate had representation.

The task
On one estate, a CF had been in existence for some time, the result of long-sustained community development. On another estate there was no lead-in time and the council expected the groups to fast track the setting up of a CF. It was a struggle for the council-funded Community Development Officers (CDO's) assigned to work with existing group members. The groups had energy and motivation for making things work, but most were simultaneously immersed in a fierce power struggle. There was a lack of democratic accountability and an underlying racial tension.

Work with the Forum
Over an 18-month period, the Forum hosted a number of successful events and was actively engaged in delivering community safety, educational and environmental benefits to the area. The paradox for the workers was that the success had been motivated as much by the power struggle as by a concern for the overall community benefit. Also, there was the pressure of the SRB agenda, which brought involvement by council managers and members.

On-going contact

On-going contact was maintained with the forum member groups by the CDO's in various ways, for example:

➤ *A children's party* - which was held by the Forum in December 1999, before Ramadan and Christmas. Members of each group helped out on the day, as well as inviting children to attend.

➤ *A Showcase* of local provision was held early the following year. It was felt that practical joint projects could have the benefit of achieving tangible results, to counter the more negative meetings where issues were discussed that did not require the same 'hands on action'.

➤ *Development proposals for a nearby piece of land* - included a traffic scheme which was set to adversely affect many of the residents on the estate. There were concerns expressed by individual groups about the common threat. The CDO's encouraged the groups to link so as to develop strength in adopting a jointly informed approach whilst seeking a solution. They advised groups about making formal objections to the traffic scheme before it was presented for Council committee approval.

The Future

The CDO involvement continues, in which the workers have to act with scrupulous fairness. This is despite becoming the target of petty accusations and recrimination from time-to-time.

Pressure from managers, who are not themselves experienced in the area of community development continues, as they are contracted to deliver on the 'outcomes' of the pre-determined SRB delivery plan.

General point

It is pertinent to ask in this case study, whose interests are being served by the existence of the community forum.

UNDERSTANDING GROUPS

Val Harris

INTRODUCTION

Sometimes groups are great fun, full of energy and achieving lots; at other times they are just awful – like ploughing through shifting sands, and you just don't want to go because it's all so negative.

While any group does have a life of its own, we know that groups seem to go through certain phases; so before you give up, check out where your group may be at – there may be hope!

STAGES IN THE LIFE OF A GROUP

1. The group begins . . . enough people feel strongly about something to take some action – they join with some other like-minded people to get something done.

2. After the first couple of sessions we realise that we don't all see things quite the same way; we have different ideas for the way forward; we can feel some tensions coming and arguments starting - but we want it to work.

3. It feels as though we're getting nowhere – we keep on having the same discussions; we know we have to find some agreement and move on, otherwise we will give up.

4. We take a step back and review what we are trying to do; maybe we simplify our goals and go for the ones we can agree on; we accept that we will not agree on everything. We start to do things again, and ask new people to join.

5. Suddenly it's horrible again – people are blocking and being hostile; it would be easier to give up; the conflict comes out into the open. We begin to look at how we handle change and challenge; some people leave.

6. Then it's OK again – we're through the worst stage, and the momentum takes us forward once more. We begin to get somewhere with our goals, and we've lots of energy.

7. We have achieved many of our initial goals; we need to decide what to do next. Should we regroup - bring in more new people? Should the group close - will we move on to other things as individuals? We need to celebrate and allow people to make choices.

So groups are like a roller coaster – up and down, up and down. When they are good they are very, very good, but . . . .

DEALING WITH TENSIONS AND CONFLICTS   John Street

INTRODUCTION

There is nothing worse than an atmosphere you could cut with a knife due to tensions between two or more people. But it is part of life that we all disagree at times with other peoples' views and actions. If unresolved, tensions can be cause a serious breakdown in relationships and possibly escalate into long term problems, and even closure of projects. But, more importantly, they can destroy friendships and leave us with a lot of emotional hurt.

While tension and conflict are inevitably a part of life, do they have to be destructive? We can learn and grow through these uncomfortable moments.

Very few people who enjoy conflict and confrontation. Generally, we shy away from situations that could put us in an awkward position. We hope that if we either ignore the situation, or just accept it, then things will sort themselves out in the end. However, experience tells us that those who do not confront the tension end up with more pain.

Although the whole area of tension and conflict is not one we would generally choose to be involved with, I believe that we can control and use them for personal development and growth, strengthening our relationships. To do this, we need to learn how to use conflict as a tool, rather than something that controls us.

FACTORS TO CONSIDER

In any conflict it is inevitable that some people will feel hurt and unsure how to deal with the effects and consequences of the tension. There are some underlying factors that need to be considered in conflict situations -

- Tension generally builds up over a period of time, and often includes factors other than just the present situation.
- Because of this time delay people find it increasingly hard to confront someone about the situation.
- When conflict arises those involved will generally become defensive, being more concerned with proving they are right than solving the problem.
- Our emotions take over from the rational and, when this is the case, our response is generally negative and aggressive.
- You never know all the circumstances to any situation involving other people.

HOW CAN WE USE CONFLICT AS A TOOL ?

We need to find ways of bringing the conflict into the open so that it can be discussed

- If you have caused the conflict you need to approach the others involved – maybe after a short cooling off period – and ask to talk it through
- If you are seen as causing the conflict and someone approaches you, you

need to try and avoid acting negatively; you could suggest having a cooling off period (no more than a day) to think about the situation, and how to resolve the problem and move forward in your relationship.

- If someone is causing you a problem, you need to think about the implications of their actions and/or words, and maybe jot down some notes or draft a letter – this could just be to release your anger/frustration, or to direct your thoughts. Don't send it until you've rewritten it to take account of how the person receiving it might take it.

- You could contact the people involved and ask to talk, but remember they may be unaware that they have upset you.

- Talk to an impartial person and seek advice; a third party may need to be involved if the tensions are not resolved, so it is sometimes good to have them made aware of the conflict from the beginning.

- You may need to look at what you have said or done from the other person's point of view and admit that you got it wrong!

In order to move forward with resolving the conflict you need to:

- Remember that things said spontaneously in conflict are generally defensive words against being hurt rather than a personal attack. Tensions that arise due to situations or actions are caused by what a person has done, rather than who the person is.

- Decide if the basis of the conflict is due to a personality clash, as this requires there to be a compromise as to the way forward. This is best done with the help of an impartial third party who mediates the discussion. If you just don't like someone and no matter what you do you can't get over it, you will need to evaluate what it is about the person that you don't like.

- Recognise the areas that produce tension and try to work around them. For example - if you always argue with someone because of their attitudes towards race, class or gender, you may find that everything they say is a conflict of opinion. If this root difference is not recognised it will soon become a conflict of personality, which is harder to resolve and more damaging. Consider whether you can just agree to differ, or if it will affect your work and the decisions that direct your project. In which case you have to involve other people - especially if these attitudes are contrary to equal opportunity or health and safety policies. You may want to challenge offensive issues through debate, discussion or provision of information. It is important to use the right tactics to achieve your objective.

- Accept that conflict with other professional workers can be part of your work differences. In this instance, work related problems should be dealt with and so allow your relationship to move on. If you are able to differentiate between work and self-protection you can control the effect that conflict has upon you and choose not to take it personally.

FURTHER READING

Conflict – Joyce Huggett, Eagle Press 1998

EFFECTIVE MEETINGS

Jeff Staniforth

INTRODUCTION

'EFFECTIVE MEETINGS DON'T JUST HAPPEN – THEY ARE MADE'
The biggest investment in community organisations is not cash; it's time. Much of that time is spent either preparing for, or in, meetings. Many of us are passionate about, and committed to, the work we do, whether as paid staff or volunteers. We know the problems are huge and the resources scarce. So we need to be effective in what we do.

It is a major challenge deserving of our best efforts. We meet that challenge in our meetings, so they need to be as effective as possible.

Our meetings should be a place to:
- Take rational decisions following structured discussion
- Check the progress of actions agreed earlier
- Decide topics for future discussion
- Allocate responsibilities for taking action on decisions made
- Receive reports
- Enable everyone to make an input
- Increase personal confidence
- Develop mutual respect
- Enjoy being a part of something useful

So what reduces our meetings' effectiveness?
- Agendas are either non-existent or irrelevant
- Minutes are either non-existent or garbled
- Not meeting often enough/ meeting too frequently
- Lack of preparation
- Inappropriate emotional responses
- Offensive behaviour or language
- Arriving late and/or leaving early
- Rambling verbal reports
- Members either dominating or not contributing
- Lack of concentration
- Negative feelings at end of meeting

How can our meetings become more effective?
- Always read minutes and agenda beforehand (they need to be ready!)
- Make brief notes about what you want to say
- Provide written reports whenever possible
- Try to arrive on time and stay for the whole meeting
- Listen carefully to what people say
- Compliment people who have done something
- Put criticism within a positive framework
- Maintain a focus on business throughout the meeting
- Make your contributions effective and relevant

JEFF'S HANDY HINTS FOR MEETINGS

ASK YOURSELF

'Have I...'
- Read the minutes
- Checked the Agenda
- Made speaking notes
- Written any reports
- Arranged to be there for the whole meeting

?

TELL YOURSELF

'I will...'
- Really listen to what people say
- Leave my own problems at the door
- Compliment the work of at least one member
- Make my criticisms constructively
- Focus on business during the meeting
- Make at least one well prepared contribution
- Enjoy myself

THOUGHT FOR THE DAY

However organised we are, however focused we are, emotions can make or break a meeting.

Step back and observe a meeting; there's usually somebody anxious, angry, sulking, frustrated or irritable. Be honest, sometimes it's you. We are not robots, so these feelings are natural. Learning how to recognise them and deal with them is a major task for each of us – and not just in meetings.

ROLES PEOPLE TAKE IN GROUPS
Val Harris

INTRODUCTION

In order for people to work well together, and be more than a collection of individuals, there are a number of roles they need to undertake. These roles can be broken down into two main types:

> **Task roles:** those that help get the work done

> **Maintenance roles:** those that help to keep the group together

Both task and maintenance roles contribute to the group achieving what it set out to do. Research has shown that there at least eight main roles in groups.

TASK ROLES

♦ **The Initiator** will come up with ideas and start things off - especially useful when the group first meets. This is often the person who has brought the group together, and who may be seen as the 'leader'. It's useful to have initiators in groups, but sometimes they need to be held back a bit!

♦ **The Clarifier** will help people to be clear about what they are saying, and also helps the group to see the bigger picture: i.e. how what individuals are doing or saying fits in with the group's aims. He/she may encourage people to be more specific – especially useful if taking the minutes.

♦ **The Information Giver** provides information that helps get the task done. This might be 'technical' (i.e. facts and figures), or just inside information, (such as who's who in the council). At its best the information is relevant and useful, and offered in a sharing way rather than as if coming from the expert on high.

♦ **The Questioner** does just that – asks lots of basic, or challenging questions about what the group's doing and why, etc. It's often useful to have someone who can step back from the immediate pressures and be prepared to get back to basics. Such questioning can appear negative, but can be very helpful if done in the right spirit.

MAINTENANCE ROLES

♦ **The Supporter** gives warmth and encouragement to group members. Someone with a warm personality can be a great help to ease tensions and create a good atmosphere.

♦ **The Joker** provides light relief and an opportunity for the group to let off steam. Beware, though, that this does not become negative humour, with jokes made at the expense of the group's morale and future plans.

♦ **The Sharer** is someone who brings a more personal angle to what the group is doing, which can be a great help in allowing people to relate more informally and get to know each other. It may be sharing feelings, hopes or fears about group, why they're there, and so on.

♦ **The Group Observer** may comment on how the group is progressing, and in so doing help it through blocks and tensions. An observer may say things like 'We seem to be getting stuck here', or, 'Isn't this a bit competitive?' Done with tact and care it can be a very useful role in the group.

EXERCISE 1

What other roles can you think of?

Don't make the mistake of categorising people in groups. Over the course of time a group member may adopt many different roles. All the roles are useful, and by identifying them we can become more aware of how they each contribute to the success of a group.

EXERCISE 2

What roles do you tend to take in groups?

Which other roles do you sometimes take?

ANALYSING YOUR OWN ROLE   Val Harris

INTRODUCTION

There are a wide range of roles community workers adopt within any group. The actual role you take on will be determined by the stage of the group's development, as well as by what is deemed acceptable by your employer / management committee.

As groups have a life of their own, so your role will change over time and in relation to its situation; for instance, when a group is starting up it will need more help with the basics of how to organise itself, while later on it may need help in recruiting new members, or seeking advice on becoming involved in a partnership.

ANALYSING A COMMUNITY WORKER'S OWN ROLE IN A GROUP

Using the examples overleaf as a guide, you can clarify and analyse your role(s) with a group. List 1 gives some of the roles involved in helping a group decide where it is going, while List 2 gives some of the roles involved in building and maintaining a group. There will be many other roles you could take – these are only examples.

For each group you work with draw out a sheet like the one below:

Roles you could take	Purpose of the role	The action(s) you take	Comments on your action(s)	Changes you want to make to your role

COMMENTS

- The technique is not intended to imply that all the roles listed should be incorporated into a worker's relation to a group.
- Actual roles taken in particular situations may depend on the worker's capability, orientations and objectives, as well as on the nature and needs of the group.
- These lists (or similar ones) can be used to analyse the roles of group members as well as those of the community worker.

LIST1: Helping a group to achieve its goals

Role	Purpose	Action Taken
Initiator	To give direction and purpose to a group	Define problems; propose tasks & goals; suggest procedures and solutions
Information seeker	To find out what the group knows; encourage the group to seek more information.	Request relevant facts
Information giver	To enable the group to be better informed	Offer relevant facts
Opinion seeker	To find out individual opinions	Ask for opinions
Opinion/advice giver	To provide a basis for a group to start to come to a decision	Evaluate and elaborate group members' suggestions
Clarifier	To reduce confusion	Define terms; interpret ideas; suggest options; spot ambiguities; give examples
Summariser	To draw ideas together	Repeat and relate statements; link themes; show contradictions; offer solutions

LIST 2: Helping to set ground rules for groups

Role	Purpose	Action Taken
Encourager	To enable others to feel recognised and that they have a contribution to make; to facilitate communication	Be responsive and friendly to others; draw out a silent member; suggest procedures for discussion to allow more people to join in
Commentator	To call the group's attention to the existence of certain reactions, ideas or suggestions	Restate what others have said
Conciliator	To relieve tensions and encourage group cohesion	Inject humour; suggest compromises
Benchmarker	To make the group aware of direction and purpose	Suggest directions and targets; analyse progress towards goals
Interpreter	To explain, or interpret, what someone else has said	Paraphrase initial speaker
Listener	Provide stimulating, interested audience for others	Listen and comment constructively

COMMUNITY WORKERS' AGREEMENTS

Val Harris

INTRODUCTION

As we move in a world of targets and outcomes, it is hardly surprising that some employers of community workers, or people whose job description includes working with community groups, want to know what their workers will be doing.

One way to do this is to try and be clear about how much time the worker has to spend with a group, and to show what type of support s/he will be providing. This can be set out in a simple agreement.

DETAILS OF THE AGREEMENT

1. Name of group
2. Name of worker and employer
3. Amount of time available for support work
4. Types of activities the worker may undertake:
   - **Providing information** - legal and constitutional matters
   - **Funding and fundraising**
     - Developing a funding strategy
     - Writing funding applications
     - Providing fundraising information
   - **Management and organisational skills**
     - Support and supervision of staff and volunteers
     - Recruitment and selection
     - Project management tasks
     - Meetings: minute taking / agenda setting
     - Helping to prepare annual reports / funding reports
     - Networking on the group's behalf
     - Advising the management committee on its responsibilities as an employer
   - **Finance**
     - Assisting with financial planning: budget and cashflow forecast
     - Basic book-keeping / bank statement reconciliation
     - Financial management and reporting
   - **Training**
     - Equal opportunities of management committee, staff and volunteers
     - On other subjects?
   - **Development work**
     - Publicity
     - Recruiting new members
     - Links with other groups
     - Partnership work
5. Accountability: to whom does the worker report? How? Who holds information?
6. Is the community worker expected to attend meetings? - if so, which ones? Why?
7. How are any disputes to be dealt with?

SETTING PRIORITIES   Helen Bovey

INTRODUCTION

Many groups are clear about their objectives and priorities when first set up. For others, the task ahead can seem daunting and almost overwhelming. Setting priorities helps clarify what should be done and when, and this should help people feel more confident about what lies ahead. Prioritising, however, is not only important for new groups: it should be part of an ongoing cycle of planning for all groups. It helps avoid confusion, duplication and wasted effort.

Most importantly it:

- ensures resources are used wisely and to best effect
- gets common agreement about what the group should be focusing on over a given period of time
- helps in allocating tasks
- helps people see where they fit in, and what they can contribute
- helps to clarify what other skills/knowledge the group needs.

HOW TO DO IT

Groups need to decide how they will set priorities. There are three main ways to set about this task:

1. Establish a specific working party to discuss what needs to happen over the coming period. The working party can involve a wide range of people, including members of the committee, representatives drawn from the wider membership, 'beneficiaries' (for service providers), funders and community/support workers. How the working party is comprised will depend upon individual circumstances and the extent to which there is a need to obtain broad agreement for the group's activities.

   Ideally, the working party should meet at specified times away from the normal cycle of group meetings. It is important that, however the working party is organised, there is a clear agenda. Everyone needs to know why they are involved, the significance of the process, and the impact of what is decided. You might want to consider some form of 'away day'. ('Away days' are often led by external facilitators, who help keep everyone focused on the task at hand.)

2. Discuss priorities in one of your usual meetings. The main advantage of this method is that there is relatively little extra work involved, although the process may be best suited to straightforward situations. Limitations lie in the composition of the people who usually attend your meetings, and the danger of getting 'bogged down' in discussion to the detriment of decisions that need to be made. Such meetings can be led by the chairperson, or by an external facilitator.

3. Prepare a report outlining your proposals, and then consult with others to obtain feedback on the recommendations. The report could be written as a result of either of the two previous methods, or by one member of the group. It should then be distributed to the appropriate audience for comments –this will again depend on individual circumstances, but might

include the management committee, the wider membership of the group, beneficiaries, funders and community/support workers. Ideally, the report should have some 'authority' – it should be prepared by a senior member of the management committee, or by a group approved by the committee.

There is a knack of getting good feedback on reports. Consider the following ideas:

- ✓ always give a 'respond by' date
- ✓ ask respondents to focus on certain aspects of the report, or ask them specific questions they need to address
- ✓ remember to give an address to which comments should be sent
- ✓ photocopy the pages of the report on to larger sheets of paper with clear space around the edges – ask people to write their comments in this space using arrows etc. to indicate the aspects they are commenting on
- ✓ provide opportunities to give feedback that doesn't require good written or language skills - such as an open meeting or a one-to-one interview.

Whichever of these methods you use, remember that setting priorities does not necessarily need to be a dull process. There are a number of creative techniques you can use to generate ideas and prioritise. The following examples give some ideas, but you can try your own too!

- 'Post-it' listing: generates lots of ideas in a non-threatening way. In silence, everyone writes their ideas on individual 'post-its' (one idea per note). These are placed on large sheets of paper/card, grouped together in clusters of similar, or duplicate, ideas. You then have the basis for making decisions about which groups of activities should be prioritised.

- Pinboard questionnaires: an easy to use technique for collecting responses to specific questions about priorities. The questions can be represented by pictures, and should be displayed on large sheets of paper, foam boards or card - participants are then asked to stick a pin, or make a pen mark, against their preferred choice. Pinboards can collect responses from a large number of people, and the contributors remain anonymous. It is also a transparent process, as everyone can see how the 'voting' is going.

- Traffic light voting: a way of agreeing priorities. From a list of possible options, participants are asked to give their views on the level of priority using three coloured pens,– green for 'must happen', orange for 'should happen' and red for 'could happen' (or they could stick on coloured dots, available on sheets from stationers).

However, do not underestimate however the potential difficulties in setting priorities – since the priorities will guide the activities of the group there is scope for disagreement and tension. Try to avoid potential problems by:

- Involving as many as possible of the key people in the process – people with different roles: volunteers, paid workers, committee members . . .

- Making sure the process is a structured one which focuses on consensus rather then conflict.

SETTING PRIORITIES: DISAGREE GAME Val Harris

INTRODUCTION

The aim of this exercise is to enable a group to decide on its priorities over a period of time, and to establish an action plan. It aims to give everyone an opportunity to contribute their ideas and comments, not just those who are good at talking in groups. It requires some level of literacy, but could be adapted to symbol language without too much difficulty.

HOW TO DO IT

You will need several pieces of paper, approx. 2" by 3", with 'I DISAGREE' printed on one side: an A4 sheet of paper can be ruled to give 8-10 rectangles, written on, and then copied. Everyone in the group has several of these pieces of paper, and a pen or pencil.

Ask each member of the group to write down what they think their group should be doing in the next year (or so many months) – each idea on a separate piece of paper. The more pieces of paper people have, the longer the exercise will take, so you could limit it to, say, four main ideas if you want a quicker exercise.

When everyone has finished writing down their ideas, ask them to gather round a table. Make sure that everyone is at the same height – i.e. all standing or all sitting. On the table you will have placed the numbers 1,2,3 spread out down one side. These can represent either priorities or time scales (e.g. what we should start doing now, in 3 months, in 6 months); make sure it is clear what the numbers represent.

Everyone puts their pieces of paper upside down on the table, they are shuffled, and everyone takes some (not their own) and places them on the table under the priority/timescale of their choice.

It is still an individual choice at this point, and no-one touches the papers laid down by other people. Once all the slips are laid out everyone goes round the table and if they disagree with the priority given to any idea, or they do not understand it, they turn it over so that I DISAGREE shows.

All of the suggestions which are left facing upwards will be transferred to flipcharts and form the basis of an action plan. Only those turned over will be debated, so it is important to make sure that everyone is happy with the position and content of those left unturned.

Pick up all those that have been agreed with in the first section, and write them up as a list on a flipchart, leaving space for an 'Action' column. Then ask a group member to turn over one that has been disagreed with in the first section, and invite bids and comments.

The idea is not to get into a long debate, but to quickly check out if anyone wants clarification about what it means, and then to ask where it should be moved to – the majority view wins! It may remain where it is, move to 2 or 3, or be scrapped.

If the issue looks set to lead to a major discussion, put it to one side and come back to it later to decide how and when the discussion can be held. The idea is to see where quick consensus or majority decisions can be made, so keep the group moving on to the next one, and then the next . . . . As decisions are made, so the items are added to the flipcharts for each priority.

Work through each priority in turn and record all the decisions. After a break the group comes back together, works through the flipcharted lists and agrees what action will be taken, by whom, when, and how; e.g. it will be put on the next team meeting agenda; it will be brought to the management team's attention; two or three people will take on the task, etc.

The actual exercise should take 30-40 minutes. The discussion of action points will depend on the length of the lists, but again should be fairly quick – at this stage it's about making decisions rather than holding debates.

This idea was gathered from a workshop on 'Action for Neighbourhood Change' run by Tony Gibson at Nottingham University.

Section 6

Organising an Event

PLANNING AN OUTDOOR SPORTS EVENT   Emma Manners

INTRODUCTION

The following check list for organising an event is based on our experiences of planning, organising and running an annual community health, fitness and well being event under the title 'Burley Park Sports Day'.

CHECK LIST

The list is roughly organised in the chronological order of when the task needs to be done.

Starting nine months before the event:

- Make sure that there is a local demand for the project.
- Consult the community on what events and activities are wanted.
- Try to ensure that all groups in the community are consulted and listened to.
- Where possible set up a working group of committed young people, parents, workers volunteers and other community members.
- Look at the needs of any potential working groups and try to find the best solutions to meet these needs.
- Make sure that tasks are delegated fairly and evenly, and that are within the means of the individual. Do not set young people, or anyone else, up to fail.
- Work out what resources will be needed, cost the event and, if additional funds are required, apply in plenty of time.
- Wherever possible use the skills and interests of the young people and volunteers.

Starting six months before the event:

- Take into account national and international events, i.e. during the 1998 Football World Cup we had a massive demand for football, and similarly for the 1999 Cricket World Cup.
- Make sure you have permission from the local council for use of the land and if you need pitches marking, gates unlocking etc, make sure you speak to the right person in plenty of time. Where possible, have any agreements in writing
- If you are recruiting volunteers do it in plenty of time to allow for police checks.
- Try and have contingency plans in case activity instructors don't turn up, equipment fails to materialise, it rains etc.

In the three months before the event:

- If necessary, recruit any teams for the event.
- Make sure that publicity is distributed widely.
- Time table the event.

In the week before the event:

- Confirm all bookings for equipment and specialist staff.
- If necessary double-check with the council that the land will be accessible, and confirm times. Try to have a direct phone number for a council contact on the day.
- Send out any press releases.
- Make sure contingencies are in place in case of bad weather.
- Confirm that everyone involved is clear about their duties on the day.
- Do a clean up of the area to ensure safety.

On the day:
- If everything is well organised then all should go well. Relax and enjoy.

Afterwards:
- Clean up the park.
- Make sure that everyone's hard work is acknowledged and thank all the volunteers.
- Evaluate the event.

CASE STUDY

Burley Park Sports Day was initiated by two local young men approaching Youth Point, an information and support service for young people, wanting to see a sports event in their area as there was very little sports provision. Research and consultation in the local community reinforced this idea and a multi-agency and community planning group was set up.

The success of the first year led to the event becoming an annual part of the community diary and each successive year has improved. This improvement has been possible due to listening to feedback from the events and successful evaluation. Each year has learnt from the mistakes and built on the successes.

PLANNING A CONFERENCE / WORKSHOP   Martin F. Jenkins

INTRODUCTION

A well planned event is a successful event (and vice versa). Good planning involves:

- knowing why you are holding the event and who it is for
- organising the event to achieve the outcome you are after
- putting yourself in the audience's place
- paying attention to practical details.

The following is a list of things to think about - not a blueprint!

WHY ARE YOU HOLDING THE EVENT? WHO IS IT FOR?

Is the event being held:

- to give people information?
- to find out what people think?
- to put over a particular message?
- to involve people?
- to bring people from different sectors together?

Who is the event for:

- ordinary community members?
- workers from the voluntary/community sector?
- people from the statutory sector?
- people from the business community?
- any combination of the above?

WHAT SORT OF EVENT WILL ACHIEVE THE OUTCOME YOU WANT?

You need to think what format will appeal to your target audience **and** achieve the outcome. Bear in mind the following points:

- A lot of people value conferences and events as networking opportunities. Build networking time into the programme (e.g. long lunch breaks).
- People come to events not just to listen, but to express their views. Have a good mix of speeches and workshops - and don't have all the speeches in the morning and the workshops in the afternoon. Make participation a feature of every session.
- Effective chairing makes for successful events. Choose a chair who can resist the temptation to make speeches or summarise the last speech.
- If you have a session for questions, insist that it is for questions, not for speeches. Make people save their speeches for the workshops.
- Brief people making speeches and facilitating workshops. Make sure that they know what and who the conference is for. Make doubly sure that they know how long the speech or workshop is supposed to last.

- Listen to the people taking part in the conference. They may come up with something different from what you wanted.
- Given the choice between a high profile speaker and someone who really knows what they're talking about - go for the high profile speaker if the aim is to get people along to hear your message, but not if you want to hear their views.

PUT YOURSELF IN THE AUDIENCE'S PLACE

- Is your venue accessible? It's not just physical access to the building itself: what about public transport to get people there?
- Don't try to squeeze everything into one event. Give people as much as they can cope with, no more.
- You, and two or three others, are fascinated by the discussion. 90% of the audience are shuffling because they want the coffee break. Have the coffee break.
- The keynote speaker expresses a number of controversial views and announces that they have to leave early. Delay the next speaker and call a question and answer session.
- One person is dominating the discussion. Visibly ignore them and ask loudly if anyone else has any questions.

PAYING ATTENTION TO THE PRACTICAL DETAILS

- Send out an agenda for the conference as early as possible. Include details of how to get to the venue.
- Don't invite people just to turn up. Insist on the return of booking forms. That way you will know how many people to expect and how many teas, coffees and lunches to order.
- Insist that child-care places must be booked in advance. You don't want to organise a crèche for one child when it would be cheaper to pay that parent's child-care costs. Make your arrangements flexible.
- Ask if people have dietary requirements. Please note that meat-eaters can eat vegetarian food but not vice versa. So, either make sure that only people who have registered for dietary specialities can get those specialities, or order double quantities to account for the non-vegetarians who will go for the vegetarian food (or whatever).
- Time-keeping is important. Some people may have to get away promptly (e.g. for child-care reasons).
- There is no such thing as a 15 minute coffee break. Either schedule 30 minute breaks for networking, or insist on people getting their drinks and going straight into workshops.

AND FINALLY ...

- At the end of the event tell people what the concrete outcome will be - copies of speakers' notes and workshop flipcharts, a conference report, whatever.

GROUND RULES FOR AN EVENT Martin F. Jenkins

INTRODUCTION

It is often a good idea to set out ground rules for an event at the beginning. The ground rules should be brief enough to fit on one sheet of flipchart paper, so that they can be displayed throughout the event and referred to if necessary.

The following are based on two sets of ground rules: one for ACW conferences, and one drawn up by Jo Woolf for the London CVS Network. They can be adapted to meet the needs of most events.

THE GROUND RULES

- Start and finish on time.
- Respect each other's opinions and interests.
- Avoid offensive language.
- Avoid, or explain, jargon.
- Anything said is confidential [or non-attributable].
- Mobiles off!

COMMENTARY

Start and finish on time.

Arriving on time and keeping to the timetable are ways of making sure that you get through all the work that needs to be done and that you don't waste other people's time. And, yes, it does include cutting short that fascinating coffee break conversation so that the next session can start on time!

Respect each other's opinions and interests.

You are going to disagree with each other on some things. There's nothing wrong with this: disagreement is a democratic right, and debating the issues helps to clarify them. There's even nothing wrong with having your own agenda, as long as you are open about it. What matters is that you recognise:

- that the other person's point of view is as valid is yours and should be answered by argument, not by rubbishing it;
- that the other person may be coming from a different starting point.

Respecting and understanding where a council officer, or a business person, is coming from is a good way of starting dialogue with them.

Avoid offensive language.

Apply common sense here. Some language is clearly offensive, while other language may offend without any intention - e.g. some people may get offended if you say "chairman" rather than "chair." In the latter case, an even-handed approach may be needed - i.e. the person saying "chairman" may be asked to modify their language, but the offended person may be asked to show a little tolerance.

Language is largely habitual; we should not expect people to change at a moment's notice the habits of a lifetime. It is desirable that people should use inclusive language and say "he or she" or "they" rather than "he" - but when someone is in the middle of developing an idea, do not interrupt them while they're thinking on their feet to criticise their choice of pronouns. The idea is more important than the language!

Avoid, or explain, jargon.

Two basic principles here. Firstly, don't speak in initialese ("SCCD reports that the CEO had a positive response from GOL to the ACW proposal"). Explain what the initials stand for the first time you use them, and include occasional reminders. Secondly, think about the terms you normally use and whether they need explaining. Does everybody know what "capacity building," "empowerment," "partnership" and "community development" mean? Come to that, do you?

Anything said is confidential [or non-attributable].

This has three elements:

- If anybody defines something in advance as confidential, it is confidential and is not discussed outside the event. (But bear in mind that in a plenary session this may not be enforceable.)
- Anything said about someone's own group, work situation, etc. is confidential and is not discussed outside the event.
- Any paperwork coming out of the event should refer to general situations and ensure that groups and/or individuals cannot be identified.

Mobiles off!

It is a reasonable expectation of people attending an event that they will give it their full attention – or, at least, will not disrupt it for other people. Turning off their mobile 'phones is a symbol of their commitment to that expectation.

POINTS FOR PUBLIC SPEAKING   Martin F. Jenkins

INTRODUCTION

Standing up and giving a talk to an audience of 30 or more people is a different skill to talking in an interactive way with a small group. The two best pieces of advice on how to do it come from churches' advice to preachers.

The Methodist version is:

- Stand up
- Speak up
- Shut up

The United Reformed Church prefers:

- Tell them what you're going to say
- Say it
- Tell them what you have said

PLANNING

What are you trying to achieve?

- to give information?
- to stimulate discussion?
- to put over a message?

To whom are you talking?

- What kind of language will get through to them?
- How familiar are they with the jargon you use day to day?

How much time are you allowed for the talk?

PREPARATION

Once you've identified your purpose and audience, you need to draft your talk. How you do this will depend on how confident you are with different methods of preparation.

Structure your talk. The United Reformed Church advice works quite well:

- Start with a **summary** of what you're going to say.
- Spend most of the allotted time on a logical exposition of your argument including the facts that justify your conclusions.
- End with a **summary** of your key points.

Hint: Most of the audience will remember the summaries more clearly than the central exposition.

Can you talk from notes and get your message over within the time allowed? If so:

- Prepare notes of the key points and be ready to talk from them.
- Make sure that your notes are in a logical order.

- It may be helpful to make overhead projector slides of your notes. That way your key points are visible to the audience and you can talk round them.

Do you need to prepare the whole talk in detail? If so:

- Prepare a draft of what you're going to say.

- Write it in your natural speaking voice. Don't write "which means that" when you'd start a new sentence "That means that ... "

- Read through it **aloud** to make sure that it can be delivered in the time **allowed**.

- Get someone to listen to it and criticise it - then revise it.

- Read through it several times until large chunks of it stick in your memory.

Think about visual aids: OHP slides, maps, graphs, etc. Make sure that you have the technology to make them visible.

DELIVERY

- Before you start, make sure that the technology is working - microphones and visual aids.

- Do not launch straight into the talk. The audience needs a few minutes to get into full attention mode. Tell them a joke, or anything to get their attention.

- Check that they can hear you at the back - and if they can't, tell them to move to the front row which is always left empty. (You are under no obligation to get a sore throat shouting across empty rows of seats.)

- Avoid, if you can, reading your talk. The more you can do spontaneously - and with eye contact - the more effective the talk will be. If you've memorised large chunks of it, that will help (but keep an eye on the text to make sure you haven't missed anything out).

- If you have to use a lot of jargon, or give a lot of information, apologise. Make it clear that it's boring but necessary.

- Watch the audience rather than your notes. If the audience looks bored, cut the talk short.

- Have a definite ending. Don't drift to a conclusion.

FACILITATING A WORKSHOP   Martin F. Jenkins

INTRODUCTION

Facilitating a workshop is a different skill from giving a talk. It is not about giving people information, or putting over a point of view; it is about giving people a starting point and enabling them to put over their point of view. A good facilitator will do five things:

- set the context
- encourage people to talk
- prevent people from dominating the discussion
- keep the discussion to the point
- bring the discussion to a conclusion.

SETTING THE CONTEXT

What you need to do to set the context will depend on what has happened earlier in the event. Sometimes a keynote speaker will have largely set the context; in other cases you will need to give more of an introduction.

In any case, as a facilitator you should:

- make sure that workshop members' know what they are supposed to be talking about and what questions the workshop is addressing
- explain any ideas that workshop members need to understand
- spend not more than 20% of the allotted time for the workshop on your introduction.

FACILITATING THE DISCUSSION

Encouraging people to talk

It is usually helpful, before or after your introduction, to go round the group and ask them to introduce themselves. At the same time get someone to volunteer to take notes on the flipchart.

To encourage people to talk you can:
- go round the group asking for answers to the questions that the workshop has been asked
- ask for examples from relevant experience
- target people whose introductions suggest relevant experience and ask them to say something.

Preventing people from dominating the discussion

In most small groups one or two people are likely to dominate the discussion. Your job as a facilitator is to keep them under control. Do not shirk it: being nice to them means failing the other group members.

Among the techniques you can use are:

- Insist on asking other group members for their views

- When other group members give their views, do not allow people who have already had a lot to say add anything
- If necessary, be formal. Insist that anyone who wants to say something must raise their hand and be given permission to speak - and then only notice the hands of people who haven't said much
- In extreme cases, tell the people who have dominated the discussion that they have had more than their say and you only want to hear from other people.

Keeping the discussion to the point

You will probably need to remind the group at some points what it is supposed to be talking about. There is nothing wrong with seeing and noting the connections with other issues; it may be helpful to write down the connections. However, if you do not keep to the point you cannot report back to the plenary session - at least, not on what you are supposed to report back on.

Bringing the discussion to a conclusion

- Keep an eye on the time. About ten minutes before you are due to finish, tell the group that you need to start winding up
- Remind the group what the original questions were and draw attention to anything on the flipchart notes that answers those questions
- Do not allow new issues to be debated. Keep the group focused on the need to reach conclusions
- Get the group to agree three or four key things it wants to feed back to the plenary session
- Remind the group that the full flipchart notes will form part of the conference record - so anyone's cherished point which is not in the feedback will not be lost.

ACCESS ISSUES

Ruth Malkin

INTRODUCTION

Imagine going to a community event and finding that the front door is locked and you have to wait outside waving frantically until somebody notices you and comes to let you in. Or going to listen to a speaker only to find that the acoustics in the room are so bad that you can only make out one word in three. Or going to a social event and having a drink or two, only to find that the toilet door is locked and nobody can find the key. Or turning up at a training session only to find that all the notes that the trainer gives out are unreadable.

Most of you reading this will be thinking 'I wouldn't put up with that!' The rest of you will probably be thinking, 'that happened to me last week!' You, like me, are disabled and well used to such situations.

I've used the above examples to show the importance of access. Easy access to a venue for everyone is essential for a successful community event. However, it is also extremely rare. Given that, there are things that a community events organiser can do to make sure that the best use is made even of a less than perfect venue.

WHAT DO WE NEED TO CONSIDER?

The first thing is to gather accurate information about the venue. Most disabled people are - rightly - suspicious of a poster or flyer which reads 'this venue is fully accessible'. There is no such thing as a fully accessible building.

Access features should be concisely listed in all publicity - for example:

> ➢ 2 parking spaces for orange badge holders
> ➢ Level entrance to the building from the car park
> ➢ Stepped entrance with a handrail on the left on Y street
> ➢ Induction loop in meeting room.

If there is poor access to a building, you owe it to the disabled community to say so, even if that means that your organisation will be open to public criticism. So if there is only one entrance with a step up, say

> ➢ The only entrance has a step up, with a handrail.

That's all. You don't need to apologise, or say that you will lift disabled people in, or that it's 'accessible with difficulty', or anything else. Just be honest, and clear.

There are other things the organiser can do to make an event more accessible, even if the building is a hired space.

Contact your local Disability Rights Forum or Coalition before you book the space- they might know which are the most accessible buildings in the area. Visit the venue beforehand, and carry out a simple access survey – see the Access Checklist in the Appendix.

Some things to check:

♦ Is there a car park or any area near the front door for cars? If so are there marked orange badge spaces? (If not, consider reserving the parking spaces for orange badge holders.)

♦ Is the 'accessible entrance' kept locked? If so, this is sending a clear message to wheelchair user and people with mobility impairments that they are not wanted. Insist that the locked entrance is kept unlocked for the duration of your time in the building. Make sure that the path up to the accessible entrance is not blocked by wheelie bins, rubbish bags advertising boards etc.

♦ Is the adapted toilet kept locked? If so, make sure that it is unlocked while you are in the building - it is a myth that all disabled people who need access to it have a RADAR key . Non-disabled adults do not have to ask for permission to use the toilet, so why should disabled people? Is the adapted toilet clean and free of clutter. A number of venues, regrettably, use the adapted toilet as a storeroom for equipment. Make sure this is not the case in the venue you are about to hire.

♦ Is there a loop system in your meeting room for hearing aid users? If so, is it working? Does anyone know how to switch it on or alter the volume? If so, will that person be there when you hold your event in the building?

♦ Are there clear sign posts from the reception to the room? Are there any visual flashing fire alarms in the toilets to alert deaf and hearing impaired people of fire? If not, make sure you know if there are any deaf or hearing impaired people coming to the event, as you will be responsible for their safety in case of an emergency evacuation.

♦ Is the baby changing area accessible to disabled people? (N.B. some venues are doubling up the adapted toilet with the baby changing area - this is not good practice, as it means that the venue is less accessible to disabled people.)

♦ If you list the access in the publicity, disabled people will feel more confident that you know the building, that it is accessible, and that your organisation cares about access issues. Physical access to a building is only one aspect of making community work practices inclusive to everyone, but it is an important aspect.

♦ Events organisers' will also need to sort out accessible work practices, such as making paper work accessible to visually impaired people and people with learning difficulties; booking sign language interpreters, lipspeakers or translators; and ensuring (if food is provided) - that all diets are included; but these are beyond the scope of this article.

♦ Finally, if a disabled person complains about access to your venue, listen carefully and make a note of the difficulties so that you can either sort out the problem or add the information to future publicity. Do not make excuses, or say it's not your fault. It's certainly not ours!

LEGAL LIABILITY FOR EVENTS
Alan Robinson

INTRODUCTION

Those who organise events, conferences and the like, need to be aware of the possibility of incurring legal liability if anything goes wrong. Liability may be civil (resulting in a claim from someone who has suffered injury or loss), or criminal (resulting in a prosecution under the criminal law). Legal actions are rare and organisers can usually avoid any possibility of being sued or prosecuted by taking proper care and advice where necessary.

THINGS TO THINK ABOUT

Event organisers should take steps to find out whether any **criminal offences** are likely to be associated with the event. There are often regulations attaching to activities which involve the public, and it may be necessary to obtain a licence from the local authority. Examples are raffles and lotteries (which are regulated by the Betting, Gaming and Lotteries Act 1963), and the sale and preparation of food, (which may require the presence of someone with a food hygiene certificate). Breach of these regulations may be a criminal offence. Advice can usually be obtained from the local authority.

Most events will include making **contracts** with suppliers of goods and services, as well as (sometimes) with those attending. In arranging an event, you are likely to enter into a contract for the hire of rooms or equipment, and this should be read carefully to ensure that it represents the terms agreed and that it meets the requirements of the organisers. For example:

- how late can cancellation be made?
  - what penalty will be payable?
- what are the expectations on the organisers?
  - can they get in early to set up?
  - will they be able to leave equipment overnight?
  - who will be responsible for opening and locking up?

Do not simply sign a contract which is placed in front of you without reading it – you will be liable for it whatever it says. Take it away and get proper advice.

The other possible source of contractual disputes is over contracts made with attenders at the event, as to what they are paying for and what they are entitled to expect. This doesn't arise for example, with those who attend an open day or festival, for example, but does apply to those attending a conference or training event. Think about what people are going to be asked to pay for, and what sort of objections they may make if they think they have not had what they asked for. Steps can then be taken to minimise any possible complaints.

Outside contract, the most common cause of actions is **negligence** - which arises where someone owes a "duty of care" to someone else and that duty is broken, resulting in injury or financial loss. For example, the providers of a bouncy castle owe a duty to the children who use it to make sure that it is reasonably safe for them. The duty is not absolute - it is only necessary to take reasonable care to guard against foreseeable accidents. As long as this is done, no claim is likely. However, it is fairly simple to become liable very quickly – e.g. the person who is supervising the bouncy castle is called away to answer another query at the precise moment a child falls awkwardly and is injured. Bear the "duty of care" in mind at all times. Negligence generally concerns itself with what is foreseeable - whether those alleged to have been negligent have acted reasonably in foreseeing and guarding against injury.

In the case of a service provided by an independent contractor, it is not usually legally necessary for them to be insured, but it is usual in most cases where damage may arise. If in doubt, the organisers should ask for details of the supplier's insurance – they should in any event be themselves insured, and it would be advisable to discuss the precise insurance needs with an insurance broker who can advise on level of cover. Again, insurance is not usually a legal requirement, but it may be seen as a sensible precaution.

EXAMPLE

The summer fete will provide entertainment for local people on a field and in a marquee. An admission charge will be made. There will be displays and stalls, side-shows, and refreshments. Think about the following -

- **The contract with the field owner.** If the field is given free of charge there will probably be no problem, but if it is to be paid for, what are the terms?

- **The contract with the marquee supplier.** When will it be erected and taken down? What are the conditions of use? What must the organisers do (e.g. insure)?

- **Contracts with side-show and refreshment providers.** Do they have an agreement to use a particular site? What happens if they don't turn up? Are they insured against possible injury or damage to customers?

- **Stalls and side-shows provided by the organisers.** Will people have to pay? If so, what do they get for their money, and is that clear? Is there any likely danger to anyone, and if so how can it be guarded against?

- **Refreshments.** Who will provide them? Do they have necessary hygiene qualifications and facilities? Are they insured?

- **People are paying for admission.** This means there is likely to be a legally binding contract between attenders and organisers – the attenders are paying on the understanding that certain things will be supplied. Make clear on all publicity that the organisers do not guarantee the attendance of everyone booked, so that if there is no bouncy castle disappointed parents (and children!) do not turn their disappointment into a legal action for breach of contract – fairly unlikely, but not impossible!

- **The Occupiers Liability Acts.** These mean that the organisers owe a duty to everyone attending to take reasonable care to ensure that they are safe. If there are dangerous places, they should be marked out, and if necessary fenced off. Steps should be taken to ensure that children do not have access to dangerous machinery, hot water supplies, etc. Think what could go wrong, and have a plan to avoid it! You are not bound to guard against people who get themselves into trouble, but it saves a lot of arguments if you can ensure that they do not get themselves into trouble to start with.

FURTHER READING

The Voluntary Legal Handbook Sandy Adirondack and James Sinclair Taylor   Directory of Social Change, 24 Stephenson Way, London NW1 2DP

Expensive: but it is likely to contain the answer to that simple legal query. There is a new edition on the way.

Voluntary but not Amateur Duncan Forbes, Ruth Hayes and Jacki Reason London Voluntary Service Council, 36 Holloway Road, London N7 6PA.

Much shorter and cheaper: worth buying and consulting as a first step.

Section 7

People Management

EMPLOYING PEOPLE

Martin F. Jenkins

INTRODUCTION

Community workers often help community groups to develop to the point where they secure funding to employ a worker for the first time. This is where things frequently go wrong.

Groups can get a lot of advice and training on recruitment and selection; but recruiting a worker is the **beginning** of a process. It shouldn't be something you do very often; employing and managing a worker is something that goes on over a length of time. What you do with (or to) a worker once you've employed him/her is much more important than how you recruit him/her.

MANAGING A WORKER – WHAT DO COMMUNITY GROUPS DO WRONG?

There are two common mistakes:

1. **LETTING GO**

A community group has been running on a purely volunteer basis for a long time. It suddenly obtains a worker - and the worker is left to get on with it. Nobody takes responsibility for supervising, or directing the work. Then the worker does something that the group doesn't like - and that is seen as the worker's fault, not the group's.

2. **NOT LETTING GO**

A community group suddenly obtains a worker, but still wants to do everything itself. The chair sits in the office all the time; the worker is allowed no discretion, or initiative, and becomes very frustrated. This often happens where the management committee is made up of people whose experience of being supervised is not being allowed any initiative.

WHAT IS THE SOLUTION?

Before you recruit a worker, think carefully about how you are going to manage him/her. (Interview candidates may ask the question!)

Recognise that bringing a worker into a group that's been run on a volunteer basis is going to change the group. The worker will have new ideas and ways of doing things. How you've done things in the past isn't necessarily the right way; it's one way, and in many cases the worker's way is just as good - and it's not worth upsetting the worker by insisting on your way.

Decide what the worker's role is, and what the committee's role is. In most cases, the committee makes policy, the worker carries it out - but make sure that the worker can feed back her/his front-line experience to influence policy. Involve the worker in your committee discussions, so that they know what lies behind policy.

A worker cannot function effectively if fifteen committee members can individually give her/him instructions. There should be only two ways of giving a worker instructions:

> ➢ at a committee meeting
> ➢ through a committee member delegated to be the day-to-day manager.

RESPECTING THE WORKER'S RIGHTS

Management committees should make sure that they understand their role and responsibilities as an employer. Workers have legal rights which **must** be respected.

Employees are not volunteers. If they are employed for 35 hours a week, you cannot expect them to put in 50 hours. If they need 50 hours to do the job, the answer is not to expect them to work 50 hours, but to either:

> ➢ secure funding for an additional worker, or
> ➢ reduce the size of the job.

Employing a worker is a serious and responsible business, and community groups should make sure that they understand their responsibilities before taking on staff. The information given in this Manual is only a summary and not substitute for proper training.

FURTHER READING

Managing Staff Problems Fairly: a Guide for Voluntary Organisations by Elizabeth Potter and David Smellie: available from Croner Publications Ltd., Croner House, London Road, Kingston-on-Thames, Surrey KT2 6SR (telephone 020 8547 3333)

EMPLOYMENT LAW AND GOOD PRACTICE   Martin F. Jenkins
- WHILST IN EMPLOYMENT

INTRODUCTION

This does not cover issues such as the minimum wage, maximum working hours, etc. These are subject to changes in the law and a responsible employer will get detailed up-to-date advice.

What it does cover is the broad outline of workers' rights and good practice on the part of employers. These are issues which don't change much over the years - but do turn up on an all too regular basis in employment tribunals.

CONTRACTS OF EMPLOYMENT

All workers have a contract, whether in writing or not.

➢ A contract is an agreement between two parties - employer and employee - and can only be varied by mutual agreement.

➢ If a contract is not in writing, tribunals and courts will decide what was in effect in the contract (implied terms). The more you put in writing, the less is open to interpretation.

➢ Some terms of a contract are determined by law (e.g. minimum period of notice).

➢ A contract can include terms that improve on the legal minimum, but **cannot** offer less than the legal minimum.

Employees are normally entitled to receive, within two months of starting their employment, a **written** statement of particulars of their employment detailing:

- names of employer and employee
- date employment commenced, and details of any continuous employment
- rate of pay
- hours of work
- holiday arrangements
- rules about sickness and sick pay
- pension arrangements
- job title and employee's duties
- place of work, and employer's address
- length of notice on both sides
- length of contract (for non-permanent jobs)
- collective agreements affecting the terms and conditions of employment
- disciplinary procedure
- name of person to whom the worker should apply if dissatisfied with a grievance or disciplinary decision.

GRIEVANCE PROCEDURES

Employees have the **right** to know to whom a grievance should be addressed, and how to apply for it to be dealt with.

You need to consider:

➢ Who deals with grievances?

➢ What are the contingency plans if that person is inappropriate, or not available?

➢ How to avoid conflicts of interest.

➢ Does the procedure apply only to employees, or to volunteers and committee members as well?

➢ Appropriate timescales (a grievance should not drag on for months).

➢ Should there be a right to be represented?

➢ Should there be a right of appeal?

DISCIPLINARY PROCEDURES

Organisations with fewer than 20 employees are not required to have written disciplinary procedures.

BUT:

➢ Having written procedures makes things clearer.

➢ The fact that you have written procedures, and have followed, them is a good defence in a tribunal.

➢ If you do not have your own procedures, any disciplinary action you take will be judged by the standard of the ACAS disciplinary code.

What should a good disciplinary procedure include?

➢ It should be clear to whom the procedure applies - e.g. employees, volunteers.

➢ It should be clear who makes the decision at every level.

➢ It should give some indication of what constitutes misconduct.

➢ It should be clear that a disciplinary matter requires **investigation** before a disciplinary hearing is held.

➢ The person under investigation has the right to be appropriately represented at a disciplinary hearing, have their case heard and question the evidence.

➢ There should be a right of appeal from a disciplinary hearing.

➢ At all levels, no-one should be judge in their own cause - i.e. the investigator should not sit on the disciplinary panel. This may not be practicable in very small organisations.

EMPLOYMENT LAW AND GOOD PRACTICE   Martin F. Jenkins
- AFTER DISMISSAL

FAIR AND UNFAIR DISMISSAL

To make a claim for unfair dismissal you must:
- be an employee (not a volunteer, or self-employed)
- be under normal retirement age for the job
- normally work in the UK
- have been continuously employed for one year (unless you are claiming some cases of automatic unfair dismissal).

Dismissal is automatically unfair, if it is
- because of membership, or non-membership of a trade union, or taking part in trade union activities
- because of pregnancy
- because the employee raised a health and safety issue
- because the employee sought to assert a statutory right
- the result of the transfer of a business, or contract (qualifying period applies).

The employer's defence:

A dismissal is fair, if the reason for it is
- related to the employee's ability, or qualifications, to do the job
- conduct related to the job
- because of redundancy
- because the employee's continued employment would be illegal
- because of "some other substantial reason".

The employer will be expected to show that the procedure used in dismissal was fair.

In dismissals for misconduct, the employer must show that
- the employee was genuinely believed to be guilty of the misconduct
- there were reasonable grounds for that belief
- as much investigation as was reasonable had been carried out.

Discrimination

It is generally unlawful to discriminate on the grounds of race, sex or disability.

There are two kinds of discrimination:
- direct discrimination (e.g. "no blacks or women need apply")
- indirect discrimination (requirements which, intentionally or unintentionally place employees at a disadvantage on account of their race, gender or disability.

Discrimination cases can be brought in respect of recruitment and in-work practices, as well as in cases of dismissal.

Discrimination can be justified - e.g. only women can apply for a post with a women's group, only black actors can audition for Othello.

REDUNDANCY

There are three main redundancy situations:

- closure of the business as a whole
- closure of a particular workplace
- reduction in the size of the workforce.

A worker may be unfairly dismissed even if there is a genuine redundancy situation.

You need to consider:

- Length of service - a worker with two years' service qualifies for a redundancy payment
- Consultation - lack of consultation is almost certain to turn a redundancy into an unfair dismissal
- Unfair selection - are the criteria for who is made redundant fair?
- Alternative employment - you are obliged to consider the possibility of offering the worker suitable alternative employment
- What does the worker's contract say? Can you afford the redundancy payment?

TRANSFER OF UNDERTAKINGS

The general principle is clear:

- If you take over a business, or contract, you take over the workers with their terms and conditions of service intact

- If you want to change the terms and conditions, you have to get the workers' agreement

- Whatever the final agreement, each employee's service is continuous from the day he/she first started in the job, no matter how many changes of employer.

SELECTING AND RECRUITING PAID STAFF

Val Harris

INTRODUCTION

People are the key to the success, or otherwise, of all organisations and groups. Getting the right people can be difficult, but there are steps we can take to try and attract (and keep!) good staff. Making the wrong decision will have a major impact on your organisation, especially if you have very few staff. Remember, also, that all employment matters are covered by a comprehensive legal framework.

PRINCIPLES

Attracting and selecting the right person/ people for your organisation requires three key elements to be in place; namely that

1. you know what you want, and it is realistic
2. you have an agreed policy and procedures which will give you the best information on which to make your decisions
3. the people involved understand the processes and policies, and have had experience of, or been trained in, good interviewing.

DECIDING ON THE JOB

Whether the job is a replacement for someone who has just left, or a new post, you need to decide what you want that person to do This should be a team/ group effort; if there are too many tasks that you want the new person to do then play the disagree game (section 5) to determine your priorities. You then need to draw up the following:

➤ **A job description.** This should state
  - the overall aim of the post
  - to whom the appointee are accountable and for what
  - an outline of the key tasks you want undertaken
  - the skills and knowledge needed to do the job - don't ask for things that are not really required, or you will reduce the number of people eligible to apply (e.g. if they don't need a degree or a car, don't ask for it).

➤ **A person specification.**
  - You need to set out the **essential** and **desirable** experience, skills, knowledge, attitude and personal situations (e.g. evening and weekend working) that you require.
  - There are a number of proformas around which will help you write one.

➤ **An application form.**
  - This is to ensure that you have the essential information you need to decide whether or not you want to interview the candidate(s).
  - Don't ask for personal information unless it is relevant; e.g. age and marital status have nothing to do with a person's ability to do the job such questions cane merely feed into our prejudices.
  - Only ask relevant questions about criminal convictions if they would prevent someone from getting the job (e.g. fraud for a finance job).

- You need to decide if you will accept CV's rather than application forms; one disadvantage is that they don't give the same information so its hard to make comparisons. Also some CVs which look impressive may have been done professionally, and this could hide a candidate's poor literacy skills.

These all need to go into the **pack for candidates,** along with:

- background information on your project/ organisation
- an equal opportunities form and policy
- a covering letter.

ADVERTISING

How to decide where to advertise.

➢ Think about the person you are looking for, and where you might expect to find them e.g. if it's a local admin job, then advertise in the local paper, or the council job sheets; if it's a long term post for a project, or finance director, then you might want to advertise in one of the national papers, or specialist 'trade mags'.

➢ Think about your advertising budget - national adverts, and even regional papers, can be expensive; are there cheaper alternatives? What about free job sheets, posters, libraries, council information shops, colleges, community centres, local voluntary sector mailings?

When you are drawing up your advert:

➢ **Make sure that you do not discriminate against people** by restricting the information about the job. Draw up an advertising plan and advertise as widely and in as many different ways as possible. If you have advertised before, you may know which places worked best.

➢ **Give clear and adequate information** in the adverts and the job packs so that people can decide if it is for them. If your building is not accessible, then say what its limitations are e.g. 'There are 3 steps to the lift'.

➢ **Make your advert stand out.** Make the most of any differences, the training you provide, the sort of organisation you are . . . so that people will read it and think about it.

What to include in your advert:

- ✓ The name of your organisation
- ✓ the job title
- ✓ where the job is based
- ✓ the salary level/ scale points
- ✓ the duration of the post, if it's for a set period
- ✓ the number of hours
- ✓ an outline of the main purpose of the post
- ✓ the closing date for applications and the interview date, if known
- ✓ where information can be obtained and if informal enquiries/ visits are welcome.

➢ **Be prepared to deal with enquiries**. Are you ready to deal with all the enquiries, or requests to visit, that will come in by letter, phone and e-mail? Decide in advance who will field all these enquiries.

SHORT-LISTING

The same panel which does the short-listing should also do the interviews as this ensures that everyone has the same knowledge of the candidates. It's best to try for an odd number, as this makes decision-making easier. Try to get as representative a panel as possible so that different ideas and perspectives can contribute to the process. Also, the candidates will feel more comfortable if they see someone to whom they can relate.

Equal opportunities forms – you must decide if you are detaching them before you read the forms; removing them means that you are not being influenced in any way until you have decided who to interview. Make a summary of the main characteristics of the applicants.

The short-listing process:

- ✓ Pick out the candidates who meet the essential requirements in the job specification. If this yields too many applicants, then reduce the numbers by using the desirable criteria

- ✓ Look at who you have short-listed – have you only short-listed men? women? white people? non-disabled people? If so, go back to the pile you put on one side and re-read it. Did you miss something? Have you not fully understood what they are saying – e.g. when they describe their experiences, do they say 'help' rather than 'volunteer in their community'? Or do you need to rethink your advertising strategy?

- ✓ Check that you have a strong and diverse enough range of people to interview. If not, do you need to reflect on your advertising strategy and re-advertise? Otherwise you could risk ending up with no-one suitable.

If you decide to go ahead, work out the questions to ask, decide whether you want presentations from people, sort out your roles and send out the invites! And don't forget to let those who haven't been selected know as well.

INTERVIEWING

Now comes the most exhausting part of the process. Before anyone comes into the room just check that:

- ✓ someone is welcoming the candidates and making them a drink
- ✓ people know you cannot be disturbed
- ✓ the room is laid out as comfortably as possible for everyone
- ✓ everyone knows who is chairing, and the role they are to take
- ✓ you know who is asking what questions
- ✓ you have agreed that people can ask a supplementary question to clarify a point, or give the candidate a chance to answer it more fully
- ✓ what sort of questions are out of order, and how you will deal with them if they are asked (e.g. if someone asks a question that is not on the agreed list, will you then ask every candidate the question, or say to the candidate that she/he need not answer?)
- ✓ you have decided how you will record and score candidates replies
- ✓ you have decided who will respond to candidates' questions
- ✓ if the candidates will be making a presentation, there is equipment, such as flipcharts and overhead projector available

✓ you know what you want to say about trying to get the post refunded if it's a short term one

✓ you have a date for making a decision and who will inform the candidate this.

Remember to allow time for the panel to take short breaks and refreshments.

Points to remember

➤ The candidates hate this process as much as you do

➤ Some people are much better at writing application forms than talking at interviews

➤ Some of the candidates may be scared, feeling ill, worried about picking the children up because the interviews are running late

➤ Explain the procedures and give them time to catch their breath while you introduce the panel members.

➤ Treat them with respect, create a friendly and interested atmosphere, and try and encourage them to tell you more about themselves.

➤ At the end thank, them for coming, check they are okay with the process for claiming expenses etc. and tell them when you will be in touch.

MAKING THE DECISION

This will either be very easy, or you may have to agonise for hours. Once you have seen everyone, take a short break. Check how long people can stay. If you are using a scoring system give people time to add up their scores.

Work through the list of candidates:

➤ Are there any that no-one wants? If so, record the reasons, in case they ask for feedback.

➤ Talk through each of the candidates in turn, and see if a clear preference emerges; if so great! Record your reasons for not selecting the others, and agree who will ring them. Arrange to get references taken up if you haven't asked for them in advance (if you have, look at them now to confirm your decision, or not!). It's best to have a second choice in case your preferred person turns you down.

➤ If you have two people who could both do the job but do it very differently, think about what they would each bring and how they might relate to the team; this can take time to talk through.

➤ If the panel cannot agree, you may decide to re-interview the top two candidates again. Only work with the information you have gained, and not on your assumptions. If you only know some candidates, you need to be very careful how you use the other information.

➤ You may decide not to appoint and go for re-advertising. Starting the process again will mean rethinking the job - is it too hard, doesn't pay enough? – and your advertising strategy - you advertised when everyone was on holiday . . .

Throughout the process stay alert to the way discrimination can creep in. We are all subject to making immediate conclusions about people from their appearance, mannerisms etc. If you think that is happening, it's best to say something so that the panel can discuss it. If the matter is not resolved the panel should be adjourned and advice sought.

WORKING WITH VOLUNTEERS

Compiled by
Val Harris

INTRODUCTION

Many volunteers will be put off if matters are made too formal. However volunteers have a right to have their contribution fully valued. If your organisation decides to recruit volunteers, then you should produce a written record of the main points and principles you have agreed. This record may form the basis for producing a Volunteer Policy. A Volunteer Policy is useful both to staff and volunteers, clarifying the roles, rights and responsibilities of volunteers. The following is a suggestion of the sort of things an organisation might include in its Volunteer Policy.

KEY PRINCIPLES UNDERLYING VOLUNTEERING

➢ Volunteering is open to everyone, and every individual has a right to volunteer.

➢ Organisations using volunteer help should recognise a volunteer's rights and adopt good practice incorporating these rights.

➢ A volunteer's expectations of what she/he will gain from volunteering should shape the nature of the work and the duties to be undertaken.

➢ Volunteering complements paid work, and volunteers should not be used to cover for paid work.

KEY POINTS TO CONSIDER

The organisation's commitment
Working with volunteers costs time and money. When budgeting for them, think about the costs of
- Recruiting
- Matching
- Training
- Supervision and reviewing
- Insurance
- Evaluation
- Travel and out-of-pocket expenses
- Office overheads and administration
- A volunteer co-ordinator or manager

Think about whether or not the presence of volunteers will have implications for workspace, materials and the time of other staff besides a designated manager.

Volunteer Recruitment
Consider how you might recruit –
- by word of mouth
- through agencies, such as the Volunteer Bureaux
- by advertising in various media.

Decide who will be responsible for recruitment – a designated person, or several people?

Think about

- whether or not, and how ,volunteers will be interviewed and screened
- whether or not the interview will be conducted on equal opportunity principles
- who will do this
- what you will do if a volunteer is unsuitable
- what a volunteer will be offered as an introduction to the organisation
- whether or not you will take up references
- whether or not you need police checks.

Volunteer Tasks
Consider the tasks volunteers will do.

- Is your organisation ready, and willing, to develop exciting and innovative opportunities for volunteering based on the skills and aspirations of potential volunteers?
- Will volunteers be able to undertake new areas of work, or meet needs that are currently being unmet?
- What beneficial changes will be possible because of the extra help, new skills and experience?
- Should each volunteer have a job specification? If so, what should this contain?

Remember that volunteers are not paid employees.
"Job descriptions" may cover:

- The task
- The responsibilities
- Those with whom the volunteer will work
- Those to whom the volunteer will report
- Volunteer hours – the commitment s/he can make
- The skills required
- The location of the job
- What the task means both to the organisation and to the volunteer
- What to do if s/he can't attend
- How to stop being a volunteer.

The status of volunteers in the organisation

- How will the work of volunteers fit in with the work of any paid staff you employ, and will they be treated in the same way?
- What will the involvement of volunteers allow paid staff to do more or less of?
- What tasks cannot be undertaken by volunteers, and why not?
- What more, or less, are the main differences between volunteer and

paid tasks?

◆ Are there circumstances in which volunteers should not be involved?

◆ Will they be given information about Health and Safety procedures, Equal Opportunities procedures, and safety cover?

◆ What will be the position of volunteers if an industrial dispute arises between paid staff and management?

◆ Will volunteers be able to say 'No' if they are asked to do things they don't want to do?

◆ What will happen if some employees do not welcome volunteers?

◆ Are there grievance and disciplinary procedures which apply to volunteers?

◆ Will volunteers have an opportunity to express their views to senior management on any aspect of the organisation's work?

◆ If so, what channels will be open to them, and how will it all work?

◆ Will they have a representative on the management committee?

Support for volunteers
What will you offer volunteers to help them with their tasks?

◆ Travel expenses?

◆ Lunch, if working all day?

◆ Telephone and other costs, if working from home?

◆ Extra help with transport, if disabled?

◆ Training and supervision?

◆ Opportunities to progress?

◆ Opportunities for social contact with staff, users, and other volunteers?

◆ Accreditation?

◆ Periodic reviews of their work?

◆ A reference?

◆ Recognition and thanks?

◆ Team-support meetings?

Confidentiality

◆ Does your organisation have policies on matters which are private?

◆ Should these be adapted, or extended, to cover volunteers?

◆ Is there a policy about talking to the media – does this apply to volunteers?

◆ What about confidentiality as it applies to the information given to you by volunteers?

◆ To whom will any records concerning volunteers be available?

◆ Will volunteers have access to information – e.g. appraisal reports?

Insurance and Health & Safety
Have you sorted out :

◆ The details of Public Liability, personal accident and contents insurance covering volunteers?

♦ A statement volunteer drivers will be required to sign advising their insurance company that they are using their own cars for voluntary work?

♦ The organisation's responsibilities for Health and Safety, and details of the proper use of equipment, protective clothing, building safety, First Aid, Health & Safety training, etc.?

Volunteers on Benefit

When a volunteer is undertaking voluntary work, s/he is still regarded, for the purposes of claiming Job Seekers Allowance, as being available for work. However, it is expected that the volunteer will be available for work on 48 hours notice.

If the volunteer is claiming benefits as a result of incapacity for work, e.g. Incapacity Benefit, Severe Disablement Allowance or Income Support, s/he will not be treated as capable of work if undertaking voluntary work.

Any expenses received by a volunteer are treated as income for the purposes of means tested benefits.

Trade Unions

- Volunteers should have the right to join a Trade Union relevant to the work in which they are involved. The organisation using volunteer help should encourage volunteers to take up union membership.

FURTHER READING

Volunteers First: 'The personnel responsibilities of people who manage volunteers' National centre for volunteering UK

London Voluntary Service Council: Voluntary but not Amateur

Community Matters:

USEFUL ADDRESSES

The National Association of Volunteer Bureaux
The NAVB supports a network of Volunteer Bureaux across the country.
New Oxford House, 16 Waterloo Street, BIRMINGHAM B2 5UG
Tel: 0121 633 4555   website: **www.navb.org.uk**

The National Centre for Volunteering provides a range of courses, publications, information and a consultancy service on most aspects of working with volunteers
Regents Wharf, 8 All Saints Street, LONDON N1 9RL Tel: 020 7520 8900
Fax: 020 7520 8910 Website: **www.volunteering.org.uk**

The National Coalition of Black Volunteers 4th floor, 35-37 William Road, LONDON NW1 3ER Tel: 020 7387 1681

The National Council for Volunteer Organisations
Regents Wharf, 8 All Saints Street, LONDON N1 9RL Tel: 020 7713 6161

VOLUNTEERS: INDUCTION

Compiled by
Val Harris

INTRODUCTION

An induction period, or session, is as important for volunteers as for paid staff. It can:

- ♦ provide volunteers with information needed to do the job
- ♦ provide an opportunity to explain your policies and practices
- ♦ give volunteers more confidence when starting work
- ♦ show that you value their involvement
- ♦ help clarify and avoid potential problems at an early stage
- ♦ help set 'ground rules' which encourage all volunteers to work to the same principles – the ethos of your project.

Ideally, an induction session will be arranged for a group of volunteers; this will provide them not only with information, but also with an opportunity to meet others doing similar work. Where this is not possible, maybe because there are insufficient people starting at the same time, information should be provided on an individual basis, backed up with written material.

INDUCTION CHECKLIST

All of the subjects listed below need to be addressed before volunteers start work, or as soon as possible afterwards:

- ♦ the agency: it's role, client group, ways of working ☐
- ♦ staff structure ☐
- ♦ where and how decisions are made ☐
- ♦ roles of paid staff ☐
- ♦ roles of other agencies ☐
- ♦ roles of other volunteers ☐
- ♦ boundaries of the volunteer's own role ☐
- ♦ to whom the volunteer is accountable ☐
- ♦ who to contact in an emergency ☐
- ♦ support available: from whom, in what form (e.g. group or individual) ☐
- ♦ Health and Safety procedures: First Aid; fire precautions and procedures ☐
- ♦ Confidentiality: of information about clients; other volunteers; any sensitive information gained in the course of voluntary activity ☐
- ♦ Equal Opportunities: volunteers' rights and responsibilities ☐

♦ dealing with potential problems: e.g. being asked by clients to perform additional tasks; being asked for confidential information, etc. ☐

♦ insurance ☐

♦ relevant agency policies ☐

♦ what to do if offered presents or money by clients ☐

♦ resources and facilities available to volunteers ☐

♦ where things are kept – including stationery, tea and coffee making facilities, paper for the photo copier. ☐

Other very specific issues can be dealt with at this stage, e.g. whether or not volunteers are required to keep records.

This is also the time to ask volunteers to sign a "volunteer agreement", confirming that they understand, and are willing to abide by, the terms of the job description and agency policies. This document could also detail what the agency will offer in terms of support, training, expenses, etc.

USING OUTSIDE CONSULTANTS   Val Harris

INTRODUCTION

There are times when organisations and groups need to bring in someone from outside to help with a specific piece of work. This may be because you need a feasibility study done, and haven't the time, or the skills, to do it in-house; or you may need an independent evaluation of your project; or there may be some tensions and difficulties within your team, or committee which are hard for an insider to address and which you want an external facilitator to come and help to resolve.

BEFORE YOU ASK SOMEONE IN

As someone who often gets asks to go in to organisations and groups - usually when there is a crisis, or problem (say over lack of funding, or the suspension of a worker) - there are some points I try to clarify before I agree to work with them. These points may change over time and with events, but they give a starting point, and, hopefully, avoid some of the mis-communication and misunderstandings that can easily arise when everyone is busy and can't meet very often.

Points to clarify could include:

➤ Are you clear about why you are asking an outsider to come in?

➤ What is it you are hoping they can do? Is it **possible** for the problem/ issue to be resolved? - we don't have an endless supply of magic wands!

➤ Why can't you do it yourselves? e.g. time, skills, expertise.

➤ Have you the time to meet and brief a consultant, and be available to talk to them as the work progresses? – we can't do a good job unless we get enough information from people.

➤ Is the timescale realistic? - most facilitators/ researchers may be booked up quite a while ahead with other work; so that being asked e.g. to do a large EU funding bid within 2 weeks is not possible if they don't know the organisation.

➤ What money do you have available? Have you checked out the going rates for the work you have in mind?

➤ What facilities can you provide – or are you expecting the consultant to be totally self-sufficient and have their own office?

➤ Are you clear about how you want to receive reviews on progress? Who will be taking responsibility for checking that the work is going ahead okay?

➤ What do you want at the end? What kind of report? To whom should the consultant be reporting?

COMMON ISSUES

➤ There are a number of difficulties an outside consultant may face; these include: - they may have been told about a number of problems requiring a solution, but their role is not clear. Be clear about what you want the consultant to do - are you mainly wanting advice before doing the actual work yourself, or do you want the consultant to write the bid, undertake staff appraisals etc.?

> **Having to take in lots of information** about an organisation they have not heard about before. Think how long it takes a new member of staff to settle in and understand what is going on - the external person usually gets an hour's chat and the last annual report, or funding application. So be prepared for lots of questions to be asked as they try to understand what the situation is.

> **Keeping up to date with relevant information**. It's easy for people involved in an organisation to be up-to-date with what is happening; but if a consultant is occasionally coming in from the outside to do a specific piece of work she/he will not have heard all the news which might affect what requires to be done.

> **The goal posts keep changing**: the consultant goes in to provide some support to the management committee over staffing matters, and following a review ends up restructuring the organisation and then obtaining the funding to carry it out. The organisation needs to keep negotiating each piece of work - be clear about the financial implications, and ensure that the committee is in agreement.

EMPLOYING A CONSULTANT/ RESEARCHER/ FACILITATOR

> **How to choose a consultant**
>   - ask around other organisations/ workers
>   - use some of the directories that exist
>   - take up references - speak to the organisations who have used them
>   - think about whether their expertise is relevant - don't assume that someone who is good at research can facilitate a divided team.

> **Getting tenders for the work**
>   - If it's a small piece of work, anyone who is good will not put an effort into a tender - its lost time (and money) for them, so unless there is several days work it is not worth their while. It has to be a big piece of work to encourage them to give up a day to go for interviews etc.
>   - A direct approach by letter, asking a consultant to say what she/he would do, how, and by when, is fine. Tell her/him how many people you are approaching or if you just want them to do the job.

> **Set up a contract** which states
>   - what you expect
>   - what you can provide
>   - how much you are paying, and the agreed hourly/ daily rate
>   - what counts as reasonable expenses
>   - what the deadlines are
>   - to whom they are accountable
>   - what support they can expect
>   - how and when to make claims
>   - what reports you want, etc.

Good luck! when it works it's fine, and everyone gets something out of it.

MANAGING YOURSELF WHEN WORKING INDEPENDENTLY

John Street

INTRODUCTION

While many people work for one or maybe two organisation(s) and have some sort of management structure (however imperfect), there are also others working independently as community or youth workers. Such people can end up feeling unsupported and quite isolated, even though they like being independent.

SOME ISSUES TO CONSIDER

1. IDENTITY

When you work for an organisation, it is fairly easy to explain to others what you do and who you are, because part of your identity is in the organisation or project for which you work. This is not the case if you are independent, as you will probably try to explain who you are through your passions and whole approach.

You might say, for example, 'I am trying to make my area a better place to live' rather than 'I work for the council'. The difficulty with this is that most people don't understand where you're coming from (unless they are in the same line of work) because, to the majority of people, community workers drink tea and attend meetings. You need to work out how to explain your work to other people, particularly those in your area.

Having a good description of your work, that tells people not only what you do, but also who you are, will have a positive influence on your work and self-image. The clearer you can be about what you are seeking to achieve, and how you are working towards this, the more it benefits your profession/occupation.

2. SELF-IMAGE

When you work on your own, you can become quite negative about what you are doing or trying to achieve – especially when it all seems to be going wrong or getting nowhere – and this can have damaging effects on your self-image.

Without working colleagues who respect your work, you lose a positive support system that can sometimes keep you afloat. You need to find someone whom you trust enough to be your personal mentor/developer/supporter and who will help you make it through the tough times. This person can help you keep a better sense of perspective and also to value your expertise.

3. FREEDOM

Working alone can give you the opportunity to pick and choose the projects you want to support. You can create your own job description and direction in youth and community work, and focus on your target groups. However, this can mean that you have to take on several 'jobs' - each with its own management body and you can end up juggling between them unless you are good at time management. You also need to agree clear boundaries and reporting arrangements, so that each organisation is clear about what you are doing for them.

The freedom of independence can mean insecurity, instability and uncertainty regarding finance and income, and you could end up taking on more work than you can realistically handle. It could also mean that you take on work you don't like, just to pay the bills rather than because you are passionate about a project. Spreading yourself too thinly can cause your work to suffer, so learn your limits quickly!

4. ADMINISTRATION AND OTHER PAPER WORK

It is easy to become bogged down with paper work; or you can end up ignoring it - preferring to go to meetings or talking to people. You need to set aside time for admin, planning, evaluation, etc. and stick to it. That way you can remain effective and manage to finish some things before starting others.

5. EVALUATION

Without a clear management structure you might find you don't have to evaluate your work or write reports showing your development. Just because you do not work for an organisation where reports and self-evaluation are expected, you should not ignore your own progressional development.

You may find it helpful to have someone who can ensure that you work to correct professional practice, or challenge your actions. Without constant evaluation and supervision you may go in an unhelpful direction without even realising it. Self-evaluation is good, but not always as effective as an impartial person who is not afraid, with your permission, to give you constructive guidance and directional support.

6. SUPPORT

Although you may well be working alone, and sometimes feel very lonely, it is good to remember that loneliness does not equal isolation. There is always someone at the end of the telephone, e-mail, or just around the corner, to whom you can relate. Communication is vital; find at least one person on the same wavelength as yourself and who can understand where you are at and challenge you on your work and values.

You could also join a union - there are some with large voluntary sector/community sector sections – which would give you some legal and professional indemnity and support, as well as providing a place to meet like-minded people.

SUMMARY

If you:

- know your limits
- know your boundaries
- learn how to say 'no'
- find someone who can become your 'shoulder to cry on'/ 'challenger' and to whom you're accountable

then you may well enjoy independent working.

MANAGING TIME, WORK AND DEADLINES   Val Harris

INTRODUCTION

It often seems as if the world continues to get faster by the day. Many people feel that they can't do a good job because there isn't enough time, there's too much change, too many deadlines and they often just end up feeling swamped and working late into the night to get the next funding application in.

There aren't really any magic answers to this situation, but there are a <u>few</u> steps you can take to improve the situation. You need to decide if it's about the way you work or that there really is just too much work around.

If it's the former, then you need to look at whether your organising or planning skills could be improved; maybe you need some training to help you to be able to do things faster.

If it's the latter, then you may need to be better at prioritising and delegating (if there is anyone to pass things onto) and saying "No".

There will always be more work than we can fit into our time, but we can easily waste time, or use it less effectively than we would like; and sometimes we think things are really important and urgent but they may turn out not to be at all. When we are very busy it's hard to think through clearly what is going on and what we should be doing – we just get into reacting.

LOOKING AT THE WAY YOU WORK

➢ Check where your time goes by looking at your diary and plotting how much time you spend on particular activities; e.g. meetings, supervision, attending groups, committees, workshops . . . .

➢ Keep a diary for a week or so and log what you do with the time between the scheduled items; allocate it to headings – how much time goes on supporting colleagues, answering the phones, trying to ring people who haven't returned your calls, looking for papers lost because you haven't had time to file . . . .

➢ Analyse what you are dealing with: are there a number of time wasters - do reports not get completed because of telephone interruptions, or because you like to catch up on the office/ centre gossip; would working somewhere else be more effective.....

➢ Look carefully at all those meetings – do you have to go, can someone else go instead, can you catch up on information through the minutes; do you have time to prepare; do you get what you need from them, or are they a waste of time? Can the group/ committee manage without you – is it just habit that keeps you going (and maybe stopping others from taking on responsibility)?

➢ What tasks take you forever to do them? Would a course on how to use the Internet save you hours of time? Or finding someone who actually likes playing with the graphics packages?

➢ What tasks do you put off doing? That's often a sign that you don't know how to start them, where can you get some help or support – to deal with the impending conflicts building up in the management committee, or to write a business plan for the National Lottery application.

➤ Do you work towards the latest possible deadline? What pressure does this put other people under? Can you begin to plan ahead more so that you do your bit in time for others to do theirs? Can you request that someone does their part by a certain time so you can do your bit well?

➤ If you are honest, is some of the last minute stuff a waste of time and effort? Because you didn't have time to do it properly you won't have made a good case for funding and you might as well have slept as finish the bid at 2a.m.!

You will find it better to work through such questions with an honest friend or colleague who may see a different side to you!

TOO MUCH WORK?

If your analysis shows you are the most organised and effective person you can be and you still feel overloaded then its time to start thinking about priorities and categories like -

➤ what is essential if the organisation/ project is going to continue and to meet its aims/ any targets

➤ what needs to be done for the organisation to continue in the longer term

➤ what is important in terms of the consequences of doing, or not doing, something at this time

➤ Can a deadline be moved? Is it important to meet it? Just because there is a funding opportunity do you have to take it just then; what might be coming along later?

➤ Do you have a strategic overview/ plan for yourself, the organisation/ project, and where does the impending heap of work fit into this?

➤ Have you prepared a time line with all the key and regular events pencilled in so that you know what time you have and when, which will help you decide if you can add in that other piece of work; have you really put in planning and preparation time?

➤ Does it really have to be you that does this? We can think that it's quicker to do things ourselves rather than train up someone else but that doesn't help in the longer term as we never get out of the spiral, and it certainly isn't good community work!

➤ Can things be done differently, e.g. can you put your information into someone else's newsletter - do you need to do your own one this month? ever?

➤ Learn to think laterally and creatively, and remember that it's best to do some things well and keep your health than end up sick with no one doing the work . . . .

SUPERVISION –
ITS PLACE IN COMMUNITY WORK PRACTICE   Joyce Hatton

INTRODUCTION

The establishment of supervision as an integral and essential element of community work practice still remains to be achieved. In other related fields, such as Counselling and Social Work, supervision is a professional requirement; but equivalent structures are rarely in place for people working with communities. Even where some management and support mechanisms are in place, the experience of many workers is of ad hoc arrangements and inappropriate style.

The papers on supervision identify the purposes, different types, structures and skills of supervision in the context of developing community work practice.

OUTLINING THE ISSUES

What is Supervision?

The term 'Supervision' is used to describe a multitude of arrangements from irregular, infrequent encounters to regular, frequent, formal meetings. It is also used to describe a multitude of styles and purposes which are discussed in more detail in the other papers in this section.

What is important is that anyone involved in a supervisory relationship will have her/his own interpretation of the situation, and if this is not recognised and explored it is likely to reduce its effectiveness. In some instances, it may be necessary to separate out the management role of supervision from the support role (see paper on Types of Supervision).

The Current Context

Community workers, both paid and unpaid, are less likely than ever to be working as part of a community work team with a dedicated supervisor or manager. Many practitioners are employed as sole workers in small voluntary organisations, but even in statutory agencies it is increasingly probable there will be a single community development specialist in a multi-disciplinary team. The trend for generic management structures in large public sector bodies means that community workers are as likely to be managed by a person whose primary discipline is in an entirely different field – town planning, health visiting etc - as an experienced community worker.

The Importance of Supervision

Community workers are expected to develop, and support, groups and individuals who are experiencing exclusion and marginalisation. They, in turn, have the right to expect support in dealing with the complexities and dilemmas of the work, and opportunities to develop and reflect on their skills and knowledge. There is always some potential for conflict between the agenda of the employing agency and that of the community. That needs skilled management to resolve creatively and effectively.

Supervision 'Pyramid'

It can be useful to think of a **supervision pyramid** where, in an ideal situation, the needs of the community influence all aspects of the supervisory relationship.

SOME SUGGESTED PRINCIPLES

Appropriate supervision has a vital role to play in the development of good community work practice.   An acceptance by employing agencies and practitioners of the following principles would be a starting point for ensuring that supervision for community workers is not a negotiable luxury but an expected obligation.

➢ Supervision is an essential and integral part of community work practice.

➢ Supervision should be offered and received by all community work practitioners.

➢ Supervision should focus on meeting the needs of communities.

➢ Supervision involves both personal and professional development.

THE PURPOSE AND ROLES OF SUPERVISION

Compiled by
Barbara Booton

INTRODUCTION

Properly used, supervision, can ensure the quality and quantity of work, and also enable, train and support community workers. Historically there has been a lot of confusion, and differing expectations, about the purpose of supervision; but if the process is open, consultative, thorough and ordered it will have positive outcomes. One of the first steps in the development of a supervision process is to come to an understanding with all involved of the meaning and purpose of supervision.

The two main purposes of supervision can be identified as:

➤ To establish the accountability of the worker to the organisation or community group

➤ To promote the worker's personal and professional development

Since accountability is concerned not only with whether or not a task is performed, but also with the quality of the work, these two purposes of supervision are interwoven.

THE ROLES OF SUPERVISION

The various potential roles of supervision can be grouped under the following three broad headings:

1. The **Managing** and **Administrative** role
2. The **Teaching** and **Learning** role
3. The **Supporting** and **Enabling** role.

1. The Managing Role

This is mainly to do with the planning, distribution, monitoring and evaluation of the work tasks. An essential part of this function will be to pass on the policies and values of the agency, and give information about how its practices and procedures work. A community worker will be able to provide a better service if s/he knows how to use the agency's policies and procedures to the benefit of the community. Supervisors themselves will, therefore, need to understand policies if they are to interpret them to others. This is particularly important in relation to equal opportunities policies where the supervisor must be able to explain their implications for the day to day work, help the worker integrate their practical application, and monitor and evaluate whether they are being integrated successfully.

In addition, agreeing the allocation of work, prioritisation of it, and being involved in some of the detailed planning, would all be part of the managing and administrative role of supervision.

Monitoring and evaluating the process and outcomes of work is important. Workers need positive encouragement for their achievements, guidance to sustain their work towards certain objectives, and feedback on things they need to change or improve.

2. The Teaching and Learning role

It is unlikely anyone will embark upon the role of supervisor without learning a great deal, but it is important to remember that the learning of the person being supervised is primary.

The supervisor's role is to facilitate that learning in every way possible, whilst also recognising his/her own learning needs in relation to the provision of effective supervision. Practitioners may need to learn a range of skills, acquire knowledge and develop attitudes to enable them to carry out their work. The Supervisor's role may therefore encompass giving straightforward information, as well as tackling sensitive issues, e.g. helping, and at the same time expecting, a worker to develop anti-racist skills and awareness.

The supervisor's own experience of learning will influence how s/he imparts knowledge and understanding to others. It is important to make it relevant, accessible, appropriate, and as imaginative and interesting as possible, and to involve the leaner throughout the process.

3. The Enabling and Supporting role

Support can cover a variety of activities, such as backing-up a worker's decision, providing time by helping them to organise their work, or simply listening when it all gets on top of them. Community work can often be a stressful occupation, and supervision should attempt to reduce the impact of those stresses that will impair a worker's ability to do her/his job effectively.

In order for this to happen, it is important that an environment of mutual trust and confidence is built up in supervision. This is particularly important in relation to discriminatory issues. If a supervisor has the advantage of being say, white, male, non-disabled in addition to the role of supervisor, it is important to acknowledge that power and ensure it does not inhibit the worker from seeking support from her/his supervisor, particularly in relation to such issues as harassment.

SUMMARY

This is by no means a comprehensive list of all the roles and functions of supervision, though most of the others will possibly come under these broad headings. Most supervisors will probably emphasise one role more than another, depending upon their individual style and the agency or organisation they work in.

However the role of supervision is seen, the most vital activity in establishing a good supervisory relationship is to make their view explicit, consult others involved, and mutually agree what those roles should be, i.e. follow good community work practice!

STRUCTURE OF SUPERVISION

Compiled by
Barbara Booton

INTRODUCTION

For the sake of clarity, non oppressive practice and good practice, the processes of supervision should be carefully agreed with participants. There are a series of structures in supervision which can help prevent issues and problems arising. These are:

♦ the beginning of supervision
♦ contracts in supervision
♦ agenda in supervision
♦ records in supervision
♦ evaluation in supervision

BEGINNING SUPERVISION

1. Be clear about the purpose and outcomes of supervision before starting the first session.

2. Ensure the first session is spent clarifying and agreeing its purpose:
   ▪ What you both want to get out of it
   ▪ What the agency expects to be done in it
   ▪ What can / cannot be talked about
   ▪ Confidentiality
   ▪ Will it be recorded, and by whom
   ▪ Frequency and timings of each session
   ▪ Recognition of any power differentiations e.g. being manager, being white etc.
   ▪ What will happen i.e. just talking, or bringing written reports
   ▪ How it will be ensured it is progressing satisfactorily
   ▪ How any oppressive behaviour on either part will be dealt with.

   Most importantly *what is supervision for?* E.g. accountability, support and education

3. Discuss any previous experiences of supervision. This will provide insight into how the worker views supervision – as potentially destructive, or really welcome? It also provides the opportunity to find ways of avoiding any negative experiences previously encountered.

CONTRACTS IN SUPERVISION

Nearly all of the above can then be incorporated into a written document to form the **supervision contract**. This may seem over elaborate, but it will reduce the possibility of misunderstandings remaining – and with so many expectations resting on the process it is important to be as clear as possible. It also provides a reference point to review supervision and check that what was agreed is actually happening, or if certain things need changing.

AGENDAS IN SUPERVISION

Compiling an agenda before each supervision session is key to creating an atmosphere of trust and equality. It is important for both parties to have the opportunity to indicate what their priorities are, whilst at the same time meeting any requirements of the agency.

Some basic guidelines for compiling the agenda are:

- ♦ Be realistic about time – people hardly ever get through everything they'd hoped.
- ♦ List items from both parties – including essential items.
- ♦ Agree some prioritisation of the list.
- ♦ Give approximate timings for each item.
- ♦ Agree methods for dealing with items – discussion, listing etc.
- ♦ Discuss what to do with any outstanding items.

RECORDS IN SUPERVISION

Often regarded as a chore, it can be a useful part of the structure of supervision sessions, as well as leaving an accurate record for reference. The necessity of making a record gives an opportunity to summarise the discussions and check that there is a shared understanding of what has been agreed. Decide how the sessions will be recorded, and include it in the contract.

ASSESSMENT IN SUPERVISION

Supervision is often used as a central part of a regular, formal or informal, assessment of work performance. If so, it is essential this is made clear to the worker when the process is instituted and should be included in the contract.

Being explicit about such assessment is important, because of persistent discrimination that has taken place in the assessment of some practitioners – particularly against Black workers, women and Disabled workers. Assessment of performance should be clearly linked to the criteria specified in the job description, and form a key part of regular ongoing evaluation.

There should be no surprises; all of the work performances, both positive and negative should be shared. If this does not happen, then the worker is prevented either from gaining confidence in work s/he is doing well or being able to change aspects of their work in need of improving. This entails developing skills in giving constructive critical feedback. Not discussing opinions about performance can be dis-empowering for a worker and gives her/him no opportunity for an explanation.

TYPES OF SUPERVISION

Compiled by
Barbara Booton

INTRODUCTION

The word supervision often implies that it is an activity taking place between a manager and worker, but this is not always the case. The following is a brief description of different types of supervision that can be used.

DIFFERENT TYPES OF SUPERVISION

One-to-One Managerial Supervision

This is the more common type of supervision of a worker by a manager. If it is carefully set up, and the agenda and boundaries regularly checked, it can be prevented from being directive or oppressive. One of its major functions will be the accountability of the worker. In community work, where practitioners also see themselves as being accountable to the community, there is the potential for tension between the agency's and community's expectations. But this tension has always been there, and it is better to address it than leave it to be exposed by a crisis or conflict.

Co-supervision

This type of supervision mostly takes place between peers. i.e. two workers of equal status. Sometimes it is between two workers on the same project, or in the same department, doing different work. The essence of it is to offer each other mutual support and attention, though accountability should by no means be ruled out. It can be difficult to give this type of supervision enough structure and regularity, and although informal supervision, mentioned later, is useful, it does not offer the same measured support, feedback and assessment. Probably the most important thing is to mutually agree, and sustain, a proper time and structure for this type of supervision.

Group supervision

This is supervision of a small group of practitioners with some common work or goals. It must be small, no more than 5 or 6, as too large a group could result in nobody getting any real support or guidance from it. Again, it has to be carefully structured to ensure that everybody gets a space and all the topics are covered. Whoever draws up the agenda for such a group has to be quite skilled in consulting and prioritising. A manager, or an agreed member, could lead the group; but what would probably not work is to have no facilitator at all – which might result in a free for all and cause more stress rather than alleviate it.

Informal Supervision

This is probably what many of people get most of the time – two minutes in a corridor, or in passing during a discussion about something else. When supervision is undertaken solely in this way it is inadequate and unsatisfactory. It almost certainly does not meet the needs of the worker for support, or any of the roles of supervision outlined in the previous section.

Clearly, informal supervision is sometimes appropriate and necessary, but it should be recognised as additional to, not instead of, proper supervision. It should be brief and to the point, not drifting on to other subjects.

Crisis Supervision

People often have crises and need immediate help. What they don't need is someone who reflects back their feelings of anxiety and panic, or does not appear concerned at all. They need someone to help them clear a space, both physically and emotionally, to think about what has happened, decide what can be done immediately and help them cope with the anxiety and worry that may ensue. Some physical serenity, such as a quiet room or a hot drink, can help enormously. Often with such space it emerges that the crisis is not as bad as first feared or, if it is, the space will help plan the quick actions and strategies needed.

Crisis response is a skill in itself. These skills can be developed, but if feeling overwhelmed don't hesitate to ask for help from someone whose skills and knowledge you respect.

SKILLS IN SUPERVISION

Compiled by
Barbara Booton

INTRODUCTION

As identified in the previous section, the main roles of supervision are management, learning and support. This paper introduces some of the key skills which contribute to those functions. They are:

➢ Communication skills

➢ Teaching and Learning

➢ Constructive critical feedback

➢ Workload management.

KEY SKILLS

Communication Skills

Communication skills are integral to community work, and certain aspects of these are central to supervision. Essentially, they are the ability to listen carefully, check out what you think was said, agree with the supervisee the nature of the issue, and then move on to finding a solution. Remember that 70% of communication is non-verbal, so consider your body language. Appearing open, interested and approachable will reassure the supervisee and encourage concentration on the issues at hand.

There are also more basic elements of communication which are too often neglected: a quiet room, comfortable seating arrangement, no interruptions, no telephone.

Having regular planned supervision will also facilitate communication, allowing it to be a positive developmental process, and not just responses to crises.

Teaching and Learning

This can be one of the most positive and rewarding aspects of supervision and community work, enabling the development of someone's skills and knowledge. In order to do this effectively, you need to recognise that people learn in different ways and at different rates.

Educational theorists have written much on the principles of adult learning: some of the key points to recognise are

➢ Adults need to know why they are learning a particular thing.

➢ They need to be self-directing – to be responsible and involved in their learning.

➢ They need to be able to draw on, and reflect on, their own experiences.

➢ Their basic needs of safety, personal comfort, and respect must be met.

➢ People learn best by 'doing', and relating the learning to their own situation

It is important to begin to think how you might apply these principles in practice. For example, by providing information in a range of different ways, shadowing another worker, and drawing on the knowledge and experience of those in the local area. You may already subconsciously employ many techniques; but consciously recognising that you are facilitating learning will make it a more positive and rewarding experience.

Constructive Critical Feedback

Positive and negative feedback is essential. Most people will welcome being told how they are doing and if they need to improve their practice, but such feedback must be **constructive**. Failure to deal with criticism in an open and direct way is often destructive. Such criticism will be undertaken in several ways: aggressively, fearfully, sarcastically, or not at all.

Supervision offers the best opportunity to give constructive feedback in a positive way. In can be agreed in the supervision contract that feedback is essential and a necessary part of personal development. Discuss the ways the supervisee copes best with critical feedback, and also what opportunities s/he has for giving feedback to you about your supervision.
Some basic guidelines are:

➢ Be specific - give concrete examples of the issue you are raising.

➢ Criticise the behaviour, not the person - and then only the behaviour that can be changed; discuss ways it can be changed.

➢ Ensure it is of value to the receiver - not just 'letting off steam'.

➢ Consider the amount of feedback that can be received at any one time.

➢ Discuss the feedback, and try to come to some agreement about it.

Drawing on your own experiences of good/bad feedback will help you to think through how to apply these guidelines.

Workload Management

This is important for both the individual and the agency. A worker should be able to account for her/his time, and you need to ensure they are able to provide the best service for the community without not being exploited or undermined.
Some of the major debates around workload management are:

➢ Be clear exactly what the worker is supposed to be doing/ wants to do/ has agreed to do with someone else.

➢ The amount of time spent on a particular activity.

➢ Balancing the needs of the worker with those of the community and the organisation.

It should be agreed in the supervisory contract that all the above issues are an appropriate part of supervision, and the form in which they will be reviewed, e.g.

➢ Will they prepare a regular verbal or written report?

➢ Are you going to get feedback from groups s/he is working with?

➢ Will you regularly review the time allocated to certain tasks?

➢ Will regular work targets be agreed?

The clearer the agreement on these issues, the less likely it is that conflicts and confusions about workers expectations will arise.

FINALLY . . .

This paper can only highlight some of the main points to consider, but it will serve as a skills-check, enabling you to identify areas you need to review and update. This could be done through training, reading, and learning from peers, alongside regular practice of supervision with some good feedback.

ACKNOWLEDGING ISSUES OF POWER IN SUPERVISION

Compiled by
Barbara Booton

INTRODUCTION

Acknowledging that there are power issues in supervision is essential. This paper will introduce some of the main points to be considered. As with all the skills and responsibilities of being a supervisor, you should regularly review and update your practice.

Understanding the impact of both personal and institutionalised power is at the core of community work. Supervisory power impacts on both the supervisory relationship and also on how anti-discriminatory practice is monitored in all the workers under supervision.

The role of supervisor, whether as a peer or manager, gives undoubted power which, coupled with the power of being say male and white, illustrates the potential for abuse of this relationship. These power bases, and their potential for oppressive practice, must be openly acknowledged and discussed at the beginning of supervision.

THE MAIN ISSUES

- It is the supervisor's responsibility to ensure staff have a working environment safe from oppression and discrimination.

- It should be recognised that some staff may be asked to undertake many tasks outside their arena. For example, a request for a Disabled representative on an interview panel, or a Black perspective on a paper or policy. Check they are not overloaded, or penalised in any way, for such commitments

- Proper career development opportunities should be identified for those from oppressed groups e.g. Black people, Disabled people, women, older people etc.

- Give all workers proper feedback about their work. Don't let fears of being accused of racism or sexism, for example, stop you from enabling workers to develop their practice and skills.

- Do not assume someone is an expert about an issue.

- Do not dominate supervision with discussions on gender, race, disability etc. in order to demonstrate your own knowledge or experience when the worker needs to discuss her/his work.

- Respect and value the knowledge and experience of members of oppressed groups.

- Consider how you would deal with a situation where the supervisee experiences you as discriminatory, without using of your power as supervisor to dismiss or suppress the complaint.

- How will you support him/her through a complaint of discrimination from another member of staff or the community?

In order for to ensure the integration of anti-discriminatory practice into the supervisee's work, you need to be clear both about your own practice, and also that of the group or organisation. Equal opportunities statements and policies, codes of practice, and applied and detailed guidelines for all aspect of work ,are very important, and should be 'owned', monitored and regularly reviewed by all members of the organisation. Not all groups and organisations have them in place, but, as a supervisor you should continually monitor your own practice and that of the person being supervised.

Ways to promote good practice include:

♦ Regularly place issues of discrimination or oppression on the supervision agenda. Be specific: ask for examples of people's practices in this area, rather than vague questions about their commitment to anti-racist practice.

♦ Consider the composition of the community the organisation or group works with, and ensure it is appropriately represented in the work undertaken.

♦ Discuss the worker's own views about stereotypes and the impact of discriminatory and oppressive practices upon individuals and communities.

♦ Check that s/he can recognise the strength people from oppressed groups show in the face of such practices.

♦ Provide opportunities for workers to develop anti-discriminatory practice skills, e.g. through training.

What is necessary to achieve anti-discrimination is sustained commitment and energetic vigilance. It is an emotive and inspiring issue, requiring constant repetition until it becomes an automatic part of everyday existence. Anti-discriminatory practice is good practice, and vice versa!

WHAT DO YOU WANT FROM SUPERVISION?   Joyce Hatton

INTRODUCTION

This paper will provide some prompts for supervisees about how to maximise the usefulness of supervision. It is always an instructive exercise to think through all the things you would want in an ideal situation – this makes a good starting point for negotiations even if there has to be compromise later. All the following issues should be discussed and agreed at the beginning of supervision, and included in the **supervision contract**.

WHAT DO YOU WANT?

Commitment

Whatever your supervisory situation, it is not going to work without commitment. If sessions are frequently cancelled or cut short, or your supervisor is constantly distracted or unprepared, it is clearly going to affect their usefulness. Try and be assertive about expecting the basic courtesy, but also ask yourself if you are contributing to the avoidance. How you think about tackling the situation will depend upon the circumstances:

➤ Is there a supervision policy for your organisation to which you can refer?

➤ Could you work with colleagues to agree a policy?

➤ Are you being realistic? e.g. a two hour session once a month may be more productive than one hour every fortnight, for both of you.

➤ Can you find a more conducive venue away from interruptions?

An Honest Relationship

Effective supervision is unlikely to always be a comfortable experience. Expect honesty about your supervisor's boundaries:

➤ What should be confidential and what needs to be shared more widely?

➤ Is there an acknowledgement of power issues? If the person supervising you has the power to terminate your employment, or fail your course assessment, this needs to be openly acknowledged as well as all the issues relating to race, gender, class and other differences of perspective.

➤ Separate the personal from the professional. Expect your supervisor to be clear about the role and purpose of your supervision sessions, even though you may have a different relationship as colleagues or friends.

Ideas and expertise

Increasingly, community workers are being managed by people who may not be from a similar professional background. Sometimes in these circumstances separating the line management from the supervisory role can be the best option e.g. using a peer supervisor, or group sessions, to provide practice support. You should, however, expect your supervisor to use a range of problem-solving techniques and a willingness to seek out information from other colleagues, reference material etc.

Structure and Organisation

A good supervisor should be able to offer advice on structures at a number of different levels. Within your sessions you should expect your supervisor to give advice on structure and content, and take a lead role in this, if you are relatively inexperienced or new to the organisation. Expect her/him to know about any relevant policies that have a bearing on supervision, and to offer methods for contracting and recording them.

You should also expect supervisions to be multi-functional and offer managing, learning and support roles. In some instances these may need to be provided by more than one person.

Your supervisor also needs to be able to help you understand, and work more effectively within, the organisational structures that impact on your work situation. If your supervisor is also your manager, there will be occasions when it is appropriate for her/him to take up issues on your behalf and give you a sense of where your contribution fits into the bigger picture.

Systematic Review

Remember, however effective the relationship may be for a while, circumstances and requirements alter over time. Expect regular reviews of how things are going and be willing to adapt.

Section 8

Campaigning

INFLUENTIAL IDEAS
Julie Pryke

INTRODUCTION

The need to campaign is constantly with those involved with 'communities', whether they are geographical communities or are drawn together by one particular issue. Those involved may be community members, activists or paid workers. There have been many theorists who have been influential in inspiring people to resist oppression and to ' fight for' their just cause.

This section is here as a brief reminder of three such people whose ideas encourage and support campaigners within the community.

MOHANDAS GANDHI (THE MAHATMA): B. 1869, D. 1948

Gandhi encouraged the use of peaceful protest , non-violent direct action. He adopted and developed the technique of **'satyagraha'** (truth = force, or 'truth power') or non-violent resistance to political coercion.

He believed in the power of numbers , moral rights, and so on, he acknowledged violent resistance in extreme cases as better than cowardice - which he saw as violent to the individual's humanity and spirituality.

Key elements of his theories:-

➢ Try to persuade your opponent by reason, then publicise your case and issue an ultimatum
➢ Eliminate self-interest, in his case, through fasting and prayer
➢ Then you can consider direct action - civil disobedience - but only under these conditions
  - there must be impartial evidence of a real grievance, removable by direct action and which the victims themselves wish to get rid of (not just a 'leader' or a small minority of those affected)
  - the protesters must be self-supporting and prepared to suffer
  - demands must be kept to the minimum consistent with truth
  - the action must be called off if there is any violence.

SAUL ALINSKY: B.1909, D. 1972

Alinsky was a **PAID** campaign organiser for the oppressed. He believed that if he was paid then he was accountable to the group who paid him i.e. they could sack him, his allegiance was to them.

He founded **Industrial Areas Foundation** (I.A.F.), a team of professional campaigners who would help identify and train local people to campaign around the community's concerns. They would not do it for them.

He believed the community had to want I.A.F. to be involved and so should fund-raise to pay for them to come in, as the community wouldn't do this unless they thought their cause was worth it. I.A.F. would not work in an area without invitation and payment.

He believed that **People's Organisations must be led by the people.**

Tactics:-
Unorthodox, change fast, exciting, fun, threat (imagined or real) to the opposition.

Books:-
'Rules for Radicals'
'Primers for Hell Raisers'
'Reveille for Radicals'
'Rubbing the Sores of Discontent'

Key elements of his theory:-

➢ His view of society - **2 classes** - the 'haves' and the 'have nots'. The 'have nots' sometimes become the 'have a little' and criticise and oppress the 'have nots' instead of challenging the 'haves'.

➢ People are motivated out of **self-interest** - they work best when they can see the benefit to themselves. Good campaigns make use of this.

➢ Power - if you have no money you still have **people power** - use people in mass numbers to show the strength of your campaign.

Tactic guidelines from 'Rules For Radicals'

➢ Power is not only what you have but what the enemy thinks you have
➢ Never go outside your own experience
➢ Always go outside the experience of the enemy
➢ Make the enemy live up to their rule book
➢ Ridicule is man's most potent weapon
➢ A good tactic is an enjoyable one
➢ A tactic that drags on becomes a drag
➢ Keep the pressure on
➢ The threat is more terrifying than the action
➢ The price of a successful attack is a constructive alternative.

PAULO FREIRE: B.1921, D.1997

Freire used political education or 'consciousness-raising' to give power back to the powerless. He looked at issues of oppression - cultural invasion/ culture of silence/ false consciousness/ cultural action for freedom. His philosophy of **'consciousization'** was the fore-runner to the 'Women's Liberation' movement and the Black Civil Rights movement in the 1960s, and has since been adapted by groups and organisations world-wide.

He also stressed the value of combining reflection and action (praxis) rather than just thinking about the issue or acting without thinking things through.

Key Quotation from FREIRE

"Washing one's hands of the conflict between the powerful and the powerless means to side with the powerful, not to be neutral".

Books:- include
'Pedagogy of the Oppressed'
'The Politics of Education'
'Pedagogy of Hope'
'Cultural Action for Freedom'

Fritz C. 'Because I speak Cockney THEY think I'm Stupid'

Key elements of his theory:-

➢ **Two views of humankind**

  ▪ as **objects** (mouldable and adaptable i.e. easy for the powerful to influence)

OR

  ▪ as **subjects** "in and with the world". Freire viewed people as independent beings, able to think for themselves, able to "transcend and recreate the world".

➢ **Three levels of consciousness**:-

  ▪ **MAGICAL CONSCIOUSNESS** - accept everything that happens - even injustices
  ▪ **NAIVE CONSCIOUSNESS** - gain an insight into what's happening to you - but only as an individual
  ▪ **CRITICAL CONSCIOUSNESS** - gain an insight into what's happening, not just to you but to others - recognise the power and the structures - able to act to do something about it.

Tactics:-
  • Raising awareness through education
  • Recognising that everyone has something to offer as well as something to learn
  • Use of ' political' text
  • Use of situations within the life experience of the students
  • Problem posing/ problem solving - designed to provide information for coping with life experiences.

PRAXIS

Reflection alone = issue not progressed

Action alone = unplanned action (may progress but not in the required way

Reflection + Action = 'Praxis' = planned and evaluated progression towards the end goal

(based on Freire)

Model of how Praxis should operate:

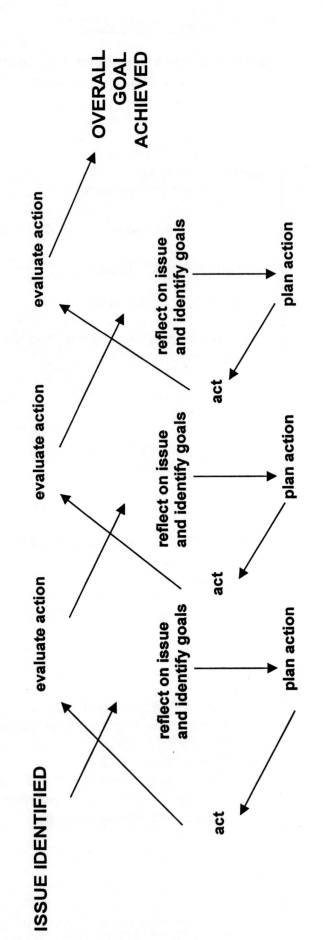

GETTING STARTED

Julie Pryke

INTRODUCTION

TO GET STARTED - <u>REMEMBER</u>

You need	**INFORMATION**	from others
They need	**INFORMATION**	from you
You need	**SUPPORT**	from them
They need	**SUPPORT**	from you

Without this your campaign won't work for you, or for them.

How do you get information and support?

You need **EVIDENCE** to support your case.

WHERE DO YOU START?

1. Find out the **SIZE** of the problem
   - ➤ is it just an issue for you, for a small number of people, for a community, or is it regional or national?

2. **IDENTIFY and get HELP & SUPPORT** from others

3. **ANALYSE** the problem
   - ➤ What are the causes & effects of the problem?
   - ➤ What needs to be done?

CAMPAIGNING ACTION

Overleaf is a diagram giving ideas of what campaigning action might involve. Then on the following pages we've expanded each line of the diagram to suggest good, bad and best practice ideas.

YOU CAN

plan

do a survey

get sponsors

use the media

work with others

know your rights

call in the experts

call a public meeting

knock on people's doors

collect names on a petition

publish a leaflet & distribute it

research in libraries, etc.

recruit local volunteers

hold a demonstration

use politicians

design a poster

pull a stunt

fundraise

use I.T.

CAMPAIGNING ACTION

Julie Pryke

INTRODUCTION

This section gives a snapshot of a number of ideas which campaigners might adopt. It is designed to 'spark off' new ideas, and is built on the experience of getting things wrong as well as getting things right. Use it during planning to get more ideas going.

PLANNING

GOOD for	➢ getting action started ➢ trying out unusual tactics ➢ sharing ideas ➢ proving need
BAD if	➢ it's not done properly ➢ it's just one person's ideas ➢ it involves violent action
BEST when	➢ it uses 'Praxis' (progress monitored & evaluated) ➢ it's inclusive of all group members ➢ it's recorded

DOING A SURVEY

GOOD for	➢ publicising a campaign ➢ getting information ➢ talking to people
BAD if you	➢ can't collate the material ➢ have no time ➢ take too small a sample
BEST when	➢ you plan well ➢ have lots of volunteers ➢ write up as a report

GETTING SPONSORS

GOOD for	➢ providing large amounts, ➢ long periods of time ➢ getting publicity
BAD if	➢ they want to alter your aims ➢ they're mean in what they offer ➢ their advertising takes up too much space on your building (for example)

| **BEST** when | ➤ you research the sponsors beforehand
➤ you agree with their ethics
➤ you sign a contract that suits **you** (and them) |

USING THE MEDIA

GOOD for	➤ launching a campaign ➤ presenting ideas and petitions ➤ taking photographs
BAD if	➤ you let them misquote you ➤ you antagonise them ➤ you don't give them enough notice
BEST when	➤ you get to know them ➤ you give them a press release ➤ you present your own materials

WORKING WITH OTHERS

GOOD for	➤ networking and identifying issues ➤ avoiding isolation ➤ spotting problems
BAD if	➤ everyone doesn't pull their weight ➤ you disagree about objectives ➤ it becomes a clique
BEST when	➤ you all share the workload ➤ you support each other ➤ you resolve differences successfully

KNOWING YOUR RIGHTS

GOOD if	➤ they have been well researched ➤ they are understood ➤ they have been put in simple terms
BAD if	➤ they are not known ➤ they are not clear to all members ➤ they have been badly researched
BEST when	➤ they are exercised ➤ they are used assertively against other parties arguments ➤ they have a legal basis

CALLING IN THE EXPERTS

GOOD for	➢ specialist information ➢ developing skills ➢ identifying resources
BAD if	➢ they take over ➢ they cost a lot ➢ they use specialised language and exclude the group
BEST when	➢ they are **yourselves** ➢ they can help with funding ➢ they 'know' people

CALLING A PUBLIC MEETING

GOOD for	➢ identifying support ➢ finding out how big the problem is ➢ for recruiting help from the community and from outsiders
BAD if	➢ unplanned ➢ one person dominates ➢ factions arise
BEST	➢ after small initial meetings where ideas have been formulated ➢ if key people are invited ➢ if used as a launch pad for campaign or challenge to authority

KNOCKING ON PEOPLE'S DOORS

GOOD for	➢ getting to know people ➢ identifying concerns ➢ getting offers of help
BAD if	➢ you've no identification ➢ you're unknown in the area ➢ it's bad weather
BEST when	➢ you can go in pairs in areas where you are known ➢ you can use community languages ➢ you have pen & paper to take notes & can give out leaflets at the same time

COLLECTING NAMES ON A PETITION

GOOD
- for publicising the campaign
- for getting to talk to people
- for presenting to the authorities
- with publicity

BAD if
- you get little support
- you word it badly
- you don't present it or follow it up

BEST when
- you present it publicly
- you record names and addresses for the future
- you involve others (including well-known others)

PUBLISHING & DISTRIBUTING A LEAFLET

GOOD if
- it tells people what you are doing
- it is easily understood (and use pictures)
- you distribute it well

BAD if
- it's boring
- it's only written in English
- it's thrown around the streets

BEST when
- it looks attractive
- it gets people interested
- it's handed over personally

RESEARCH IN LIBRARIES, ETC

GOOD
- for getting information
- for identifying evidence
- if you record well

BAD if
- you don't do enough
- you rely on second hand evidence
- you don't plan how to use it

BEST when
- it means you contact others interested in the same issue
- you get access to resources
- developing new ideas or adapting old

RECRUITING LOCAL VOLUNTEERS

GOOD if
- there are lots of small tasks to do
- you plan & work together
- you use their different skills

BAD if
- they're not clear about their role
- they are overworked,
- they are unappreciated

BEST when
- they are offered support
- they're given a contract
- they are recognised as <u>VOLUNTEERS</u> and as part of the team

HOLDING A DEMONSTRATION

GOOD if it's
- well organised
- well publicised
- well attended

BAD if
- it's poorly attended
- it becomes violent
- it attracts bad publicity

BEST when
- the media are present
- it has police consent
- it attacks the right target

USING POLITICIANS

GOOD if
- they depend on local votes
- they understand your issues
- you get to know them well

BAD if
- they support other interests
- they are "too busy" to respond
- you make an enemy of them

BEST when
- you identify their key interests & skills
- you involve them in your publicity campaigns
- you ask questions in Parliament or Council

DESIGNING A POSTER

GOOD	➤ for raising issues ➤ for advertising events ➤ if it's straight-forward
BAD if	➤ it's confusing ➤ it's poorly presented ➤ it's just lying on a desk!
BEST when	➤ it's simple and easily understood ➤ it's fun ➤ it has logo or a recognisable theme.

PULLING A STUNT

GOOD if	➤ you do something new ➤ you get maximum publicity ➤ you use the idea to fund-raise at the same time
BAD if	➤ it goes wrong ➤ you damage people or property ➤ you get bad publicity for it
BEST when	➤ it's FUN ➤ everyone knows what to do ➤ you video, take photos or use audio-cassette to record it

FUNDRAISING

GOOD if	➤ it's planned carefully ➤ you approach more than one source ➤ it's well presented
BAD if	➤ it's done without consultation ➤ it is too greedy or dishonest ➤ it underestimates actual costs
BEST when	➤ you keep accurate records ➤ you build in safeguards ➤ you are accountable to funders

USING INFORMATION TECHNOLOGY (IT)

GOOD for
- ➢ researching issues and making links with others
- ➢ producing publicity
- ➢ e-mailing supporters quickly

BAD if
- ➢ it excludes some people
- ➢ you neglect "snail-mail", phone calls etc.
- ➢ it costs too much

BEST when
- ➢ everyone has access (not just one 'expert')
- ➢ people receive training & practice
- ➢ it records successes and collects evidence

WRITING A GRANT APPLICATION   Julie Pryke

INTRODUCTION

This section offers a brief idea on how to fill in applications for grants from a variety of sources in order to fuel part or all of your campaigning work. Further advice is given in Section 10 – Funding; use this section as a quick checklist.

CHECKLIST

➢ **Identify** the most appropriate charities for your need

➢ **Find out**
- when they meet to make decisions
- who you have to contact
- whether phone enquiries are acceptable,
- how much they usually give out in grants to each applicant
- what the conditions of the grant are: i.e. criteria & areas of interest - groups/ individuals, women, children, arts, poverty, historical buildings etc.

➢ **If you still qualify**
- ask for an application form (if they issue them)
- take several copies of the blank form
- practise your bid on them.

➢ **After you've practised**
- Fill in the original form,

  OR

- If they have no form, write your letter of application using the following guidelines:-
  - **Proposed outline** : concise summary - include the sum requested
  - **Introduction** : aims/objectives, brief history, management structure etc.
  - **Definition of need** : description of problem, statistics, support/links with other agencies/ Local Authority etc.
  - **Methods** : how you will achieve the objectives
  - **Goals/ outcomes** : target what will be achieved - by when.
  - **Evaluation** : how you will monitor & evaluate your success.
  - **Budget** : capital and revenue expenditure, allow for inflation, but don't be too greedy or exaggerate too much

- **Any other information** : constitution, support, annual report, financial statements, etc.

- **Who and where** : who should the money be paid to? Name and address of bank account, which agency will manage the budget, registered charity number if you've got one (or that of the managing agency).

FINAL POINTS

➢ Don't just apply for money for the sake of it

➢ Keep a copy of the final application

➢ If they ask for two sides of A4 - give them two sides of A4!

➢ Be prepared to answer written or phone queries

➢ Be prepared to monitor and evaluate, meet targets

  then...!!

➢ Enjoy it - good luck!

SUCCESSFUL CAMPAIGNING   Julie Pryke

INTRODUCTION

This section aims to give additional ideas which will help campaigns to become successful. If used by groups, they can make life easier and leave more time to enjoy the campaigning action. The key role is the 'Trouble-Shooter' – a person who can anticipate problems or barriers raised by the opposition, and also offer solutions which may be acceptable to them whilst still meeting the needs of the campaign.

SUCCESSFUL CAMPAIGNERS . . .

> Keep everything **CLEAR, SIMPLE & LOGICAL**

 > **APPOINT** people to different roles -

  ♦ **trouble-shooter - the KEY ROLE** (to anticipate problems & look for solutions)

  ♦ **chairperson** (for meetings)

  ♦ **secretary**

  ♦ **treasurer and/or fundraiser**

  ♦ **publicity officer**

  ♦ **researchers**

  ♦ **volunteers**

  ♦ **supporters**

DO'S AND DON'TS

✓ **DO** consider rotating roles and gaining extra skills

✗ **DON'T FORGET** that one person who can address & post 10 pieces of mail is worth 10 people who grumble they haven't received any!

✓ **DO** involve other people and make best use of their individual skills

✗ **DON'T** undervalue them or lose their interest

✓ **DO** share out tasks as much as possible

✗ **DON'T** expect too much

✓ **DO** offer support

✗ **DON'T** pressurise their supporters

✓ **DO** help others to enjoy it

REMEMBER TO . . .

> ➤ **RECORD** at every stage
> ➤ **DOUBLE-CHECK** the information
> ➤ Ensure campaigns are **ACCURATE** in their claims
> ➤ Make **RECOMMENDATIONS** which are feasible
> ➤ Offer a **FACE-SAVING** solution
> ➤ **ROLE-PLAY** difficult situations beforehand
> ➤ Get **FUNDING**
> ➤ Pay **EXPENSES**
> ➤ Send **COPIES** to everyone
> ➤ Act **QUICKLY**
> ➤ Use **EYECATCHING** ideas
> ➤ Promote **POSITIVE IMAGES** of your own group
> ➤ **TIMETABLE** and plan ahead
> ➤ Inform the **POLICE** of plans where necessary
> ➤ Remember **ALINSKY's** tactics, etc. etc.........

WHAT HAPPENS NEXT?
Julie Pryke

INTRODUCTION

You've run a successful campaign   You need to wind up the group

You've not been successful this time   You want to fight on

You want to "call it a day"

How can you

> ➢ Complete the work you have done?
>
> ➢ Finish off the campaign satisfactorily?
>
> ➢ Get people to feel OK about responding next time?
>
> ➢ Interest funders in the future?
>
> ➢ Avoid that 'let-down' feeling when it's all over?

YOU NEED TO ...

> ➢ **RECORD THE WORK** as you go along; use writing – reports + records of
>   - who helped
>   - who supported you
>   - photos
>   - press reports
>   - video recording
>   - banners and posters
>   - financial records
>   - songs
>   - poems
>   - plays etc.
>
> ➢ **REVIEW AND ANALYSE THE WORK YOU'VE DONE AS YOU GO ALONG**
>   - what worked
>   - what didn't
>   - and why?
>
> ➢ **EVALUATE THE CAMPAIGN WHEN IT'S FINISHED**
>   - Whether you met your aims and objectives,
>   - What was achieved?
>   - Was there conflict within the group, if so

- why?

- was it dealt with in a satisfactory way?

- Can you produce satisfactory accounts and reports for funders and group members?

- What have you learnt from the work?

- Could you do it better next time?

➤ **FIND OUT WHAT THERE IS TO CELEBRATE** –
- End the campaign, or this part of it, with a party, festival or meal

- Even if you haven't achieved everything you'd hoped for you will still be able to find "plenty of plus points".

- Proclaim your success to the world –
  - inform the media etc. and you'll attract support for the next stage or the next issue.

- Let people know you appreciate their efforts.
  - Show the video,
  - exhibit the photos, posters, banners,
  - produce the play,
  - sing the campaign song,
  - have a 'play-in' on the new play equipment, a duck race on the newly cleaned river - whatever seems appropriate.

➤ **KEEP A 'WATCHING BRIEF' ON THE ISSUE** –

- e.g. if it's around a health or environmental issue you may need to keep meeting for a while (it doesn't have to be at such regular intervals),

- plan what you might do next time,

- be able to respond quickly if necessary.

➤ **KNOW HOW TO CONTACT EACH OTHER - NEXT TIME!**
                                              NEXT time!
                                                    next time!
                                                          next ti...

THE ROLE OF THE PROFESSIONAL   Julie Pryke

INTRODUCTION

One of the most important points you need to consider before embarking on campaigning work in future employment is that as a 'professional' you have a particular role to play. You also hold your own set of ethics and values.

In addition, as a paid worker or contracted volunteer you will also have your own management structure to which you are answerable. Yes, even as a volunteer you may well be constrained by the agency policy, particularly if it is one which has a policy on the use of volunteers and has outlined to you clear expectations of your work for it.

So I'd like to outline, briefly, what I see as the factors you need to consider, at least as a starting point. This is not to put you off any future campaigning, but rather to make you aware so that you can think around the various issues and give the best service for your community members within the perimeters/boundaries defined by/for you.

WHY SHOULD YOU BECOME INVOLVED?

Many youth and community workers would feel themselves unable to consider working in this way with their community, either because they see themselves as managers of a building, e.g. the Youth Club, or as service providers. They may feel that it is a role for others to undertake, that it is too 'political', or that they do not have enough knowledge or experience. They may have too much other work in hand, or they may have genuine anxieties about how their work would be received by their employers.

I would argue that

◆ as a professional working in the 'caring' professions, it is almost impossible not to respond positively for a request for support and skills development from people within the community with whom you work, particularly if these people are expressing basic concerns over social, environmental and economic issues of direct relevance to their lives

◆ all youth and community work involves some element of 'political' education

◆ helping others work through the process of collective action is just as important as the achievement (or not) of their goals.

With a supportive worker, individuals can achieve a great deal, both in terms of self-development and in acquiring valuable resources for their community.

HOW FAR CAN YOU SUPPORT WITHIN THE TERMS OF YOUR EMPLOYMENT?

Consider the following points:

◆ Be honest with your community. If they are aware of the constraints you are under, then they will be able to work around them with you.

◆ Be honest with your employer about your work – he/she may be extremely supportive, also better for your health and self-esteem, and less stressful! If you cannot become fully involved, offer as much support as you are able and question the policy of non-involvement in a positive way - you may be able to alter the policy for the future.

- ◆ As an employee who wishes to engage in 'political education'/community action, you must take care to act as a model employee in every way - employers may not wish to high-light their non-support for your action (you may have a lot of popular support they wish to keep). However, they may choose to look carefully at other areas of your work and identify any breaches of contract on which they can act - poor time-keeping, unexplained absences, use of resources for personal reasons etc.

- ◆ Work within the general obligations of your contract, as well as carrying out the specific duties involved - i.e. obey any reasonable and lawful instructions, ask permission in writing to attend demonstrations or to attend them in your own time. You should not cost your employer time and/or money in campaign work which is merely about your own concerns. If, however, you are employed as someone with a campaigning role, or have expressed access to resources as part of your work, then this is acceptable, provided you are working within your contract.

- ◆ Make sure accurate minutes of meetings are taken and that these are circulated to all who attended as soon as possible. Even if another note-taker is present it is still OK to do this yourself if you have concerns over the accuracy or perspective of the minutes, or you feel that these are being edited in a biased way. Do, however, bear in mind the question of confidentiality and whether this has affected what has been put on paper rather than said verbally. Beware of breaching confidentiality, you do have a duty to your employer as well as your community, and you may find that your ethical considerations may not be accepted under employment law.

- ◆ Work out your objectives clearly. Do not assume that your employer is equally clear - you can use this to your advantage of course! Plan, record and evaluate - this can be a good way of selling the campaign to your employer in retrospect. Be clear what methods you will use - if these involve facilitation and skills development, rather than leading from the front, this can again be a positive and legitimate part of your work.

- ◆ Use supervision as a positive mechanism to check out your role/agency's stance.

- ◆ Do not 'take over' the campaign - it's not yours, it belongs to the people for whom it is an issue. Help it to succeed for them through you - not you through them! Remember, a good leader is the last to accept the praise and the first to accept criticism (as a paid worker isn't that part of your job also?)

- ◆ Be aware of your employer's constraints - it may not be in your own best long-term interests to negatively target their main funder.

- ◆ Look for support from colleagues and the union.

- ◆ Use as many links as possible through your employer in a positive way.

- ◆ Remember Alinsky's 'Rules for Radicals', relax and have fun!

Finally, don't be depressed by all of the above. They paint the worst possible scenario. They are things to be aware of, and planned for not excuses for lack of action.

USING THE INTERNET
Julie Pryke

INTRODUCTION

One of the reasons community groups begin to use the Internet is as a campaigning tool. This chapter aims to give you points to think about, and also some tips to enable your group use it effectively. It is important to remember that it is only one of a number of tools available, e.g. personal contact, meetings, door-knocking, surveys, publicity stunts etc., etc. The Internet is best used in addition to, rather than instead of other methods, as you cannot always be sure who you are reaching through the net or when it will be read.

USES OF THE INTERNET

* **What can the Internet be used for when campaigning?**
  Researching information, informing others about what you're doing, networking (contacting others with similar concerns/interests), and contacting experts are all possible through the 'Net'. So is publicising events, getting support for your campaign and contacting influential others (e.g. Government Ministers). Finally, it's possible to hold debates and 'virtual' conferences, use the 'alternative' media, publish articles and so on.

* **Information**
  When you are starting a campaign, whether it is for something you need or against something you don't want to happen, you need information on which to base the campaign. If it's a local campaign, you would probably start off by finding out how many people are concerned, and then use the 'Net' to obtain statistics.

  If it's damp houses, you might want to know how many people in your town live in such houses and the attendant problems (e.g. you might need to find out about asthma and its causes plus the symptoms and effects on children). You might also need to know whether minority ethnic members are over-represented in the statistics. All this kind of information is available using the right search tools. There are some examples in the 'Further Reading' section; but experiment, try different ones until you find those which suit you and you'll soon be an expert in using the web.

  You may have lots of information on a very specialist area and want to share it with others - having your own web-site would be one way of doing this. Most service providers allow you to have a certain amount of space free of charge, and even give lessons on how to do it.

  You can use public areas to appeal for contacts with others having a similar experience, or add your e-mail address as a link from your web-site or, by agreement, through some-one else's.

  You can contact experts who might be able to advise you, help provide an investigation, an 'expert witness' or undertake particular research. Be warned, you may have to pay a fee, but you might also find that, if they are particularly interested or have links with Universities or Colleges, they may be able to give you a service free of charge or know someone who can.

*   **Publicity**
    Use your own website for publicity e.g. photos you've taken, a poster for
    an event, a quiz which gives information or playing a video you've made -
    with a voice over as a bonus! The Internet can be linked to many other
    devices through Digital cameras, Scanners and other tools. Ask your
    community IT provider for advice. Don't spend lots of money without trying
    things out first - an unused gadget is never worth the money!

    Publish your own articles on the campaign on the 'Net'- others may need
    your help and ideas.

*   **Contacts**
    Contact your MP if he's on e-mail and ask for his support, fill in petitions on
    line, write to well-known celebrities with web-sites asking for support. But
    don't forget about personal & written contact - many people prefer this.

*   **Media**
    There are lots of contacts with the media – on the 'Net', the 'BBC', 'The
    Guardian', 'Red Pepper', plus many small, but widely read 'alternative'
    papers produced by activists in the 'not-for-profit' sector who may be
    concerned about particular issues. For example 'Schnews'
    (http://www.schnews.org.uk/) provide information on 'New Age Travellers',
    'Road Protestors', The Criminal Justice and Public Order Act.
    'Undercurrents' produce videos of action and cover world-wide events.
    They also accept material from <u>you</u>!

    When using the media, remember that however friendly and sympathetic
    they seem to be they want a story - rehearse it, polish it, feel confident
    about it and then approach them. Give them a written copy of what you've
    said so that they don't misquote you.

    Finally, don't forget you can hold live debates, use 'Instant Messages' and
    hold 'virtual' conferences (in other words you don't have to travel - you do
    it through your PC), some of these can include video conferencing. Again,
    you can get advice from community groups with experience.

EXAMPLES OF WEBSITES

Undercurrents
A producer of video magazines and community information on the Internet -
see above. (http://www.undercurrents.org/)

C.A.R.F. (Campaign against Racism and Fascism)
Provides up-to-date information by sending you a magazine via e-mail; the
subscription is free. In October 2001, for example, they produced a petition on
the web against the voucher scheme for asylum seekers which was sent to
the Home Office.
(http://www.carf.demon.co.uk/)

B.C.S.P. (Bradford Community Statistics Project)
An example of a project, based in Bradford, which helps community groups
identify relevant statistics, through the 'Net' and other sources, to back
campaigns.
(http://www.geocities.com/community_statistics_project/)

F.O.E.(Friends of the Earth)
Run national and local environmental campaigns Worth looking at local branches for ideas
http://www.foe.co.uk/

C.P.A.G.(Child Poverty Action Group)
A national charity which campaigns on behalf of children against poverty. Lots of campaign ideas. Again, look at the local branch web-sites.
http://www.cpag.org.uk/

SEARCH ENGINES

Below are some search engine addresses which may help to get you started. But remember, they all have different ways of searching, or may look at different areas. Sometimes you will find this very frustrating and time-consuming. Don't let it worry you too much. Leave it, go back to it later. The same search at a different time might produce better results or different key words get you instant results.

AltaVista: http://www.altavista.com/ Good general information

Ask Jeeves: http://www.aj.com/ Ask a question

Clever Search: http://cleversearch.hypermart.net/ Searches through several engines

HotBot: http://hotbot.lycos.com/ Very friendly site

DPPC Library, Electronic Sources:
http://www.brad.ac.uk/library/dppc/electron.htm Very comprehensive list of search engines, plus lessons on how to use them.

Section 9

Funding

WHAT DO YOU WANT MONEY FOR?

Martin F. Jenkins

INTRODUCTION

There are four stages to fundraising:

1. Decide what you want to do
2. Work out how much it will cost
3. Decide how to raise the money/ to whom to apply
4. Write the application.

This order **cannot** be changed. You **cannot** miss out any of the stages.

HOW DO YOU DECIDE WHAT YOU WANT TO DO?

Be clear about who makes the decision. It could be:

➢ the staff
➢ the chair
➢ the whole management committee
➢ the fundraising sub-committee -

but, whoever it is, make sure that they have the authority to make the decision on behalf of the group.

Base your decision on need. Can you answer these questions:

➢ What is the problem we want to solve?
➢ How do we propose to solve it?
➢ What is the scale of the problem?
➢ How do we know our solution will work?
➢ Are we the best group to take on this work?

Before you rush to develop a project, do some research. Find out how big the problem really is and whether your solution will work. For example: has a similar project worked elsewhere? Do we have the skills to deliver this project? Is there another group that could do it better (and could be convinced to do it)?

Decide what work you really want to do. **Do not**

➢ invent work to meet a funder's criteria, or guidelines
➢ develop a project just because funding is available for that kind of work
➢ move into a totally new area of work because funding is available.

Hint: When, just because funding is available, an organisation starts moving into new areas of work which have nothing to do with its original objectives - it needs to look, not at funding, but at why it exists.

ONCE YOU'VE DECIDED WHAT YOU WANT TO DO...

Do you want to raise money for one piece of work, or a single project? **Go to next section.**

Do you want to raise money for more than one piece of work, or project? **Then answer the following questions:**

➢ Can you handle running (or fundraising for) more than one project? If **No**, go to next question.

➢ Is there one project which is more urgent, or important, than the others? If **Yes**, deal with that one first. If **No**, go to next question.

➢ Is there a logical order? If **Yes** - We can't run project B without project A, so we have to fundraise for project A first - the next step is obvious. If **No**, go to next question.

➢ Is there one project for which it will be easier to raise money? If **Yes**, start fundraising for that project. If **No**, start wherever you like.

CASE STUDY

As Development Officer for the local Council for Voluntary Service, I attended a meeting of a group concerned with access issues. They wanted to promote two projects as part of the town centre redevelopment:

➢ increasing the Shopmobility scheme from part-time to full-time

➢ a drop-in centre where carers could leave people with Alzheimer's disease while the carers did their shopping.

Like the council officers present, I saw the logic of the first project, but queried the need for the second. There was no apparent evidence for it; the local Alzheimer's group had been invited to the meeting, but didn't attend.

In the end, we found out that one member of the access group's committee who was a carer for someone with Alzheimer's had suggested it, and the rest of the committee would not have dreamed of offending her by rejecting the idea.

Lesson: One person is not a survey. Don't rely on anecdotal evidence; find out how much need there really is.

WRITING A BUDGET

Martin F. Jenkins

INTRODUCTION

You've decided what you want to do. Now you have to work out how much it will cost.

The key principle is:

Don't be afraid of numbers.

Numbers are the key to a successful project. If you get the numbers right at the start, you won't run into problems running the project. Whatever their commitment to other values, funders want to know whether you can deliver the results (**numbers**) for the budget (**numbers**). If you can't convince them of the numbers, you won't get the funding.

WHAT YOU NEED TO WORK OUT

- ➤ How many clients do you want to help?
- ➤ How many staff do you need to do the work?
- ➤ What will you pay the staff?
- ➤ What are your running costs?

Hint: Don't base your budget on what you think the funders will give. Base it on what you would like in an ideal world. The funders may haggle you down; but it's better for you if they haggle you down than if you have to try to haggle them up.

WHAT SHOULD BE IN YOUR BUDGET?

- ➤ Salaries (including employer's National Insurance, annual increments and inflation increases, pension contribution if applicable)
- ➤ Rent and rates (don't forget the automatic 80% rate relief for charities and the discretionary 100% relief)
- ➤ Gas and electricity
- ➤ Equipment - initial purchase costs and maintenance/replacement
- ➤ Office costs - postage, telephone (including installation), stationery
- ➤ Printing and photocopying
- ➤ Training (at least £500 per employee)
- ➤ Volunteer expenses
- ➤ Travel expenses
- ➤ Insurance
- ➤ Professional fees - e.g. auditor.

Use basic guides, such as local authority pay scales and office equipment catalogues, to work out your costs. Do not underestimate the value of the Argos catalogue!

HOW TO FIND SOURCES OF FUNDING
Martin F. Jenkins

INTRODUCTION

You know what you want to do. You know how much it will cost. Now the question is: what is the best way of raising the money?

The key to answering this question is **realism**. You can't fund three full-time workers through car boot sales. However, don't forget that raising money is not the only thing a group exists for. Groups can fall apart because a few people are busy writing funding applications and the rest of the group has nothing to do but wait for the money. That is when volunteers go off and do other things.

Never let fundraising divert you from community development!

HOW MUCH DO YOU WANT TO RAISE?

IS IT A FAIRLY SMALL SUM (SAY £500)?

It can take nearly as much work to write a grant application for £500 as for £10,000. If there is a local small grants programme, or community chest, with an easy application process, it is worth applying to it. If you are facing a twelve page application form, think about other options.

Small sums like this can be raised through fundraising events such as car boot sales, social events, jumble sales, etc. These have advantages above and beyond the money raised:

> They get the group known in the community, and can help to recruit new members.

> They help the group to come together because the group is working together.

> Group members involved in organising an event acquire new skills - e.g. planning, organising, publicity.

> They can be fun!

IS IT A ONE-OFF, SMALLISH CAPITAL SUM (E.G. OFFICE EQUIPMENT)?

> Is it worth approaching companies for support and/or sponsorship?

> Might a company give you second-hand equipment?

> Can you offer them a marketing opportunity?

Companies generally have a simpler process for giving money than charitable trusts. However, you still need to do research to find out what their policies are and who to contact.

Bear in mind also that companies are commercial organisations and will look for a return on their investment. This will be in terms of publicity - e.g. the minibus will need a sign saying "Sponsored by Joe Bloggs plc."

Always consider whether, or not, you want to be associated with the company you are approaching. How will your users feel about sponsorship from, say, a tobacco company? Do you want to accept money from a major local employer just as it lays off thousands of staff?

DO YOU NEED PEOPLE RATHER THAN MONEY?

You should consider the short-term secondment of an employee from a company. Contact **Business in the Community** for details.

DO YOU NEED A LARGE AMOUNT OR REVENUE FUNDING OVER A NUMBER OF YEARS?

Your options in this case come down to:

> ➤ local authority funding (most of which is already committed and reducing)
> ➤ central government funding (as for local authority funding)
> ➤ regeneration, or European, funding (only a practical option for established groups with some reserves)
> ➤ the National Lottery distributing bodies
> ➤ charitable trusts (by far the most likely option).

To choose the Trusts to apply to, you can:

> ➤ read all of the 3,500 entries in **The Directory of Grant-Making Trusts**
> ➤ use the **FunderFinder** computer programme (your local Council for Voluntary Service ought to have it). **FunderFinder** should produce a list of about thirty trusts which seem likely to fund your project. **Do not apply to them without research. Read the entries in the reference books before you do anything else.** Then:
> ➤ eliminate the Trusts which clearly say that they don't fund projects like yours;
> ➤ identify the six to eight Trusts most likely to fund your project (because they say that they do, or they've funded similar projects)
> ➤ get hold of any information which those six to eight Trusts provide.

Hint: Charitable Trusts fund about 25% of the applications they receive **which meet their criteria.** Make sure you meet the criteria, write a reasonable application, and you're most of the way to getting the funding.

FURTHER READING

The Directory of Grant-Making Trusts (3 volumes), published by the Charities Aid Foundation

A Guide to the Major Trusts (2 volumes), published by the Directory of Social Change

The Directory of Social Change also publishes **regional** guides to smaller grant-making Trusts.

HOW TO APPLY FOR FUNDING   Martin F. Jenkins

INTRODUCTION

Writing the funding application is stage 4 of fundraising. If you have done stages 1 to 3 properly, this is actually the easy bit. A well thought out project equals a good application.

I have written about applying to charitable Trusts, but the same principles apply whatever funder you're applying to.

CHECK OUT THE TRUST'S REQUIREMENTS

DOES THE TRUST ENCOURAGE YOU TO TALK TO THEIR GRANTS OFFICER BEFORE WRITING THE APPLICATION?

➢ Then talk to the grants officer! If you don't, your application is almost certain to fail.

DOES THE TRUST HAVE AN APPLICATION FORM?

➢ Answer all the questions - including the ones you'd rather not answer.

➢ Answer the questions the form asks, not the ones you think they should have asked.

➢ If you can't provide information, say why (e.g. "we can't send 3 years' audited accounts because we've only been in existence 18 months").

DOES THE TRUST ASK YOU TO WRITE A LETTER?

➢ Read the Trust's request for information **carefully** - and supply what it asks for.

➢ Write to a **named person**. It proves that you've done your research.

➢ Keep it short (a good application can be expressed on 2 sides of A4).

➢ Don't include lots of supporting material they haven't asked for. They won't read your last 10 annual reports!

➢ Get the details right. If you're writing the same letter to 5 Trusts and change the name in the address, change it in the body of the letter as well.

➢ Describe your organisation and project in the body of the letter - not in enclosures.

Use a logical structure. The following is a good guide:

➢ Start by saying how much you want, and what you want it for.

➢ Describe your organisation (**not** the project for which you want money). Say what you do, and what your track record is. Convince the funder that your organisation can be trusted with money. (All in one paragraph.)

➢ Say what the problem is your project will solve. Who are the people that need help? How many of them are there? How do you know all this?

➢ Describe the project - what it will do, and how this will address the need you have just described. Make sure you clearly link the **solution** with the **problem**.

> ➢ Set out, or enclose, your budget.

Don't make assumptions. The Trust knows nothing about your work, and probably nothing about your area. Tell them what you do, and what the area is like - but keep it short.

Write in **plain English,** and **avoid jargon**. Funders will judge your application on its quality and whether they understand it - not on the number of words used and/or how long they are.

Key points to remember:

> ➢ Funders are unlikely to be familiar with the specialist words you (or your staff) take for granted (e.g. "respite care," "flexible day care").

> ➢ Do not say, "If there are any points on which you require explanation or further particulars we shall be glad to furnish such additional details as may be required by telephone," when what you mean is: "Please ring if you have any questions."

> ➢ The longer the sentences, and the longer the words, the more likely you are to write nonsense by mistake. As G.K. Chesterton observed, short words make you think about what you're saying.

Remember to sign the letter and include all necessary enclosures.

If you are not asking for the full cost:

> ➢ Tell the trust what your plan is for raising the rest of the money.

> ➢ If there are options for what they might fund, give them enough information to make a decision (we could begin work without post X if we had post Y or post Z).

> ➢ If you already have a pledge of money, tell them (they are more likely to if somebody else has already agreed to fund you).

Before you send off the application, get someone **who has nothing to do with your organisation** to look at it. You are too committed to what you want to do to assess the application objectively.

If there is a deadline, make sure that the application is sent off in good time to meet it.

Assume that if the Trust says something in its guidelines, it means it. "You must" does not mean "We'd like you to, but it doesn't really matter if you don't."

FURTHER READING

Writing Better Fundraising Applications (2nd edition, 1997) by Michael Norton and Mike Eastwood, £12.95 (+ £2.50 p&p) from the Directory of Social Change, 24 Stephenson Way, London NW1 2DP. The essential short (144 pages) guide to writing a good application.

Avoiding the Wastepaper Basket (2nd edition, 1998) by Tim Cook, £5.50 from London Voluntary Service Council, 356 Holloway Road, London N7 6PA (also available from the Directory of Social Change). The former Clerk of the City Parochial Foundation tells what it feels like to be on the receiving end of applications - and the mistakes to avoid.

BUSINESS PLANS/DEVELOPMENT PLANS   Jeff Staniforth

INTRODUCTION

This is an attempt to look at the reality lying behind the mythology surrounding Business Plans/Development Plans, together with a brief look at how they can become an essential and enjoyable process in community organisations.

MYTHOLOGY AND REALITY

Mythology

- Business Plans are not relevant to us, we are a community group
- It is just something to keep funders happy
- Write it and file it
- Too technical for us, we need to pay an expert to write it for us
- It will distort our ethical voluntary base by importing business ideas

Reality

What's in a name?

Community groups have scarce human and financial resources. It makes sense to plan carefully how to secure, maintain and increase them. Forget the title, look at the process. Call it something else if that will avoid the frisson of horror and despair evident in many groups when the topic is raised. The favourite re-title is 'Development Plan'. Although not strictly accurate, it ensures that most people will be sufficiently relaxed to engage with the process. When completed, you can repackage it as 'Business Plan' for those bodies which insist on it.

Who is it for?

If written only when funders demand one, it represents an enormous waste of potential management of resources. Such a plan will seem unreal to you, and probably also to a potential funder. Even if a funding bid is successful, an unreal Business Plan neatly filed away is a ticking time bomb, primed to explode when your funder reports don't match the promises.

A genuine Business Plan/Development Plan is there primarily to help you to achieve your aims. A funder's needs should be coincidental. Far from being filed away, it should be seen as an evolving process which is monitored, evaluated and changed regularly.

Experts

You are the experts. You know your history, what you are aiming to do, how you want to do it, the likely difficulties, and how much it will all cost. Using an external facilitator is often useful in developing an overview of the process, bringing objectivity into the planning, suggesting new ideas and helping with conflict resolution. Depending on the level of internal expertise, it may be advisable to import someone to do the financial bits. Do not hire someone to go away and write your Plan, it will end as theirs not yours. Do hire someone to come in and help you write your Plan.

Ethics

There is nothing contradictory between concepts of community empowerment and planning. We have a record of intense use of scarce resources which would scare most businesses away. The traditional business style headings in Business Plans can be replaced by everyday language e.g. 'Who is it for?' instead of 'Target market'; 'Our aims' instead of 'Mission Statement'

WHAT SHOULD BE IN A BUSINESS PLAN?

A Business/Development Plan is usually produced for a period 3-5 years ahead. Typical contents (preferably with each item on 1 side of A4) should, though not necessarily in this order, include the following:

♦ **'Who we are'** This should be a brief history of the organisation

♦ **'Our aims'** Outline what you want to achieve in the next 3 years, and why there is a need for the work

♦ **'What do we offer?'** Describe clearly what services or products you offer now and intend to offer in the future

♦ **'Who is it for?'** A precise definition of the community/communities (whether of geography or interest) your services are for

♦ **'Target timeline'** Graphic or list representation of what you will do, and when; and the results envisaged

♦ **'Past activities'** Prove you have a track record by listing significant previous pieces of work, including funding

♦ **'Working in partnership'** Show that you know what other organisations are doing, and how you fit in with them

♦ **'SWOT analysis'** Describe how you have estimated your strengths and weaknesses, and identified opportunities and threats

♦ **'Policy statements'** Health and Safety, Equal Opportunities, Volunteers, confidentiality etc.

♦ **'Our management' structure and systems'** Applicable to organisations with either paid staff or volunteers, or both. Needs to explain your structure of decision-making, description of personnel functions (including job descriptions) and financial operating systems

♦ **'Our forward strategy'** Show you have thought about life after funding and considered income generation

♦ **'Financial projections'** Detailed Income and Expenditure and Cash Flow forecasts

CASE STUDY

I was asked, as an independent consultant with experience of business planning in the voluntary sector, to write a Business Plan for a Credit Union Steering Group. After meeting with the whole group a small group was set up. It met weekly for 6 weeks. Each member drafted a section of the Plan, all of which were discussed by the group. I chaired the group, took notes, did some drafting, and edited the drafts into one document. The steering group accepted the final draft. They have used it to register the Credit Union, amended it for funding bids, and evaluated relevant parts of it quarterly. It clarified policies, increased the confidence of the members and gave them a sense of ownership.

MAJOR FUNDING BIDS   Jeff Staniforth

INTRODUCTION

Many community organisations now have to submit complex multi-annual funding bids to major national funders, often for amounts up to £500k. This section is designed to assist the process by a brief look at planning, preparation and submission. It is assumed that you already know what you want the funding for.

PLANNING

Give yourself plenty of time; too many bids are a last minute scramble against the clock. This is when an existing Business/Development Plan really shows its worth, especially if it includes or has led to a Funding Strategy (see the 'Business Plans/Development Plans' in this section).

- You will need 3-4 months if you have an existing strategy, 5-6 if you haven't.
- Build a relationship with your funder if possible.
- Decide whether you can complete the process in-house, or if you need outside help with part or all of the process. In either event, you will need to schedule considerable time for it.
- Be clear about which members of your organisation will be responsible for different elements of the bid.
- Make sure your legal status is clear, and documents relating to it are up-to-date. You may want to change the legal status to take advantage of new funding opportunities. Don't forget to allow time for this, if relevant.
- Make sure your accounts are audited, and that you have proof of any other current, or future, funding arrangements.
- Take a deep breath and move on to preparation.

PREPARATION

Research is vital.
- Make sure you have read and understood the proposed funder's aims and requirements.
- Read the application form carefully, and list all the items of information you will need.
- If you will be referring to third party aims, e.g. a Regional Development Plan, ensure you have actually read and understood the relevant documents.
- Gather relevant statistical information relating to your bid e.g. levels of deprivation in target community.
- List and contact other statutory, voluntary and private organisations working in the same field to ensure your bid is complementary and does not duplicate work.
- Arrange for letters from them in support of your intended bid.
- If matched funding is involved, negotiate agreement on the level of

funding early.

- Networking with other community groups, even those bidding for the same funds, will bring benefits of shared experience that outweigh any loss of competitive edge.

- Expand the outline activity described in your Business Plan with as much detail as possible. You will have a clearer image of the project's shape, and it is easier to leave out detail in the bid than to work it out at the last minute.

You are now ready for the actual submission.

SUBMISSION

- It's obvious, but the first step is to treat the application form as a sacred object until you have completed all the work.

- Don't forget to make copies and use them for drafting.

- Write out a completion timetable, then double it (seriously); thinking and drafting always take longer than anyone thinks.

- Develop your own style of drafting. Some people prefer to sit down with their information and write a complete draft before anyone else sees it. Others prefer to settle like a hen on a nest, focus on one question at a time and circulate drafts for comment. You should use whatever style you are most comfortable with; writing funding bids can be a lonely and stressful occupation.

- Answer the questions asked, not the ones in your own head. Precise, clear, simple language lets your funder know exactly what you mean.

- Don't panic when problems occur; you can usually talk them out with funders or others in your network.

- Be prepared to be flexible; there are usually last minute changes needed to some elements of any bid.

- If you are using outside help, make sure briefings are comprehensive, your facilities fully available, and that you retain control. Read drafts carefully, and be honest about them. The bid will be in your name, and you will have to deal with results.

- Once the draft is completed to your satisfaction, transfer it to the application form, check thoroughly that all accompanying material e.g. Business plan, audited accounts etc. is included, and make sure the bid is in the hands of the funder in good time.

ASSESSMENT

Virtually all major bids are subject to rigorous assessment. This can take the form of a visit to your organisation, in which case careful preparation is required. Some such visits have apparently become more testing, negative experiences than formerly.

- Make sure all the relevant people are present and in command of their information

- A rehearsal using an external 'friend' is a good idea. Keep detailed notes of the encounter.

Other forms of assessment are 'open assessment' by scoring, where you at least learn your strengths and weaknesses; and 'internal assessment' where you just learn the result. Whatever the system, you will eventually (usually later than advertised) get a decision.

If '**No**', most funders will let you know quickly.

- You must have a back-up plan for a negative decision, either alternative funding sources for new projects, or cut-backs/closure for existing ones, or a mixture of both. It is not fair to staff, volunteers or users to be unprepared for this.

If '**Yes**', don't relax - now the real problems begin.

- Lack of preparation is potentially damaging.

- Access to the funding agreed will often depend on the provision of regular detailed information. Make sure you have the systems in place to cope with this need.

- Always work on the basis that next week an auditor will arrive to exercise the funder's right to check how you are spending their money. This means clear audit trails for everything you spend.

Finally, don't let any of this put you off applying for funds your organisation needs for the achievement of its aims. A well-organised approach to funding will produce positive results.

CASE STUDY

Case Study A   I was appointed to apply for a Lottery grant for £250k for an organisation which had worked for some time with adults with learning disabilities. The manager spent one hour with me talking about the project, and promised to supply documentation as requested. She became quite annoyed when, after not receiving the material, I said it was difficult to make further progress as time was getting short. She insisted I write the bid as best I could within the original time limit. I did. She could not find time to meet me to discuss the draft, but simply copied it to the Lottery Board. At the assessment visit, she could not answer most questions convincingly. I was blamed, and someone else got the money. She was out of work, and her community lost a potentially good project.

Case Study B An organisation working mainly with young people in deprived communities had worked out exactly what it wanted, but knew it did not have adequate in-house time to write a bid. I had three 2-hour briefings, and was weighed down with documentation. They amended drafts rapidly, and felt able to change significant areas of the original concept. They romped through the assessment process, because they were familiar with all aspects of the bid, and had rehearsed the meeting. They were flexible enough to alter some elements of the bid in response to funder comments arising from the assessment. Knowing the track record of the funder, they had allowed for a delay in decision time and arranged bridging funding. They eventually got the grant, thanked me for my input and got on with the job of helping their target community.

CREATIVE WAYS OF ACCOUNTING FOR YOUR MONEY TO FUNDERS.

Emma Manners

INTRODUCTION

Working for a charitable organisation, I have found that funding, both attracting and maintaining it, is key to project development. Experience has shown that each funder seems to have different criteria for accounting for the money and how it is used.

Here are some examples of accountability that can help people in thinking about what information they need to collect, as you never know when requests may be sprung upon you.

OUR EXPERIENCES

We were not initially told of any requirements attached to money we received from a Partnership Trust for a drugs peer education group. One of the partners never contacted us again, whereas the other, a commercial company, coerced us into speaking at a national conference on alcohol education in schools. Then, several months later, another department in the company wanted a report on group progress and photographs of group activities. Fortunately, both of these were available from project evaluation.

A different partnership funded a community health and fitness project. From the beginning we knew that it required budget breakdowns, receipts and periodical evaluation reports; but, as the project progressed, we were also required to host a media-covered presentation event and to take two young people involved in the project, together with a display of the project, to a national conference in London. As a gesture of goodwill, we also invited a representative of the funders to present awards to young people in the project.

A commercial trust that funded a community inter-generational photography project requested a report, and when informed of the project exhibition open night wanted the press present to photograph a cheque presentation.

The project core funders want quarterly monitoring forms submitted showing statistics, events, case studies, budgets and the annual audited accounts. They also like to see any reports and evaluations; and they come out to monitor contact work.

Occasionally we will get small pots of money for which we only have to supply receipts; in the case of a local student rag they only wanted us to attend a presentation evening, but this is rare.

Our project has found that it is always better to take photographs, write reports and be prepared to smile for the local paper; or to tell the media what wonderful work the funders have enabled the project to do. It is good practice anyway to properly evaluate projects, write reports and deliver good public relations.

CHECK LIST

Things you need to keep, and things you should keep 'just in case':

- ➢ Financial records, including all receipts and accounts for petty cash
- ➢ Planning and development notes and plans
- ➢ Minutes of meetings
- ➢ Reports
- ➢ Evaluation and monitoring records
- ➢ Any feedback from media participants and professionals e.g. written, recorded, visual, video
- ➢ Records of all contacts, statistics and case studies
- ➢ Photographs of any events and activities
- ➢ Press releases and cuttings
- ➢ Contact numbers of any participants who can be contacted at short notice
- ➢ A posh frock (or suit!) and a big smile for presentations, speeches or photo shoots!

Section 10

Monitoring and Evaluation

MONITORING AND EVALUATION IN COMMUNITY DEVELOPMENT	Jacky Drysdale and Rod Purcell

INTRODUCTION

Community development is about helping people to make positive change in the quality of their lives. This process should involve people in the identification of needs, exploring the solutions to problems and evaluating the success of these activities. Monitoring and evaluation are therefore part of the learning experience for individuals and groups. It should be a continuing process that runs through any piece of work. It must not be seen as a one-off activity to be undertaken by experts at the end of a funding cycle. Paid workers have a role to play in evaluation, but many local people can also contribute to the evaluation of projects.

The following is one way of ensuring that the principles and practice of community development are carried through into the process and experience of evaluation and monitoring.

We have broken this into sections to illustrate the various stages of evaluation and monitoring. However, we have written it in such a way that a proper evaluation can be completed by simply working through the sections in order. The case study shows how this can be done.

The sections are:

1. Basic ideas
2. Planning for Evaluation.
3. How to Measure the Achievements of Community Development.
4. Gathering Information.
5. Telling people about the results
6. Jargon Buster.

Note: This model has been developed from Monitoring and Evaluation of Community Development in Northern Ireland (Barr, Hashegan and Purcell 1997) which has become known as Achieving Better Community Development (ABCD).

PART 1. BASIC IDEAS.

In keeping with the principles, values and definitions of community development, evaluation should be a process that involves everyone concerned. People who have a legitimate interest, and for have a stake in the work being undertaken by a community group, should have a say what needs be evaluated, and how this might be achieved. These partners could include local people, service users, funders, local interest groups, workers and agencies.

Evaluation is always part of good community development practice. The ability to clearly define aims and objectives, and to measure the achievements (or gaps) against agreed criteria, enables people to have a greater impact on planning, a clearer direction for current and proposed work and also allows for the accountability required by funders, local people and supporting agencies. Evaluation should not be viewed as a burden and additional work, but as a useful planning aid for new work, development and growth.

The quality of community development can be determined by looking at the processes which empower individuals, groups and communities; what is produced by the work; and the effects which result from the activities. In addition, in days when Best Value and Value for Money are important considerations for funders, it is necessary to be able to identify the contributions available, in order to consider the value for money of the activity.

By having a system in place that enables these parts of the work to be measured, local people and professional workers can learn from each other's experience. This can further strengthen the power base of community groups and individuals, and promote sustainability, rather than a dependence on professionals.

Community development often just concentrates on demonstrating the process of community empowerment, rather than taking a good look at how this is achieved in practice, and what the actual products and effects of work undertaken amount to. For community development to be really effective it is essential to have specific aims and objectives, and a clear outline of the skills and knowledge that help to build a stronger and more empowered community.

This means that community groups can be held accountable for achievable aims, measured in appropriate ways, rather than intangible good deeds and personal growth, and political change. All too often, in top down evaluation the techniques and indicators are picked by funders with no knowledge of local conditions or experiences. These indicators often have no relevance to the work being undertaken, and exclude local people because of complex concepts or language. (see the Jargon Buster section)

FURTHER READING, USEFUL WEBSITES

Monitoring and Evaluation of Community Development in Northern Ireland (Barr, Hashegan and Purcell 1997) which has become known as **Achieving Better Community Development** (ABCD).

There is a range of evaluation material on the Internet at. www.scdc.org.uk including downloadable copies of the above book.

Information on **PRA** can be found through the Institute for Development Studies at the University of Sussex. www.ids.ac.uk

Information on other participative approaches to evaluation and monitoring can be found through ELDIS at http://nt1.ids.ac.uk/eldis/pra/pra.htm

Training for Transformation by Anne Hope and Sally Timmel is published in 4 volumes by Intermediate Technology Publications,
103/105 Southampton Row, London WC1B 4HH.

The Reflect Mother Manual on participative approaches is published by Action Aid, Hamlyn House, Archway, London N19 5PG.

PLANNING FOR EVALUATION

Jacky Drysdale
and Rod Purcell

WHY DO YOU WANT TO EVALUATE?

You may be required to evaluate by funders or other agencies, but remember that evaluation is a learning and empowering activity for groups and individuals too. Use this opportunity and don't get caught up in responding to requests without benefits. Try to make sure that different reporting times can be met to avoid duplication of information collection, or reporting e.g. quarterly reports, annual funding cycles, tri-annual policy reviews.

WHAT DO YOU WANT TO EVALUATE?

You may want to evaluate a programme, project or policy. It is important that you are clear about exactly what you intend to evaluate, and place a clear boundary around that activity. There is no point in trying to evaluate everything you have done. Focus on the essentials.

WHO HAS AN INTEREST IN THE WORK, AND WHAT DO THEY CONTRIBUTE?

At the start it is important to identify who has been involved in the work and what they have contributed. This is also the time to negotiate with funders about what should be measured, and how this can be done. People need to be encouraged to take an active interest in this stage of the process to ensure that all interests are covered. All those with a direct interest in the work should be involved in planning the evaluation.

WHAT IS THIS PIECE OF WORK TRYING TO DO?

The clarity of aims and objectives is central to any successful community activity, although for a variety of reasons, often relating to changes in funding criteria, these are often unclear and imprecise.
The aims and objectives of the activity can be clarified by answering the following question.

WHAT DOES THE ACTIVITY INTEND TO PRODUCE, AND WHAT ARE THE LIKELY EFFECTS OF THE WORK?

This should include, for example, number of courses offered to various groups of people, experiences / satisfaction of people using the services, hours of service provided, effects on the environment following a neighbourhood clear-up day, reduction in deaths following road safety campaign.

Objectives can be measured in a number of ways. Firstly, it is important to distinguish between **outputs** and **outcomes**. An output is just something that the project has direct responsibility and control in delivering. The project can therefore be credited with success if the output is achieved, but has to take responsibility if it is not. In contrast, an outcome is something that happens as a result of the work of the project, but which is subject to a number of factors outside the control of the project. Sometimes outcomes are called impacts.

Funders often want answers to questions about outcomes that may flow from the work of the project, but tracing a direct relationship is not possible. These difficulties need to be identified and discussed at an early stage. Without discussions projects may inadvertently accept responsibility for outcomes beyond their control e.g. reducing unemployment.

WHAT DO YOU DO WITH THE RESULTS?

The information needs to be assessed once it has been collected. It can be useful for an outside person to review the material. Very often local people can miss something because they are too close to the work. Outsiders can also ask the difficult questions management committee members and workers may find difficult.

Finally, you need to think about what this information tells you about your aims, objectives, outputs and outcomes, where you are succeeding and where changes are necessary.

IN WHAT FORMAT WILL THIS INFORMATION BE USEFUL TO THE VARIOUS PEOPLE WITH AN INTEREST IN THE PROJECT?

Evaluation reports can be used for a number of purposes. For example:

  ➢ to see if the work is being effective
  ➢ to help plan changes / future development in the work
  ➢ to report back to funders
  ➢ to provide evidence for further funding
  ➢ to inform possible changes in local government services and policies.

Clearly, the information should be presented according to the needs of the audience. e.g. an abstract might be made for the initial discussion by a group's management committee; a printed report made for the AGM and to send to funding bodies; a press release sent to local papers to show the success of the group; posters and slide shows planned for recruitment of more members, etc.

MEASURING THE ACHIEVEMENTS OF COMMUNITY DEVELOPMENT

Jacky Drysdale
and Rod Purcell

INTRODUCTION

Not only should evaluation in community development be directly linked to the outputs and outcomes, it also has to answer four key questions that are the core of any community development process:

1. How has the work changed people's lives (personal empowerment)?
2. How does the work include disadvantaged people (positive action)?
3. Are active links made with agencies, organisations and individuals relevant to the work (building community organisations)?
4. How was the focus of the work chosen? Is it still relevant for local people (power relationships and participation)?

HOW HAS THE WORK CHANGED PEOPLE'S LIVES?

When looking to demonstrate personal empowerment there are a number of things that you should consider. These include looking for confidence, knowledge, skills, strong community leadership, managing budgets and projects. When you know what you are looking for you can then decide what is particularly important to this work, and how useful information that illustrates this can be collected.

HOW DOES THE WORK INCLUDE DISADVANTAGED PEOPLE?

This looks at issues relating to oppression, discrimination, equal opportunities and social exclusion. You can look at the existence, or absence, of policy statements, the transfer of policy statements into action to deal with oppression. Issues of how power is allocated may also be relevant here.

DOES THE GROUP DEMONSTRATE LINKS WITH AGENCIES, ORGANISATIONS AND INDIVIDUALS RELEVANT TO THE WORK?

Do minority groups participate? What are the networking arrangements for the group/activity? What links are there to agencies with an interest in this activity?

HOW WAS THE FOCUS OF THE WORK CHOSEN?   IS IT STILL RELEVANT?

Were local people, or communities of interest, involved in identifying needs? This could be achieved through Training for Trainers, REFLECT, PRA, or a variety of other participatory techniques.

If local people were not involved, can they contribute to a re-examination of the needs and issues for future planning?

WHAT ARE INDICATORS, AND WHY DO WE NEED TO USE THEM?

The answer to all the above questions should relate directly to the aims and objectives outlined for the project. However, you need to be able to measure your achievements. To do this you should select an indicator against which you can collect information. For example if you have set up an after-school programme a good indicator would be the number of children attending the club.

Indicators should be

- simple
- tell you something of value
- be based on easily collected information.

Many people make the mistake of either having too many indicators or using those requiring complicated means for collecting information. The case study at the end of this section illustrates this process in more detail.

WHAT IS THE DIFFERENCE BETWEEN MONITORING AND EVALUATION?

Evaluation usually takes place at the end of a project.

However, it is important to identify changes at regular intervals. This allows the project to know if the work is succeeding. This periodic checking of progress against the agreed indicators is called **monitoring.**

GATHERING INFORMATION

Jacky Drysdale
and Rod Purcell

INTRODUCTION

Ideally, the plan for evaluation should be developed at the start of the project. This is because evaluation is directly linked to the objectives set out for the work. Secondly, it is important to be able to identify changes over time. This initial information, collected against the indicators at the start, is known as the **baseline**. Without a baseline it is impossible to know what the changes have been. If the work of the project is already underway it is important to undertake a baseline study as soon as possible.

WHAT INFORMATION DO YOU NEED TO GATHER?

You need to gather information so that you can answer the questions asked in the previous section in a meaningful way.

As far as possible, evaluation should be as much about using existing information in a planned way as creating new methods of data collection. Very often the information you need is already being collected for another purpose, or could easily be collected through simple administrative changes or by local people. Knowing what information already exists is an important starting point. However, be careful not to select an indicator just because information is at hand.

Using a variety of different kinds of information gives a broader understanding of the nature of the work. Information can be collected in a variety of ways, numbers and st,atistics, surveys, opinion polls and vox pop can all be useful. Focus groups and other recorded discussions, can be fruitful. The documentary evidence available through minutes of meetings, funding applications etc. also has a part to play. You can observe groups of people, especially around issues of confidence and change.

It is important to note that indicators for outputs and outcomes may be either **qualitative** (based on people's feelings and understanding), or **quantitative** (based on statistics). A good evaluation will use both, as it is important to know not just how many people received a service, but also what their experience was like.

HOW CAN THIS BE DONE, AND WHO CAN HELP?

It is commonly thought that experts trained in such matters are the only people who can undertake evaluations. It can be useful having an experienced outsider to advise on how an evaluation might be produced, or to review the results. However, local people can undertake community development evaluations themselves. In doing so, the educational and empowerment aims of community development can be furthered. In this way evaluation becomes part of the group's activity, and helps them to make decisions and manage their own affairs.

CASE STUDY

Jacky Drysdale
and Rod Purcell

INTRODUCTION

This is a simple case study of a local community health project. It shows how the evaluation of the project can be developed through answering a number of specific questions.

WHO HAS AN INTEREST IN THE MONITORING AND EVALUATION OF THE PROJECT?

Interested parties in an evaluation of the work of the community health project included the following:

- Local people
- Members of the community health group
- Health Board /Trusts: in particular GP's, health promotion and health visitors
- Local Authority: especially officers from Social Services, Leisure Services and Education
- Local elected member
- Men's health group
- Well women's group
- Schools
- Police

It is important to rank these interests into those who have a direct involvement in the planning of the evaluation and those with a lesser interest. The latter group may wish to see the results of the evaluation, but are unlikely to want, or need, to be directly involved. This will ensure that all interests, consumers, funders, etc. have their interests included in the evaluation process. This makes it more difficult for organisations to distance themselves from the results of the evaluation at a later date.

In this case a planning group was formed, which included project management committee members, project staff, a worker from health promotion and a representative from the Social Services.

WHAT IS TO BE MONITORED AND EVALUATED?

The planning group worked through the process of:

Aims ⇨ Objectives ⇨ Output / Outcomes ⇨ Indicators ⇨ Data

One of the **aims** of the health project was the improvement of children's health.

As part of good community planning, the project has identified a number of **objectives** that break up the aim into manageable parts. The objectives are:

1. To provide exercise for local children
2. To encourage schools to remove confectionery from the tuck shop and replace with fruit snacks

3. To promote breast feeding support groups for new mothers
4. To monitor environmental issues affecting children's health, especially in respect of road safety.

HOW DO WE MONITOR AND EVALUATE THESE OBJECTIVES?

As described above, we need to link the objectives of the project to the outcomes and outputs.

The selection of objectives need to

◆ be relevant to the core activity of the project
◆ reflect the principles of community development outlined above i.e.

- personal empowerment
- positive action
- building community organisations
- power relationships
- participation.

See Table 1

HOW DO WE MEASURE THE SUCCESS OF THE OUTPUTS AND OUTCOMES?

It is necessary to identify a range of **indicators** we can use to tell us what the outputs and outcomes have contributed to the community. Table 2 shows how indicators can be used to illustrate the effectiveness of outputs. A similar process can be used to provide indicators for outcomes. **Qualitative** indicators are shown in **bold**. **Quantitative** indicators are shown in plain text. All of the information detailed in the tables was collected by local people.

WHEN SHOULD MONITORING AND EVALUATION TAKE PLACE ?

The plan for the evaluation was drawn up during the first year of the project, once the objectives had become clear. The baseline information was collected about 5 months later. Because the project now had defined outputs, outcomes, indicators, identified sources of data and baseline information, it was possible to undertake short monitoring exercises every year. This annual monitoring allowed the project to check if its work was on course to meet its objectives and identify difficulties.

Towards the end of the five-year funding cycle the project was able to undertake a full evaluation of its work. As the baseline and annual monitoring information had already been collected, the evaluation exercise was a simple task.

WHAT DO WE DO WITH THIS INFORMATION ?

The report was printed and sent to everyone identified at the initial meeting. In addition, the community health group used selected results of this evaluation in a number of ways. This included future planning work within the group, funding applications, and for recruitment and advertising purposes.

Table 1 : **Monitoring and Evaluating the Objectives**

Project Objectives	Planned Outputs	Planned Outcomes
1. To provide exercise for local children	a. Swimming club 3 nights per week b. Junior football team I night per week c. After school club developing a sports programme	a. fitter children
2. To encourage schools to remove confectionery from the tuck shop and replace with fruit snacks	a. providing information to schools on low fat / sugar alternative foods b. arranging fruit delivery to schools	a. improved diet
3. To promote breast feeding support groups for new mothers	a. providing breast feeding support in hospital b. ensure breast feeding information is available during ante-natal appointments c. breast feeding support group information at post natal checks	a. improved health of babies
4. To monitor environmental issues affecting children's health; especially in respect of road safety	a. campaign to reduce traffic speeds past schools b. monitoring accident rates for RTA's involving children	a. safer roads

Table 2 : **Measuring the effectiveness of outputs**

Outputs	Indicator	Source of Information
▪ swimming club 3 nights per week	a. number of children attending the swimming club over a 3 month period.	a. club records
▪ junior football team I night per week	b. number of children attending the football club over a 3 month period	b. club records
▪ after school club developing a sports programme	c. number of children participating in after school club sports activity	c. club records
	d. children's comments on their sporting activity	d. interviews with children
▪ providing information to schools on low fat / sugar alternative foods	a. changes in sales of sweets and crisps	a. shop records
▪ arranging fruit delivery to schools	b. changes in sales of fruit and healthy snacks	b. shop records
	c. children's comments on their buying habits	c. questionnaire to children
▪ providing breast feeding support in hospital	a. changes in number of mothers breast feeding for at least 6 months	a. statistics from health visitors
▪ ensure breast feeding	**b. Mothers' comments on the value of breast feeding their children**	b. interviews with mothers
▪ information available during ante-natal appointments	**c. Mothers' commenting on the usefulness of information provided**	c. focus group with mothers
▪ breast feeding support group information at post natal checks		
▪ campaign to reduce traffic speeds past schools	a. activities undertaken by the group	a. group minutes
▪ monitoring accident rates for RTA's (road traffic accidents) involving children	**b. attitudes of relevant officials to road safety issues**	b. interviews with selected officials
	c. dissemination of collected statistics	c. group minutes

INVOLVING PEOPLE
Irene Kakoullis

INTRODUCTION

Monitoring and evaluation are integral processes in the development of the services we as youth and community workers offer: and, most importantly, ensure that we are meeting the needs of the participants involved and our aims and objectives.

People can be involved in monitoring and evaluation in two ways:
- they might be asked to contribute to, or facilitate, the process
- they may be monitored as participants in a project or activity.

Empowering people, by encouraging them to be key players in the evaluation process, is beneficial to all involved – especially if they are responsible for actually facilitating a session or activity. Planning ahead with a group raises levels of confidence and prepares a group in advance (even for negative feedback).

POINTS TO CONSIDER

- What are your original aims/targets/ anticipated outcomes? (Set realistic targets).
- What information do you require? (e.g. what participants have learnt, statistical information, information regarding how attitudes may have been changed).
- Who is participating? (e.g. to encourage young people the process might be made more informal and fun to participate in).
- Ask the participants what their ideas are.
- Are there literacy difficulties within the group?
- To whom are the monitoring and evaluation being presented? (i.e. funders, management committees).
- How much time and resources is allocated for monitoring and evaluation?
- Are any resources required for monitoring and evaluation? Can participants use specific resources e.g. video camera?

You must remember to ask participants to self-evaluate their own skills and achievements. Questions could include:
- What were my goals?
- Did I achieve them?
- If not, what stopped me?
- Did I listen to other people's views?
- Did I encourage good discussion?
- Did I answer questions clearly?
- Where there benefits to other young people?

- ♦ What was the most/least enjoyable activity?
- ♦ How could I improve future sessions?
- ♦ How could I improve my skills?

CASE STUDY: YOUNG PEOPLE'S PEER EDUCATION PROJECT

Peer educators in our group are responsible for their own monitoring and evaluation to ensure that they are meeting the targets they set out at the start of the project. Young People identify their own aims: in our case, they chose to provide drugs education to other young people.

During the training programme the workers facilitated with the participants, young people were asked to evaluate each session. They were also responsible for maintaining a register monitoring how many young people attended. This encouraged the young people to feel comfortable with the monitoring and evaluation process. Prior to the group delivering their own drug education sessions, we ran a workshop on the relevance to monitoring and evaluation, and the group were asked to consider the point listed above.

The members of our peer education group developed a number of fun methods of monitoring and evaluation their work.

- ♦ Graffiti wall
- ♦ Recording young people's opinions, using a video camera or Dictaphone
- ♦ Easy to read appealing questionnaires.

They designed their own 'user friendly' monitoring forms and agreed to de-brief after each session with a large helping of Caffeine!

FURTHER READING, USEFUL ADDRESSES

Address:
Youth Point, The Cardigan Centre, 145 - 149 Cardigan Road, Leeds LS6 1LJ

Books:
Harvey, M. **A Framework for Peer Learning,** Youth Clubs UK 1998.
Harvey, M. **Know the Score-youth to youth drug education,** Youth Clubs UK 1999.
Health Education Authority **Health Promotion with Young People: An Introductory Guide to Evaluation,** HEA 1998.
Health Education Authority **Positive Participation,** HEA 1998.

RECLAIMING THE EVALUATION AGENDA   Gersh Subhra

INTRODUCTION

The evaluation data required from practitioners operating in the Community Work sector has largely been governed, not by those carrying out this work but those who fund it. This has related to the type, amount, format and emphasis (qualitative or quantitative) of evaluation material being generated. The agenda shaping these requirements ought to be a shared process and consequently there is an urgent need for practitioners to re-claim the initiative. They need to assert how to demonstrate the impact and value of what they are trying to achieve with the many communities with which they work. The evaluation material required and generated ought to be consistent with:

- the value base, philosophy and methods of working used in this sector
- the ability and capacity of the agency to undertake evaluation
- the level of funding provided for the project work and evaluation
- a recognition of the fundamentally informal educational purpose of this work and the intangibility of its effects .

A six stage process is suggested as an assertive challenge to the culture of evaluation in which community work finds itself.

THE CURRENT SITUATION

Evaluation, as an activity, has been influenced and utilised by many disciplines interchanging ideas to produce a practical and conceptual tool that is confusingly yet fascinatingly, multi-faceted. This has produced a series of contrasting features including:

- Being seen to be about 'outsiders' (or external stakeholders) checking-up and assessing other peoples work, contrasted with what ought to be a self-designed educational tool for use in empowering those engaged in Community work

- 'Neutral' and 'objective' calculations which attempt to demonstrate 'value for money' contrasted with practitioners not wanting to 'play the numbers game' and trying to hang on to the merits of process oriented practice

- The emphasis on quantitative and mechanistic performance indicators, inputs, outputs and outcomes which contrasts with an approach that examines the qualitative impact on people, communities and social change

- The dominant agenda set on a top down basis by funders and/or employers in a search for accountability, rather than allowing evaluation to be developed 'organically' by communities

- A need to value formative evaluations which aim to look at developments as they occur and feed into the decisions and practices of agencies as opposed to the emphasis on summative evaluations which take place once a project is complete and 'objectively' assesses the outcome.

- The increasing use of evaluation as a managerial tool, which reinforces control and, some would argue, dilutes the adversarial nature of community work.

The evaluation agenda has to be 'reclaimed' by Community Work and other related fields. This is not a plea for reducing accountability to funders/employers, or lessening the priority of evaluation as an activity. On the contrary, it is an argument which aims to encourage the production of evaluation data that more accurately reflects the real impact of community & youth work, and encourages a higher profile for evaluation within organisations, by integrating it even more closely into activities such as supervision and planning.

The other debate relates to the critical question of exactly what evaluation is primarily for – accountability to managers or funders; or for learning and development within the organisation? It is not an either/or outcome, but the question that should be raised is which of the two purposes should have priority. Some evaluation requirements have become so technical and specialist that they yield no educational or learning benefits for the organisation or community.

A STRATEGY FOR RECLAIMING THE EVALUATION AGENDA

This is an attempt to make evaluation into a learning and educational process and is linked to future planning, in contrast to something that is done grudgingly and expediently for an external party. Although the framework is presented in stages, these should be considered simultaneously.

Stage one: Formulate an Evaluation 'Manifesto'
A manifesto which begins to describe your organisation's approach and thinking should include both a theoretical perspective and a practical indication of how you view evaluation. The following statements provide a starting point, and should draw on the fundamental principles already within your agency and its work, and those generally of Community Work. The manifesto needs to assert

♦ That subjectivity has validity and different perspectives which can be utilised

♦ Evaluation ought to be integrated into the fabric of the organisation's operations, and seen as essential rather than optional, and voluntary rather than coerced.

♦ Evaluation is a valuable planning tool which helps to validate work, acknowledge effort, shape priorities and generate material for a variety of uses, other than just to meet the information needs of say, the funders.

♦ That qualitative evaluation methods do not aspire to tell the whole story.

♦ Not all of what community workers achieve can actually be measured or easily presented.

♦ The current climate of under-funding/scarce resources will impact on the priorities of agencies, and choices are inevitably made about the relative amounts of time spent on supporting communities as opposed to gathering and preparing material for evaluation purposes. Consequently there may be a loss of data.

♦ A core part of community work is adversarial and aims to enable others to challenge institutions and policy makers, including those providing the funding. This naturally limits the openness with which this type of activity can (or should?) be evaluated or presented.

♦ If one of the aims of community work is to enable communities to participate, then evaluation must be included. This will result in lots of narratives, subjectivity, multiple realities and an acknowledgement of uncertainty - this is important when issues of 'academic' rigour are raised, as neither community members nor workers are necessarily planning or evaluation experts.

♦ The nature of community work can often generate more questions than answers, and highlight needs rather than meet them. This may not be what funders want to hear, but a lack of clarity and a highlighting of further needs is often the outcome.

♦ Evaluation takes time! If funders or employers want the material, account needs to be taken of this and resources made available to generate it.

♦ Evaluation of community work has to take into account the context of the work - including the dynamics of funding, legislation, policies and the tensions of inequality within British society.

♦ Community work agencies may not have a high level of capacity or experience in evaluation techniques, and therefore need to include a level of capacity building as a part of negotiating the evaluation requirements of funders.

Stage Two: Assessment of your Evaluation Capacity
The essential assessment of the resources made available to your organisations for evaluation purposes should consider the approach, interest, capacity and skills of the workers, volunteers and management committee. This could include examining:

♦ Who, historically, has had the responsibility for it?

♦ How can evaluation become a more democratic activity by involving the staff team, management committee, other volunteers, student placements or community members?

♦ What is the predominant attitude to evaluation within the staff team and management committee?

♦ What is the level of interest amongst the staff team in this area of work?

♦ What resources does the agency want to commit to this type of activity? Utilisation of students, volunteers and/or secondment placements, as well as partnerships with Universities and research assistants, are all ways of increasing capacity. These different resources will, by definition, provide a rich mixture of perspectives contributing to the quality of evaluative analysis.

Stage Three: How does Evaluation integrate into the policies and practices of the agency?
It is important to assess how closely evaluation priorities and activities integrate into the various functions of an organisation's operation and general strategic planning. Examples include planning, policy making, supervisory and appraisal systems, equal opportunities policies and systems, staff development and training, public relations, and fund-raising. Each of these areas offer opportunities for evaluation to feature significantly, and an audit may uncover some useful ways in which the profile could be raised. For

instance, linking evaluation to supervision and appraisal may be slightly contentious, as evaluation has often been thought of as a mechanism for checking-up on workers.

However it is suggested here that supervision, as a regular organisational activity, should be seen as a mechanism by which workers can actively discuss, generate, contribute and store evaluation data with their managers. The nature of this data can include anecdotal material, case studies, spin-off benefits, attitudinal changes in the individuals being worked with, and impacts on deep-seated community issues. This sort of material is regularly discussed in supervision is not necessarily confidential; but is it ever called, or seen as, a source of evaluation data?

Similarly, appraisals may involve workers providing accounts of impacts that they have made in the preceding year; and could include case studies, summaries, and progress reports that could easily be adapted into evaluation material.

Stage Four: Negotiate the Evaluation Requirements
This is a crucial part of the 're-claiming of the agenda,' and may well take some funders by surprise! Whilst it is recognised that many funders and other external 'stakeholders' have pre-identified evaluation and proforma requirements, it is worth putting this up for re-negotiation. It may be worth checking what the sponsor wants the evaluation information for. Is it

♦ to try and calculate value for money?

♦ for (the sponsor's) public relations purposes?

♦ to encourage your agency to learn and develop clarity about the work being undertaken?

♦ just an administrative exercise that allows the agency to demonstrate accountability to the funder?

♦ a relatively mechanistic evaluation framework because they are unfamiliar with what qualitative data to ask for?

The format, approach and type of `data` required, will naturally vary, depending on which of the above is shaping the sponsor's thinking.

The strategy suggested is one which involves a presentation of your manifesto, and the type and quantity of data collectable in relation to your capacity.

An example illustrative of this need to flag-up the intangible aspects of community work could be the time some agencies spend in building relationships of trust with say, young people whose life experiences lead them to be suspicious of authority, adults and organisations. No-one can argue that this aspect is not essential or that it takes time. It is a pre-requisite for further work: but how do you

♦ Recognise and acknowledge within an evaluation framework the complexity of the skills demonstrated by the worker in engaging with a young person showing extremely challenging, perhaps aggressive, behaviour?

♦ Measure it?

♦ Identify its outcomes?

- Remember its role when, say three months later, the focus is on the more tangible things your agency is doing with that young person?

Stage Five: Organisational monitoring and data-collection tools
Monitoring and data-collection are inextricably linked with evaluation. The quality of the data collection critically determines the quality of the analysis presented within the eventual evaluation reports. Consider then –

- Is there a range of collection tools, or templates, various people in your agency can use?

- Have time and resources been invested in training these people to generate evaluation data?

- What is the quality of monitoring, information recording and retrieval systems?

- Is there scope to establish an evaluation portfolio, in which a wide variety of material can be located?

- Does it make use of audio-visual, artistic and other forms of communication?

- What data is being lost? Valuable work can usually be remembered, but it may not have been evaluated at the time. Are there systems within your agency that allow the value of this type of work to be retrospectively acknowledged? For example, are there annual reviews which give time and space to this reflection?

Stage Six: Matching evaluation activity to changing objectives
Evaluation is commonly thought of as an analysis of how much progress has been made in achieving the original objectives of the project. Objectives, however, are not static or limited in number, and are usually added to (formally or informally) by the variety of stakeholders involved in funding and implementing the work. What starts out as a single objective can change into a multiplicity of aims that may actually be competing with each other. Projects can take different directions for a variety of reasons.

- Is this complexity of objectives shown by the ways your agency has for collecting data?

- Is your system flexible enough to accommodate changing objectives?

- Is the evaluation work being undertaken appropriate to the actual objectives, or does it relate to out-dated ones?

JARGON BUSTER

Jacky Drysdale
and Rod Purcell

COMMON SENSE DEFINITIONS OF THE JARGON

BASELINE

Recording of the situation at the start of the piece of work

DATA

Information that is collected to show what has been achieved

EFFECTIVENESS

Measuring outputs of performance against targets set

EFFICIENCY

The ratio of the inputs to the outputs and outcomes which involve not only costs but also issues of management, resources, structures, methods of working and procedures which need to be measured both quantitatively and qualitatively

EQUITY

This is equal opportunity in action. Making sure that the work does not affect some people less favourably than others

EVALUATION

Is more than monitoring; it makes judgements about the success or failure of a project/organisation in an informed way: it attempts to assess whether the objectives are being achieved. It involves quality as well as quantity issues.

INPUTS

All the resources used to plan and carry out a piece of work. Includes staff, skills, knowledge, budgets, equipment and the influences of policy or legislation

MEASURES and INDICATORS

A way of measuring what has been achieved

MONITORING

The regular checking and recording of progress relative of the work compared to the plan. The systematic collection and recording of information to help an organisation know how it is doing: it helps to account for the work of the organisation.

OUTCOMES (or IMPACTS)

What happened as a result of the outputs e.g. more people able to claim benefit, more people able to seek work, improved housing conditions

OUTPUTS

Real things that have been achieved by the work, e.g. advice services provided, crèche facilities organised, information presented as part of a campaign

P.R.A.

An approach to identifying community needs through research, education and collective action. It uses local knowledge in an interactive way, which involves keeping checking the information being gathered with local people. It believes that local people should be fully involved in the process, and should own the information gathered.

PROCESSES

This is the way in which inputs are applied to achieve the objectives of the work, e.g. by encouraging community participation, building contact between groups

QUALITATIVE

Approaches to collecting information which reflect peoples feelings, and understanding

QUANTITATIVE

Approaches to collecting information which are mainly statistical

REFLECT

A particular style of training and research which

- Explores and analyses the causes of power in equalities and oppression
- Recognises that individual transformation is as important as collective transformation
- Sees gender equality as essential for social transformation

Section 11

Partnership Working

THE PURPOSE OF PARTNERSHIPS

Lydia Meryll &
Paul A Jones

INTRODUCTION

Partnership working aims to maximise the contribution of groups, agencies and organisations (statutory, private sector, voluntary and community) by bringing them together to undertake joint projects within agreed structures (see next paper).

Since the late 1980's, it has been suggested that effective area regeneration depends on organisations collaborating and working to shared objectives. The current government sees partnership working as key to effective neighbourhood renewal.

WHY WORK IN PARTNERSHIP?

Potential Problems

Some community organisations have been suspicious of the notion of "partnership working". Common problems have been:

♦ the domination of statutory agencies, the private sector and large voluntary organisations on partnership programmes, to the exclusion of the community voice.

♦ partnerships being no more than temporary token arrangements to secure external funding.

♦ community organisations feeling ripped off by large statutory organisations who claimed their resources as "match" for extra funding, without any reciprocal benefit.

Potential Benefits

Properly understood and managed, partnership working between statutory, voluntary and community organisations can result in enormous benefits for communities. Large organisations and bureaucracies are slowly realising that "top-down" and/or single organisational approaches to community development and area regeneration do not work. To develop sustainable communities, all the organisations and groups in those communities have to be involved in the decision making and activities of any initiatives.

Benefits of partnership working include:-

▪ **Clarity of purpose** – organisations working together can clarify the key issues for a community or neighbourhood. Negotiating can be hard, but the process of trying to set priorities can result in overall strategic plans. Shared thinking, and the co-ordination of projects, can prevent individual organisations pulling in different directions.

▪ **Inclusion** – the skilful use of Visioning Days, 'Planning for Real' exercises, and facilitated group discussions, can help achieve agreements on the purpose and priorities of the partnership. Community workers should ensure that unaccountable local leaders do not silence the voice of marginalised groups, e.g. single fathers or asylum seekers. A look at the population details of an area will help identify the under-represented groups.

- **Local ownership** – Commitment to, and local ownership of, initiatives and services will be increased if those affected are involved as genuine partners from the beginning. This should ensure that things are done **with** local people rather than **for** them.

- **Maximising resources and expertise** – close collaborative working on projects and programmes will enable organisations to share their expertise and skills, and may avoid duplication and waste of resources. Some funding bodies will fund partnership programmes rather than separate small organisations.

- **Connections and linkage** – partnership working can help develop networks within the community which promote understanding, and may lead to new ideas and initiatives. For example, a science project in a primary school linked up with an allotment project where Asian grandparents shared their knowledge with the children. This led to a healthy eating initiative which affected the eating patterns across a whole estate, giving rise to a demand for vegetarian cookery classes.

- **Synergy** – (Greek word meaning *"working together"*) refers to the potential of organisations to be more productive as a result of coming together. This is evident in some developing Health Action Zone initiatives, e.g. where doctors are beginning to connect with allotment societies, parent and toddler groups, health visitors, educators and local youth groups.

- **Added value** – all the resources committed to the development of a community can be recognised; the unpaid time, commitment and skills of volunteers can be valued, as well as the professional expertise of local authority officers. The cost value of volunteer time can often be match-funded against grant allocations.

- **Equality and citizenship** - effective, inclusive partnership working respects equally the voice and the ideas of all partners. Community workers need to ensure that *all* participants are heard as equals.

- **A sustainable future** - community based actions and initiatives are often time limited. Partnership working can sometimes offer the opportunity for longer term planning and resourcing, e.g. a time-limited partnership programme may create a local development trust as its successor, which enables all the stakeholders in a community to continue their collaborative working and ensure the future development of actions and initiatives.

FURTHER READING

Involving Communities in Urban and Rural Regeneration: a guide for practitioners. 2nd Edition (1997)   DETR.

'Rich mix'. Inclusive strategies for urban regeneration   Sue Brownill and Jane Darke (1998)   The Policy Press

Including young people in urban regeneration. A lot to learn? Suzanne Fitzpatrick, Annette Hastings and Keith Kintrea (1998)   The Policy Press

A place for the community? Tyne and Wear Development Corporation's approach to regeneration   Hilary Russell (1998)   The Policy Press

Partnership against poverty and exclusion? Local regeneration strategies and excluded communities in the UK Mike Geddes (1997)   The Policy Press

STRUCTURES AND MODELS

Lydia Meryll &
Paul A Jones

INTRODUCTION

Partnerships are about more than working with others in a collaborative way. Groups and organisations may meet, share ideas, and even work together informally on a whole range of issues, but they still may not be "working in partnership".

Partnership working usually involves some kind of contractual arrangement between participants who operate within a formal or semi-formal arrangement in which roles and responsibilities are identified and agreed. How formal any individual partnership arrangement is depends on a whole range of factors.

Some of the traditional ways in which organisations and groups work together, sharing ideas and resources, cannot strictly be regarded as partnerships.

PARTNERSHIPS ARE NOT . . .

- **networks** – organisations and groups may operate in networks which have a certain structure, common aims and even a lead organisation pulling together the network, but have no contractual arrangement.

- **alliances** – as with networks, alliances are looser arrangements than partnerships. Alliances usually have a common purpose, and even particular objectives, which bring allies together, but rarely have any formal/informal contractual arrangements between participants.

- **co-working** – organisations and groups can co-work to common goals without any form of structural /contractual arrangement.

- **a service level agreement** – where service providers are sub-contracted to deliver a specific service to a larger organisation/agency, with targets and outcomes specified by the commissioning organisation

- **project teams** – project teams may form part of partnership working, but are not in themselves partnerships. Teams may be brought together to work on specific projects and tasks without any formal, contractual arrangements between the organisations from which the project participants are drawn.

ESSENTIAL INGREDIENTS OF A PARTNERSHIP

- **Partners** drawn from at least two different organisations, agencies, departments, companies, or groups. People within the same organisation may co-work, or be part of a project team, but not part of a partnership.

- **Clear objectives** – a partnership is usually linked to an identified and measurable task or series of tasks.

- **A formal or semi-formal structure** – this clarifies the roles and reporting relationships of the partners in relation to the task/tasks. Where a constitution is adopted and staff employed, the allocation of responsibilities must be precise.

- **A contractual arrangement** – almost always written and agreed. The contract forms the basis of the partnership – it may be a formal legal document or a written agreement. There may be costs/fees associated with distinct tasks within the overall project.

- **Protocols,** or agreed ways of doing things – partnerships depend on basic agreements around how the partnership is to operate, e.g. agreed ground rules about confidentiality.

- **Measures of success** – all partnerships need to know whether or not they are achieving what they were set up to do. They need some form of agreed criteria by which progress can be measured. Often these are called performance indicators, milestones, or benchmarks. However, less formal (but still measurable) criteria may be used by some partnerships. Time needs to be allocated to involving all participants in deciding what is meant by success, and how they will measure it. The criteria may need to be reviewed through the same consultative process to ensure that sustainability is achieved.

- **A time line** – partnerships can in principle operate for many years, but they are usually time limited. A partnership has each objective normally linked to specific time scales.

- **A lead organisation** – partnerships usually identify a lead organisation within the partnership to co-ordinate and ensure the implementation of its actions. It is important that this lead body does not over-power the others and ensures that respect for each voice is maintained. One partner usually takes responsibility for the payment of staff, fund holding and accounting.

- **Paid staff** having clear job descriptions, lines of accountability, support and supervision arrangements, and fair and open terms and conditions of service.

- **Voluntary workers** have an equally clear role definition, means of support training and supervision, and agreement on areas and scope of responsibility.

FURTHER READING

Bailey, Nick. **Partnership Agencies in British Urban Policy**. (1995) UCL Press.

Roberts P. and Hugh H., **Urban Regeneration – a handbook.** (2000) Sage

DIFFERENT TYPES OF PARTNERSHIP

Lydia Meryll &
Paul A Jones

INTRODUCTION

The structure of partnership arrangements ranges along a continuum from highly formalised partnerships to looser arrangements. There are many models of how partnerships operate in practice, and no single blueprint fits all circumstances.

♦ **Bureaucratic** partnerships.

♦ **Hierarchical** partnerships with the lead organisation keeping a tight hold of proceedings.

♦ There are partnerships that are based on a definite **legal structure,** or recognised constitution - they can be limited companies, industrial and provident societies, or development trusts.

♦ **Flexible** partnerships that adopt models of development reflecting innovation, flexibility and change. Some are based on agreements worked up by the partners themselves. Others bring together groups and organisations in partnerships deeply committed to democratic and participative styles of working.

One key difference between the various kinds of partnerships is the level within each organisation from which the members come together. Chief Executives or departmental leaders with policy overviews will bring one kind of suggestion to the table. Partnerships made up of people who deliver services in the community, or who receive those services, will reach conclusions of a different kind. A mixture of these two groups, along with the private sector, may achieve the more innovative and practical solutions.

EXAMPLES OF PARTNERSHIPS

♦ **Strategic Partnerships** – these may be regional, sub-regional or local.

- **Single Regeneration Budget (SRB)** Partnership Programmes bring together representatives from the community, voluntary, private and public sectors with the specific purpose of area and neighbourhood renewal. They can include churches, mosques, housing associations, etc.

- **Health Action Zones** bring together local authorities, health authorities and the voluntary sector.

- **Education Action Zones** bring together Local Education Authorities, schools and colleges, parent organisations, youth forums and neighbourhood groups who will be affected by any changes and can benefit from opportunities in lifelong learning.

♦ **Development Trusts**

- Development Trusts are organisations engaged in the economic, environmental and social regeneration of defined areas or communities, and which are made up of representatives of the local community, business community, voluntary, public and private sectors - as in the SRB's above.

- ◆ **Local Coalitions**

  Medium term

  - E.g. a local health project which brings together the Health Authority, local Community Association, local schools, the Youth Service, local doctors and Social Services to organise a Young Persons' Health Clinic.

  Short term

  - E.g. Summer play schemes which bring together local residents, the Leisure Services Department, the Youth Service, the Parent and Toddler group and the Community Association to run a specific project for young people in the summer holidays.

- ◆ **Joint Venture Development Partnerships**

  - Physical regeneration projects involving housing associations and local authorities. These partnership projects, aimed at improving the environment and housing stock, often involve tenants and residents associations and local business.

FURTHER READING

The Guide to Development Trusts and Partnerships Wilcox, D. : Development Trust Association, 20 Conduit Place, London W2

Local Evaluation for Regeneration Partnerships: good practice guide Tym Roger and partners: Regeneration Division, DETR, 4/G5, Eland House, Bressenden Place, London SWIE 5DU

"The National Evaluation of Health Action Zones", Personal Social Services Unit report (2000): University of Kent at Canterbury. http://www.ukc.ac.uk/

ACCOUNTABILITY

Lydia Meryll &
Paul A Jones

INTRODUCTION

One of the key issues around partnership working is how the member organisations will report to their 'customers' and get feedback on the quality of their service. This can be done through surveys and focus groups, as well as by consulting area forum groups, or Ward councils.

TENSIONS AND DIFFICULTIES

Community-based partnerships can become sites of tension when people give different weight to the various forms of accountability. For example:

- volunteer activists are likely to feel most accountable to the individuals in their patch.
- local reps of groups may see their role as reporting to their committee, rather than the wider community .
- a regeneration manager may be very aware of the targets to which s/he has signed up with the regional funders.
- local elected members may feel accountable to the strategic plan agreed by committees in the Town Hall.

The role of the community worker is to highlight these differences and allow stakeholders to discuss the tensions, and seek ways of resolving difficulties.

RELATIONSHIPS WITH FUNDERS

Where a partnership is getting public funding, funders require accountability:

- for public money.
- to the Charity Commission.

The services of professional accountants need to be costed into all financial forecasting and budgeting procedures. Community representatives, along with any paid staff, can learn how the figures are added up and future spending needs predicted.

Public money must be carefully administered. Spending is usually associated with targets which have been built into initial funding applications, often before local people became involved. Targets, and milestones for achieving them, need not be inflexible; it is usually possible to renegotiate them.

INTERNAL ACCOUNTABILITY

Partnerships can also involve internal accountability between staff and volunteers. Damaging suspicion about unfair treatment can often be triggered by the lack of simple tools, such as holiday charts and weekly time-tables, which show where people are working. Accountability is about everyone being seen to pull their weight. Open access electronic diaries are increasingly being used by staff across partnerships. An ongoing debate is often needed to agree, and then review, appropriate protocols. The key word here is **'Transparency'**

USING A STAKEHOLDER MAP

Community workers involved in partnerships often feel they are being pulled in several different directions - they seem to be accountable to many bodies, and have much expectation placed upon them. It is useful, therefore, to map out where the tensions lie.

1. **Make a Stakeholder Map**.
   - Choose ONE issue to consider, e.g. the redevelopment of a local playground.
   - Who are the active partners already wanting to be consulted?
   - Who are the silent partners whose views ought to be sought?
   - How much power do they already have?
   - How much authority do they have to make decisions?
   - Is there a lead agent with responsibility for delivering the project?

2. **Locate yourself on the map**.
   - Where do you stand?
   - What are the tensions as you perceive them?

Use the map as a tool at the next meeting to test out your perceptions and discuss the difficulties. You can use it to help clarify roles before you all decide what needs to be done to create a more inclusive way of operating.

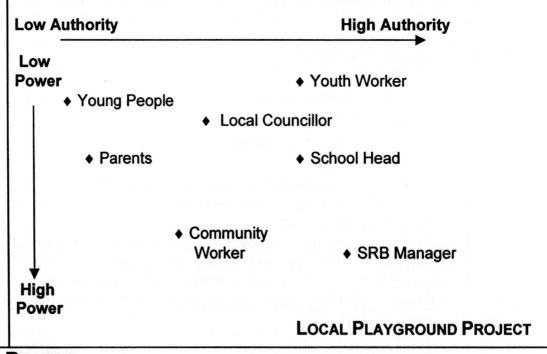

LOCAL PLAYGROUND PROJECT

FURTHER READING

From Thatcherism to New Labour - History of the Youth Service in England Davis. B. : Youth Work Press, Leicester (see chapter on accountability). (1999)

Community Economic Development, Twelvetrees, A. : Community Development Foundation   (1998)

INVOLVING LOCAL PEOPLE

Lydia Meryll &
Paul A Jones

INTRODUCTION

The current Government expects local people to be involved in all service delivery as a part of the Best Value standards and procedures for local government officers. It advocates community involvement, as it believes that this enhances the effectiveness of regeneration programmes through:

- better decision making
- more effective programme delivery
- ensuring longer term sustainability of regeneration .

(DETR 1999 Regeneration Research Summary No 25
Involving Communities in Urban and Rural Regeneration)

But how is this to be achieved in practice, especially when local people may have become sceptical about being "consulted" in the past, or local councillors feel they have been bypassed? There is a tension between traditional representative democracy and new forms of participative democracy. How does a community worker manage these tensions, and at the same time enable local people to feel genuinely empowered by these new opportunities for involvement?

PARTICIPATIVE DEMOCRACY: The active involvement of people in local decision-making

Issues to be aware of:

- **Clarity:** for "The Community" to be actively involved in decision making, and the delivery and monitoring of quality of a service, the extent of "Involvement" needs to be clarified from the start.

- **Involvement** of local people can mean anything from seeking one-off views from a group/individual, to having a constant series of meetings and discussions about the progress of a project with as many people as want to be involved.

- Community workers need to develop **a range of strategies** which ensure that local people, who are not usually asked their views, can get involved in a small group before they engage with more formal settings.

- Community workers can play a part in **clarifying the roles** of local community members. They can help make sure that minority voices are actively sought out, and heard.

- **On-going involvement** There are numerous examples of Partnerships where advice and involvement was sought at the beginning of the project, but only token involvement was sustained.

- The **full engagement** of local people is not always welcomed by the staff and managers of partnerships.

- **Equal access to information** – e.g. the increasing use of Bulletin Boards for posting information and getting feedback could mean that local people with IT skills and access to the Web can engage as fully as they want to with a project, but other people may be left out, or ignored.

REPRESENTATIVE DEMOCRACY: involvement through an elected representative

- The involvement of people in decision-making is determined by their link with their elected representatives, or by key individuals from an area who have been picked out to stand as representatives on various boards.

- The elected member(s) may be supported, or opposed, by voluntary officials who belong to strong community organisations, such as a Tenants' Union. This allegiance can lead to the social exclusion of many minority groups and disabled people.

- The establishment of new Executive Groups in many local councils has left ward councillors unsure of their role. They no longer have power in the many Committees which used to exist to make local policy. In the DETR Draft Guidelines for Preparing Community Strategies (June 2000), they are told that it is their job to be involved:
  - as representatives of their wards, leading and listening to formal and informal discussions and consultations, and representing these community views to the executive
  - as members of overview and scrutiny committees
  - as members of area and neighbourhood forums and committees
  - as council representatives on outside bodies.

- Local representatives may be given no support to canvass the rest of their community and seek out minority views. They may be seen to be 'set up' in this role, and alienated from the rest of their community.

- It is vital for social inclusion that the less strong voices are well represented, and that these representatives develop confidence in voicing their concerns and influencing local policy.

EFFECTIVE PARTICIPATION REQUIRES . . .

- Individuals volunteering to take on roles as representatives for their community, with an understanding of group dynamics and the power structures which surround them.

- Support for representatives to continually engage with their peers as they gain increased knowledge, different professional 'languages' and confidence.

- Knowledge of how, and when, to use techniques for broader consultation. Peer-led and peer-owned community audit techniques can help with this. The community worker can arrange training in constructing surveys and questionnaires.

- Updating the needs of a community as they change over time. This can be done through focus groups, surveys using questionnaires, and interviews; and may include engaging schools, youth groups and community groups in a **"Planning for real"** exercise in which people visually construct physical and environmental solutions to the needs of their neighbourhood.

- Training to enable members of communities to acquire skills in community participation and development.

FURTHER READING

Anastacio, J., Gidley, B., Hart, L., Keith, M., Mayo, M. and Kowarzik ,U., **Reflecting realities: Participants' perspectives on integrated communities and sustainable development.** Published for the Rowntree Foundation by The Policy Press (2000)

Burns, D., and Taylor, M., **Auditing community participation: An assessment handbook.** The Policy Press (2000)

DETR **Preparing Community Strategies: Draft Guidance to Local Authorities** (June 2000)

Packham, C., **Community auditing as community development.** Community Development Journal. Vol. 33 No 3 pp. 249-259 (1998)

Percy-Smith, J. and Sanderson, I., **Understanding Local Needs**, Institute for Public Policy Research. (1992)

Percy-Smith J., (1996) Needs Assessment in Public Policy. Open University Press.

DECISION MAKING

Lydia Meryll &
Paul A Jones

INTRODUCTION

A partnership involves a range of people and organisations, with the aim of improving the quality of decision making, and ensuring the effective implementation of programmes and projects.

In all partnerships, questions arise about why and how decisions are made, and by whom. Multi-agency partnerships are often designed so that local people and community groups can have a real say in the decisions that affect their lives.

However, the reality of decision making can be far from the ideal. Local community groups may feel marginalised in formal meetings by skilful, experienced and vocal professionals. At other times, one or two key community activists may dominate proceedings, so that less confident local participants are excluded from contributing effectively.

RELATIONSHIPS BETWEEN PARTNERSHIPS

Partnerships come about through a need to collaborate - but it is important to recognise that organisations, groups and individuals come with their own interests, aims and agendas. Sometimes these may be open, at others, more hidden. Community representatives and activists need to be able to map out what these agendas may be.

In the early days, when relationships are being forged and consolidated, diverging interests can lead to tension over the direction of the work and the different roles organisations will take. This is why it is very important to establish at the outset a shared understanding, not only of what the partnership is trying to achieve, but also of how it will go about achieving it. It demands honesty and trust among participants for decisions to be made that will be owned and implemented by those involved.

INFLUENCING THE DECISION-MAKING PROCESSES

Effective participation in partnerships depends on influencing the processes of decision making; and this depends ultimately on the power of organisations, groups, or individuals. The bigger agencies have the resources, the connections, and the position to give them an overriding influence.

Potential Problems

♦ Some community participants may feel uncertain about working in partnership. They may not have had experience of working in this way before or they may feel that their voice will count for little. If they lack confidence or feel intimidated then their ability to work in the interests of their community is negated.

♦ Community groups and activists are often sceptical of multi-agency partnerships, because they know that they have little power in comparison with professionals from statutory agencies and the private sector.

◆ In some multi-agency partnerships, community representatives are not genuinely expected to radically influence the major decisions. Here community reps have been recruited simply to give an inter-agency partnership the necessary "community" respectability and rubber stamp decisions.

In order to change such situations, it is important to know how to build and mobilise influence. This requires the reps to have relevant information and knowledge, and a range of skills in organising, planning, networking and handling meetings. Community workers have a particularly important role to play in enabling the reps to develop the confidence, capacity and skills to participate effectively in decision making processes.

Some suggestions to ensure an influence on decision making processes:

◆ establish, communicate and share a vision – community leaders feel strongly about their communities, and need to communicate a vision of what the partnership has to offer to others. Other members are influenced when confronted by someone who believes passionately in their community.

◆ question assumptions and old ways of doing things – think creatively about issues and ways of influencing decision making. Most people, when presented with a problem, will try and find solutions based on tried and tested modes of reasoning. Influential thinkers think "out of the box". They challenge assumptions and are ready to think and try out new ideas.

◆ have reasoned and logical arguments - passion, on its own, is not enough. If we want to have influence, it is important that our vision and passion about what we want to achieve is expressed clearly, logically and backed up with evidence and sound arguments. Write it down. Brief written recommendations carry weight.

◆ think strategically - it is important to think though the action steps that enable a goal to be achieved. To influence the decision making process means thinking ahead and giving consideration to tactics and strategies. Flowcharts and diagrams can be taken to meetings.

◆ be open, friendly and a good listener - having a positive attitude to members of the partnership not only creates an atmosphere in which mutual understanding can take place, but also results in other participants taking us more seriously.

◆ be assertive – if it is important not to be aggressive and hostile. It is equally important to be able to express ourselves in a forceful manner. Community participants must insist assertively that their voice is heard.

◆ make contacts and build alliances – influencing the decision making process happens as much outside meetings as within them. Networking and making contacts is the foundation for building alliances and coalitions with people, and mobilising their support in the decision making process. It is a good investment of time, but it may need to be costed and allowed for.

POWER CHECK LIST

To check what power your group may have, tick the relevant boxes:-

♦ **Position power** – Does your partnership *need* recognised community involvement in order to access resources and funding? ☐

♦ **Expert and information power** – does your partnership programme depend on up-to-date knowledge and information about local communities to be effective? ☐

♦ **Connection power** – do you have access to other groups and networks in the community which are invaluable to the partnership programme? ☐

♦ **Reward and Coercive Power** – is your group in a position to either reward the partnership programme with positive feedback about its impact in the community, or undermine it in formal evaluations if the process has been inadequate? ☐

♦ **Personal power** – community representatives and activists are often well known and respected leaders in the community, with the personal dynamism and charisma which is itself a source of power in the decision making process. Their vision, planning, communication and creative action can have a positive unifying effect on people. Their action is based on a set of evident values and beliefs, and they are committed to achieving clear goals. Does this apply to you? ☐

♦ **Negotiating power** – are you in a position to modify the preferred options, and so allow common agreements to be possible? The art of the community negotiator is to be flexible and open to persuasion, while, at the same time, endeavouring to ensure that whatever is agreed is fully in the interests of the community. ☐

♦ **Bargaining power** – are you prepared for an element of give and take to achieve an outcome? Influencing decisions in the interest of the community may mean that certain desired outcomes have to be forsaken in exchange for others; and this means checking back with a group, or the wider community. ☐

FURTHER READING

Transforming Leadership, Anderson, T.D. : Blackhall (1998)

 "Social and Community Issues" (Chapter 6) , Jacobs, B. and Dutton, C. *in Roberts P. and Hugh H, Urban Regeneration – a handbook* Sage (2000)

Problem Solving in Groups, Robson, M. : Gower (1995)

Effective Problem Solving,   Whetten, D., Cameron K., and Woods M. :

Harper Collins (1996)

CHECKLISTS FOR WORKING IN PARTNERSHIP

Lydia Meryll,
Paul A Jones &
Val Harris

INTRODUCTION

If your group, or a group you are supporting, is thinking about entering into a partnership, this checklist may highlight areas you need to think about.

CHECKLIST

Checklist if you are initiating a partnership	✓
1. Are you clear of the purpose of the partnership – why is it you want to work with other groups?	
2. Have you consulted and discussed the idea widely in your group?	
3. Have you decided you own vision of the partnership – is it realistic?	
4. Have you a draft a mission statement outlining what you want to achieve?	
5. Are you clear about which other organisations to involve as partners?	
6. Are you clear about the role your organisation wants to take?	
7. Have you taken advice on the different kinds of contracts or agreements?	
8. Have you drafted a discussion document on how a shared project could develop outlining its aims, objectives, outcomes, directions, possible targets and milestones?	
9. Have you started by bringing your potential partners together for negotiations ?	
10. Have you set out the minimum conditions for involvement of full partners ?	
Checklist if you are asked to join a partnership	✓
1. Do you understand exactly the purpose of the partnership?	
2. Have you discussed, as group, how being a partner would add value to what your organisation wants to do?	
3. Have you consulted people who you trust and who know about the partnership? Have you checked out where the power lies in the partnership and who are the key players?	

4. Do you know how decisions are made? Will your voice be heard in the important meetings? Will you get enough information to make decisions?	
5. Have you found out about the history of the lead organisation and how participative and responsive it has been with other partners?	
6. Have you looked at the annual reports and financial statements of other organisations involved? What other information might you need?	
7. Have you consulted widely about the benefits of taking part both in and outside of your organisation? What questions are people raising?	
8. Don't sign anything without thinking it through. You can say no!	
9. Do you know how much time it will take? Have you costed it carefully including the time and expenses of volunteers?	
10. Have you checked if you will get any extra resources to service the partnership as well as deliver any new services? Is this written down anywhere?	
11. Have you people willing to get involved with the partnership and its meetings? Have you thought about how people can be selected/ elected?	
12. Have you thought about what new skills you need to develop to participate in the partnership fully and how you will learn them?	
13. Are you clear about the legal structure being proposed and what it means for your organisation and representatives?	
14. Are you sure about the options for getting out, if the partnership does not work for your organisation?	
15. How will your representatives remain accountable to the organisation and its members?	
16. How will the partnership monitor and evaluate its progress? Will that involve local peoples views?	
17. Go for it! – and make your voice heard in the partnership as much as possible.	✓

REGENERATION: CAPACITY-BUILDING
Martin F. Jenkins

INTRODUCTION

"Capacity-building" is a term that is being heard more and more, particularly in the context of regeneration. Sometimes it seems to mean community development; sometimes it seems to mean something else, or nothing at all. I suggested at the 1999 AGM that ACW should rename itself "The Association of Capacity-Builders." I was only half joking! This section attempts to identify the skills and issues associated with "capacity-building" - but without being quite sure what it means.

WHAT IS 'CAPACITY-BUILDING'?

It is building the capacity of someone to do something. More helpfully, the bidding guidance for Round 5 of the Single Regeneration Budget defines "community capacity-building" as

> 'organising a partnership's procedures, and providing adequate training and administrative resources for community representatives, so that the local community can fully participate in the regeneration of the area.'

The **aim**, then, of capacity-building is the **full participation** of the **local community**. How is this achieved?

Organising a partnership's procedures

Most regeneration partnerships are led by local authorities; the systems are set up by local authority officers. The procedures therefore reflect local authority practice. This can get in the way of community participation. Some of the barriers are:

- meeting structures (very formal, based around written reports)

- meetings largely made up of men in suits

- everything conducted in the language of bureaucracy (including abbreviations)

- everything happens in work time, without reference to volunteers who may work or have childcare needs.

The skill a community worker requires in this context is the ability to engage with the officers who (without thinking) create these procedures and get them to recognise how these procedures exclude the community. You may also need to empower community members to challenge the procedures.

Hint: The business members of a partnership may be as unhappy with local authority habits as you are.

Adequate training

Community representatives will need some training (or advice/support) about being an effective representative. As a community worker, you may be called on to provide it. In order to do so, you will need to have a good understanding of how local authorities and other bureaucracies work.

It is, however, more likely that the regeneration partnership will offer community representatives "training" / "induction." You may need to beware of this. There is a real risk that they will be sucked into the partnership's bureaucratic ways and co-opted into the bureaucracy.

Acceptance of training implies acquiescence in how things are done. As one grants officer put it: "Instead of training people to jump through the hoops, we should be asking why the hoops are there."

Administrative resources

Council officers come to regeneration partnerships with a number of resources:

- typing pools

- photocopying

- administrators to do research

- contacts in other departments

- networks with other agencies.

Community representatives have none of these.

As a community worker, you cannot substitute for the resources council officers benefit from as members of a large organisation. Your job in this context is not to substitute, but to demand that community representatives are as adequately resourced as the statutory agencies.

Hint: All this back-up for council officers is being recorded as match-funding. Ask for access to the same back-up on the basis that it increases the match-funding.

FINALLY ...

Capacity-building is not just about enhancing the community's capacity. Civil servants have acknowledged that **all** sectors need capacity-building - especially the statutory sector. Statutory agencies tend to see capacity-building as training community representatives to work to their procedures. The government's definition of capacity-building makes this one point out of three. As a community worker, you may well feel that the other two points need more attention.

NEIGHBOURHOOD AGREEMENTS   Joe Micheli

INTRODUCTION

A neighbourhood agreement is a document which sets out a commitment on service delivery by service providers to local people. It details ways in which people can have a say in how an area is managed, how services can be improved through better links with residents, and how special projects can be identified to benefit an area.

CASE STUDY: A COMMUNITY DEVELOPMENT APPROACH

One example of a neighbourhood agreement is in the Foxwood area of York. A community profile was carried out to ascertain local peoples' concerns. An expressed needs survey was undertaken - followed by a series of focus groups, some specifically for young people.

Alongside this, events were arranged that responded to the concerns of the residents, including a summer festival, community safety conference, establishment of a detached youth work project, and development of new youth facilities. Existing community groups were also helped to find funding to carry on and/or expand the valuable work they were already doing. The outcome was that local people realised that the Neighbourhood Agreement would be a way of improving things for themselves, which would not be tokenistic consultation but one in which they would have a powerful voice.

Residents, supported by the community worker, have taken the lead in the negotiations; and also in identifying and working on local initiatives that will benefit the whole community. Working groups are held regularly in the local Community Centre. Service chiefs attend when requested, to provide information and discuss the service improvements residents would like to see.

The residents have formed themselves into a constituted body, called the Foxwood Community Action Group, accountable to all residents in the area. Great efforts are made to encourage new people to join the group. Every opportunity, such as community events or meetings, is taken to talk about the Agreement and obtain the opinions of other people. A recently launched residents' newsletter, keeps everyone informed about what is going on and gives them the opportunity to get involved or just pass comment.

THE VALUE OF THE NEIGHBOURHOOD AGREEMENT

The agreement is a living document that will change as residents' priorities change. It is a mixture of information residents think vital, service improvements, local initiatives and monitoring. It is divided along subject lines that make sense to residents, not along service demarcation lines. Even though it is in it's early stages, it has already meant that service improvements have been introduced and that residents, by working together, have been able to attract funding for vital improvements to the area.

Monitoring
Residents did not want to be buried under mounds of paperwork - detracting from the real issues and designed to meet the needs of the service providers.

The monitoring meetings are based on personal contact, with written information providing clear and concise feedback on the topics in the Agreement. Emphasis is placed on qualitative monitoring, so that the real benefits and improvements to quality of life can be assessed. As with all parts of the Agreement, the residents have the upper hand on the monitoring body.

The Community Work Skills Course
From the outset, it was realised that the key to the success of the Agreement was building up the capacity of the residents. There was nothing to fear, and everything to gain, from having a properly informed group of residents with the confidence and skills to constructively challenge authority and get their views across. So a Community Work Skills Course has been instituted.

WHAT IS THE FOXWOOD NEIGHBOURHOOD AGREEMENT?

The Foxwood Neighbourhood Agreement aims to build good working relationships with service providers in Foxwood, and to improve the quality of life for everyone living in the area.

The agreement covers the following services:
➢ Community policing
➢ Cleansing
➢ Jobs, training and enterprise
➢ Housing
➢ Services for young people
➢ Welfare benefits

Who are the partners to the agreement?
➢ Foxwood Community Action Group(acting on behalf of all residents)
➢ City of York Council
➢ North Yorkshire Police
➢ Bradford & Northern Housing Association
➢ Railway Housing Association
➢ Joseph Rowntree Housing Trust
➢ Detached Youth Work Project

These partners provide services to Foxwood, as set out in their individual agreements.

What are the aims of the Foxwood Neighbourhood Agreement?
➢ To tell residents who their service providers are
➢ To try to improve services through regular feedback from residents, joint working between service providers, and special initiatives involving residents
➢ To tell residents the service levels they can expect, and ask whether or not these are being met
➢ To give residents the opportunity of monitoring services through the Community Action Group
➢ To provide good customer care
➢ To support community development
➢ To bring standards up to the level of the best provider, within the available budget
➢ To strengthen the partnership between residents and service providers.

Section 12

Running a Training Session

PLANNING & PREPARATION

Helen Bovey

INTRODUCTION

Training often looks easy to outsiders. This is because they are witnessing a good trainer, someone who understands how to put training sessions together, about how people learn, and how to make sessions relevant in their practical application back within the group. Most importantly, a good trainer is probably very well prepared.

ASPECTS TO CONSIDER

There are a number of aspects to consider in planning any training session. Each must be given equal weight and careful consideration.

Initial Analysis : Who wants the training? Who is it for?

♦ Find out the perspectives of the various stakeholders, including, the person asking you to run the event, the organisation funding it and the participants themselves.

♦ Be prepared to negotiate between the different objectives of the stakeholders; know what the priorities of the organisation are.

♦ Don't try to please everyone by agreeing to everything suggested.

Aims and objectives

♦ Find a suitable trainer.

♦ Work with the trainer to produce very clear aims and objectives.

♦ The objectives – or learning outcomes – describe very specifically the changes expected in participants by the end of the training event. Be realistic about what can be achieved.

♦ Make sure all the stakeholders have seen the aims and objectives before the event.

Resources

♦ Look at the options for venues, refreshments and other costs (signing, translation, travelling expenses for participants, hire of equipment etc.).

♦ Produce a budget for the event.

♦ Assess whether you can afford to employ trainers or if it has to be done 'in house'. Always get estimates which include preparation and delivery time, photocopying, travel and other expenses. Find out the maximum/minimum number of participants the trainer will work with for this fee. What cancellation charges might you incur?

♦ Consider 'selling' places to another organisation to make up any shortfall in the budget.

Logistics

♦ Find a comfortable venue – you cannot overestimate the importance of good heating/ventilation, comfortable seating, good lighting and good refreshments.

♦ Check the venue is accessible. Does it have adequate parking, and can it be reached by public transport?

♦ Is the venue suitable for the kind of training being planned? For example, is there enough room to move around, is there wall space for displaying finished work, can a crèche be provided?

♦ Work out how much time is available for the session – be realistic about what can be achieved in the time you have.

♦ Find out the maximum and minimum number of participants likely to attend.

Publicity and bookings

♦ Produce relevant publicity which indicate whether the training is just for your group or open to others.

♦ Ensure the images used and language are inclusive.

♦ Remember to include course title, aims and objectives, together with cost, location, date, accessibility, crèche facilities, payment methods and booking arrangements.

♦ Set up an efficient system for dealing with enquiries and handling bookings.

♦ Acknowledge bookings and keep records so you have a running total, and don't exceed your maximum number of participants. Keep a reserve list if necessary (people always drop out at the last minute).

Planning the programme

♦ Find out as much as you can about the participants – consider sending out a pre course questionnaire or speaking to people individually.

♦ Consider the previous learning experiences of participants – will this affect how they respond to this session?

♦ Choose methods that suit the course aims and objectives, the group, the venue and the time available.

♦ Be prepared to be flexible – have some activities 'up your sleeve'.

♦ Consider the pace, flow and structure of the session. Produce session plans.

♦ Don't be too ambitious. Be clear about why each part of the session has been included, and check back over your objectives to ensure you can achieve them all.

♦ Write an evaluation form to check whether the objectives have been met.

♦ Make a checklist of all the resources you will need.

Before the session

♦ Distribute a final programme, map/location/transport details and list of participants about 10 days before the event.

♦ Double check your equipment – does it all work, have you got spares?

♦ Check the booking for the venue – have you booked extra workshop rooms and hired equipment; have you confirmed numbers and agreed refreshment times?

♦ Check all the handouts are prepared and copied.

♦ Practise – particularly if you are trying some activities for the first time.

VENUE CHECKLIST
Helen Bovey

INTRODUCTION

There is a theory about human needs that has a great deal of resonance for anyone who has attended a training event in uncomfortable surroundings. This theory, Maslow's hierarchy of needs, states that individuals' physiological needs have to be met before they can move on to self development and really make the most of learning opportunities.

HOME OR AWAY?

There are many variables to consider in choosing a venue for your training. Start by considering whether the training should take place in your usual meeting place/premises, or in an alternative venue. There are good arguments for going to another venue.

♦ Participants are less likely to be interrupted by urgent phone calls and messages.

♦ They can concentrate more if they don't rush back to their desk, open the mail or answer the telephone during session breaks.

♦ They have the real luxury of space and time to think about the concepts and issues raised during the session.

♦ For some people being away from their usual surroundings removes a 'safety net' i.e. they cannot resort to a particular mind set that otherwise causes difficulties.

There may be cost implications if you don't hold the training on your premises, but you might find that you can access training rooms free of charge, or at very low cost, via other voluntary bodies or the local authority.

DETAILED PLANNING

The following points are equally relevant whether you hold the session in your premises or go elsewhere:

♦ Is the venue 'neutral'? Some people, for example, had negative experiences at school and associate all school/college premises with emotions related to these experiences.

♦ The venue probably needs to be appropriate to the participants. Be wary of being 'too posh'; use the kind of premises people feel familiar with: and use this opportunity to show the participants they are valued.

♦ Consider the location. Is it accessible (see the Access Check List in the Appendix)? Does it have adequate parking, and can it be reached by public transport at the time you hope to start?

♦ Think about the size of room you will need. This will depend on the seating arrangement you want, how much space is needed for participants to move around, and how many people will attend. A room that is too big is as difficult as one that is too small.

♦ Do you need extra rooms for small group working? If so, how big do these need to be? They should always be fairly close to the main training room to avoid losing time in moving people around a building.

♦ What time can you access these rooms to prepare before the training starts? You will need plenty of time to familiarise yourself with the rooms, the equipment, the building layout, and fire and emergency arrangements.

♦ Will staff at the venue put the seating and equipment out for you? This will affect how much time you will need to put aside before the session starts.

♦ Are you allowed to stick completed work on the walls? It is always a good idea to display flip chart sheets and feed back summaries on the walls as you progress through a training session. All good training venues should recognise this fact and let you do so!

♦ Think about the refreshments needed (and your budget). Can they be provided by the venue? If not, whose responsibility is it for buying them in – theirs or yours? Who is responsible for clearing up?

♦ What equipment does the venue have and what will you have to bring? Ask whether you need to book equipment separately and whether there is a separate hire charge.

♦ Make a checklist of your specific needs. Produce a shortlist of venues, and then go and visit them. Sit on the seats, check whether the lighting is adequate, assess the warmth/ventilation of the building, and see if there are any distractions such as background noise. Check whether staff are welcoming and pleasant. Can you access a photocopier or telephone during the event? Check whether the fire alarm test is due, and who else is using the venue that day – it's no fun competing with a drumming group!

♦ Know your budget, then find out all the costs – training room hire, workshop room hire, refreshments per head (remembering to include the trainer[s]), and the hire of equipment. What will the payment terms be? What cancellation costs will you incur?

SESSION OUTLINES   Helen Bovey

INTRODUCTION

Planning and preparation are essential to the delivery of good training. Session outlines are just one part of the planning process.

WHAT IS A SESSION OUTLINE?

Outlines help the trainer plan the session and act as the main reference point.

Ideally your outlines should summarise the following aspects of the session:

- ◆ Start and finish times.
- ◆ The amount of time available (in minutes).
- ◆ Name of the topic being covered.
- ◆ The learning outcomes for the session.
- ◆ Summary of trainer activities.
- ◆ Participant activities.
- ◆ The learning points to be covered/brought out in the session.
- ◆ The resources needed.
- ◆ Name of the lead trainer (where training delivery is being shared).
- ◆ The handouts pertinent to each session.

The outline should be in a format which makes sense to you, but you also need to consider the following points:

- ◆ Title the outline so you know to which session/event it relates.
- ◆ Number the pages.
- ◆ Put the outcomes at the top, so you can check whether you are likely to meet them.
- ◆ Use note form, not lots of wordy description.
- ◆ Don't be over complicated. You need to be able to work out at a glance what to do next.
- ◆ Put in times for breaks, and allow time at the end for review / evaluation.
- ◆ Make the notes look tidy – this will re-assure the participants!
- ◆ Consider leaving a space so that you can write some immediate notes about how the session went/improvements for next time etc.

Don't start by writing the session outlines. Rather, make notes and diagrams on rough paper first and only move on to the outlines once you have a clear picture of the overall format of the session.

PART OF A SAMPLE SESSION PLAN OUTLINE

The Main Outcomes are:

Time	Min	Topic / Trainer Activities	Participant activities	Learning points	Resources
9.15	15	**Tea / coffee / registration** Direct participants to complete question boards while having tea / coffee.	Complete question boards: • How much consultation do you presently undertake? • How effective do you think this is? • Do you think there should be more or less?		Name badges Blank sheets of paper Question boards: on flip paper "Principles of a community based approach" "Techniques"
9.30	10	**Introduction by the chair**			
9.40	15	**Welcome / introduction to the course** Introduce trainer Go through aims and objectives and focus to the course Give out manuals Analysis of question board exercise	Listen / question Comment	Add to principles sheet: • Don't consult where the outcome is already decided • Don't consult inappropriately • Prioritise on what to consult Add to techniques sheet: • Question / pin boards • Get people talking / doing asap.	Aims & objectives OHP Programme OHP Manuals

Continued . . . .

TRAINING METHODS
Helen Bovey

INTRODUCTION

Training should not be a passive experience. If learning and change are to take place they must be delivered so that new ideas can be converted into understandable and useful information by the participants. It is not enough just to present a set of facts, as we know that

- ◆ people learn in different ways, so the training methods used should take account of these different learning styles and preferences, and keep participants interested and alert
- ◆ participants will bring different prior experiences of learning and different personal priorities

So aim to employ a variety of different approaches in each session.

METHODS

Each method has its own merits and drawbacks. You will need to consider the right range of methods for each training situation.

The lecture
- ◆ The most formal training method, where participants sit still and listen to information from the lecturer.
- ◆ Enjoyed by people who like to 'collect information', and are not irritated by sitting still with no interaction.
- ◆ Often over used, particularly by trainers worried by the idea of 'uncontrolled' interaction with the group.
- ◆ Good for putting over new information quickly if the following guidelines are used:
  - ✓ no longer then 20 minutes
  - ✓ careful structure – tell them what you're going to say, say it, summarise it
  - ✓ give space for people to collect their thoughts, and encourage questions afterwards
  - ✓ no more than 7 main points or slides
  - ✓ provide handouts
  - ✗ don't simply read out the points on the OHP which are already in a handout – be more relaxed and 'informal'.

The demonstration
- ◆ Useful for training people in practical skills – e.g. using equipment and technology.
- ◆ Can take one of 3 forms – performance demonstration (showing), teaching demonstration (explaining) or interactive demonstration (working together).

Interactive training
- ◆ The trainer facilitates participants to learn for themselves – to discover, practise, discuss, learn through mistakes, develop, explore and refine.
- ◆ It needs planning, to ensure everyone takes part while you control the direction of the participation.

There are a number of ways of facilitating interactive learning:

Discussion

♦ The role of the trainer is to:
  - set the topic, keep the discussion focused
  - make sure everyone has the chance to speak summarise what has been said at regular intervals
  - keep to time
  - help avoid conflict
♦ Many participants enjoy this learning method; the people who struggle are those who don't like to commit themselves to a point.

Small group work

♦ The group splits into smaller groups (or pairs) to discuss a specific topic, quick list ideas. or work on a problem or case study.
♦ The groups can be self managed, or facilitated by a trainer.
♦ Suits people who prefer to work in a smaller group, and those who like to enter into more analytical discussion/debate.
♦ Each group should have the opportunity to share the key points of their discussion with others.

Role play

♦ Role plays mimic real situations and allow participants to practise new skills or behaviours in a 'safe' environment.
♦ Many people dislike the idea of role plays, but they can be very powerful tools when set up carefully
  - always try to work with real examples where you know a lot of facts and variables
  - write down and display the objectives, characters, scenario, timing, tasks, and feedback looked for
  - give participants time to prepare
  - run a well managed feedback session which deals sensitively with the 'actors' feelings.

Activities

♦ Use different kinds of activities to engage participants' interest and to make learning points. These could include:
  - drawing   - cartoons   - mimes
  - statues   - using pictures / postcards
♦ They must have a clear objective, otherwise they can appear silly.
♦ Activities are particularly good for exploring emotions, reviewing learning points, injecting fun and humour, and giving participants the opportunity to move around.

Individual learning

♦ There is always a place for individual learning opportunities. Space for working alone and reflection should be made on every course.
♦ Always be clear about
  - the objectives for the time spent working alone
  - the timescale
  - whether help is available
  - what they will be asked to do once they have finished.

WAYS PEOPLE LEARN   Helen Bovey

INTRODUCTION

Learning is not simply about giving and receiving information. Rather, it is a complex process that hinges on a number of factors. To facilitate learning the trainer therefore needs to take these factors into account.

POINTS TO CONSIDER

Warm-Ups
If the brain is 'warmed up' before a training session the facts presented will be retained more effectively. This warm up can take the form of

♦ a recap on existing knowledge/experience in the subject matter

♦ 'limbering up exercises' for the brain – riddles, word or memory games.

Warm-ups can also be games to

♦ help people to relax, and leave everyday life and problems outside the group

♦ encourage the group to work together.

Learning period
♦ Taking frequent short breaks increases the ability to remember.

♦ Ensure the breaks involve a change in physical position.

♦ The start and end of a session are the parts remembered best – present the essential information at these points.

♦ The memory surges into action a few minutes after being presented with new information. It starts organising and making sense of the facts – capitalise on this surge by setting tasks that use the information as quickly as possible after presenting it.

Outstanding elements
♦ Surprising or unusual information is more likely to be remembered clearly. When introducing new facts make the opening statement or visual image more vivid, use imaginative examples, or make your language more exciting.

Individual learning styles
♦ There is a view that individuals differ in the way they respond to, and therefore learn from, different activities or approaches. In 1986 Honey and Mumford defined 4 basic learning styles:

- **Activists** ~ like to get on with things, low level of need for detail, prefer doing to reading, like group activities, giving and receiving feedback.

- **Theorists** ~ like to take time, like detail, feel unsafe without handouts, etc., prefer to work alone, like receiving feedback but slow to give it.

- **Reflectors** ~ like to look at all sides of the picture, like to discuss and explore issues rather hear details or read about them, like group activities, like giving and receiving feedback.

- **Pragmatists** ~ like to get things done efficiently, want details if they

are useful, like leading group activities, prefer factual feedback.
♦ Trainers therefore need to plan sessions or events that will 'hit the right buttons' for individuals with any of these learning styles.
♦ Trainers also need to be aware of their own preferred style – to avoid the tendency to design events that would meet only their own needs and not those of all the participants.

Presentation styles

♦ Consider how information is presented to participants. People generally remember:
- 10% of what they read
- 20% of what they hear
- 30% of what they see
- 50% of what they hear <u>and</u> see
- 70% of what they say
- 90% of what they both <u>say</u> and <u>do</u>

Guidelines for effective learning

To put all these ideas into practice and ensure that participants on your course learn effectively, follow these principles:

✓ 'warm up' participants minds before starting a session
✓ watch out for sensory overload – sequence information, input in a clear and ordered manner, allow no distractions
✓ take frequent breaks
✓ present important information at the start of sessions, recap at the end
✓ repeat critical points at least 3 times, in different ways
✓ back up important information with reading materials
✓ link new information with existing knowledge
✓ encourage discussion and debate to enable people in their own words describe issues and concepts
✓ use realistic case studies and role plays
✓ the chance to practice skills should follow the input of information as quickly as possible
✓ visual memory is strong
✓ spend time helping participants transfer the learning into the 'real world' outside the training room
✓ use varied techniques throughout sessions

FURTHER READING

The Institute of Personnel and Development produce an excellent series of books under the name 'Training Essentials'. There are a number of very useful books in the series, particularly:

Psychology for Trainers, Alison Hardingham, IPD, 1998

Delivering Training, Susan Siddons, IPD, 1997

USING PEOPLES' EXPERIENCES   Helen Bovey

INTRODUCTION

Learning is always most effective when related to participants' previous experiences, and their work and lives outside the training room. This is sometimes described as 'experiential learning'.

It is also important to value people's experiences and to use them as a springboard from which further learning can take place. Some courses and qualifications now actively encourage people to go through a process of reflecting on their previous experiences; this is known as 'the accreditation of prior learning', often called APL in short hand.

FIVE STAGES YOU CAN TAKE

There are 5 stages to actively using people's previous experiences in training events.

1. **'Priming' participants prior to the training event**

    ➢ Ensure all participants see the course aim, objectives and programme beforehand.

    ➢ Ask them to think about the course and how it will relate to their experiences; what do they want to get from each session?

    ➢ Encourage them to come with a checklist of questions or issues relative to individual sessions, together with examples from their own experiences.

2. **Find out information about participants' experiences before the event**

    ➢ Find out as much as you can about participants' experiences, and use this information to help shape the final details of the programme.

    ➢ If the training is for members of a group or organisation, find out about their group and its problems / activities.

    ➢ Use pre-course questionnaires or interviews to ask about people's experiences as they relate to the event.

    ➢ Use 'pin board' activities at the start of the event to gather more information.

3. **Use participants' experiences in delivering the course**

    ➢ Where possible use real examples and anecdotes to illustrate issues and information – both from the participants' and your own experiences.

    ➢ Use techniques which help participants bring their experiences into the course – problem solving activities, case studies, sharing information with others, and providing mutual support and help.

    ➢ Always ensure permission is sought before using participants' experiences in the course – agreeing ground rules at the start of the event can help decide appropriate/ inappropriate references.

4. Provide opportunities to reflect on experiences

➤ Within the structure of the course, provide opportunities for participants to reflect on their experiences in the context of what they are now learning.

➤ This can be done on an individual level, with trainer help, in pairs or small groups.

➤ Offer help where this reflection may be difficult. Pre-prepared review sheets with questions and bullet points can be helpful.

5. Help participants plan their future experiences

➤ Learning does not take place only within the confines of a training course. The important part of the process lies in the participants' ability to put the information they obtain from a course into practice in their 'real world'.

➤ Every training event should give participants the opportunity to plan how they can do this.

➤ This planning should focus on the following points:

- WHAT can I do as a result of being on this course?
- HOW should I do it?
- WHEN should I do it?
- WHO else needs to be involved?

➤ Where possible, provide some follow up to help participants reflect further in their attempts at implementing the learning from the event. A very simple way of doing this is to ask participants to write a self addressed letter at the end of the training event – it should include their action plan, and any other relevant information they want to incorporate. The trainer then sends this letter to participants at an agreed time after the event, say 6 weeks.

➤ Consider whether it is appropriate to bring the participants together again some time after the training event. This will encourage them to try and achieve the actions they've planned, and also further the sense of collective support which will have developed throughout the course.

EVALUATION

Helen Bovey

INTRODUCTION

It is always important to evaluate the effectiveness of training, although this is not always as straightforward as it may seem.

The first step in preparing to evaluate training is writing good objectives. Think of the objectives as 'learning outcomes' – i.e. what differences do you realistically expect in participants' skills, knowledge and behaviour as a result of the training event?

Objectives should therefore be written in 'active' language. Right from the beginning think about how these objectives can be measured. The following outlines just one approach to presenting your objectives.

By the end of the course participants will:

- Understand the principles of community work
- Have practised conflict resolution skills
- Have considered how the course will impact on their own work.

MEASURING THE SUCCESS OF A TRAINING EVENT

You need to measure the success of a training event against a number of criteria. These will differ in individual circumstances, but some of the common measures will be against the following;

- Were the course objectives met?
- Was the venue appropriate and acceptable?
- What was the trainer like? Did s/he demonstrate principles of equality?
- Did the course meet participants' needs?

WHEN TO EVALUATE

Interim review/evaluation

It is always worth doing interim reviews during a training event, particularly where it lasts for a day or longer. These will give the trainer some feedback on progress against the objectives, together with issues about comfort factors (such as lighting, meals, ventilation etc.).

Reviews can be built into other 'warm-up' activities at the start of sessions, and can be a fun way to open the day/session. Use your creativity to think of ways of reviewing or try the following examples:

- A quick round, with everyone mentioning one important/useful thing which has stuck in their mind from the previous session; and one thing they still have questions about.
- 'Post-it' reviews, where everyone fills in post-its under 3 headings and then sticks them on a flipchart sheet. The headings reflect progress, confirmation, omission.
- Draw a snake on two pieces of flipchart paper stuck together lengthways. Ask participants to stick post-its on - with things they like about the course above the snake, and those they want changed below it.

End of course evaluation

There should be some mechanism for obtaining feedback at the end of a training session or event. This is a good time to find out about the venue, the trainer or resources; but not so effective for assessing whether learning has taken place.

A number of methods are possible. The most common is an end of course questionnaire. Questionnaires should be as simple as possible, and address any issues you are concerned about. Lengthy wordy responses should be avoided. Use a straightforward scoring system, like the following:

Indicate your feelings about the course by circling the appropriate grading for each question.
1= unacceptable   **2 = fair**   **3= good**   **4 = excellent**
1   2   3   4
a) how do you rate the training room?
b) How do you rate the course content?

Using an even number of options ensures that people commit themselves to a considered response rather than always opting for the middle of the scale!

This technique can be used for individual questionnaires to each participant, or placed on a flipchart sheet for people to complete as they leave the room.

Another approach is called the 'talking wall'. A number of flipchart sheets are placed around the room with questions addressing the pertinent issues and participants add their comments or scores to each sheet. This approach can be useful in avoiding any kind of written responses, if diagrams rather than words are used.

You might want to know what worked for people, so you could either ask them

What should be kept / changed next time the course is run?

Or, for a course running over a period of time, to complete   "One thing that has affected the way I work is . . . "

Post-course evaluation

Questionnaires completed some time after a training event has finished will test more accurately whether the new skills acquired on the course have been integrated into participants' work/lives – i.e. whether the required learning has actually taken place.

However, there can be problems with post-event responses, and there is no way of estimating the extent to which other external influences have affected the way such questionnaires are completed.

A combination of approaches

Given the limitations of both end-of-course and post-course evaluation, a mixture of the two is probably the best approach. Whatever happens, it is crucial for the trainer to see the results of questionnaires, since these are the basis of any course amendments and improvements for the future.

Section 13

Project Management

UNDERSTANDING VOLUNTARY SECTOR ORGANISATIONS

Gersh Subhra

INTRODUCTION

It is sometimes hard for people outside, and even inside, the voluntary and community sectors to understand how voluntary and community sector projects are developed. This section attempts to explain the key stages any new project needs to engage with.

THE CORE ACTIVITIES OF VOLUNTARY SECTOR ORGANISATIONS

The core activities of voluntary sector organisations should be seen as being part of a cyclical process, and indeed the current climate facing the voluntary sector means that workers have to find ways of dealing with aspects of all the various stages simultaneously.

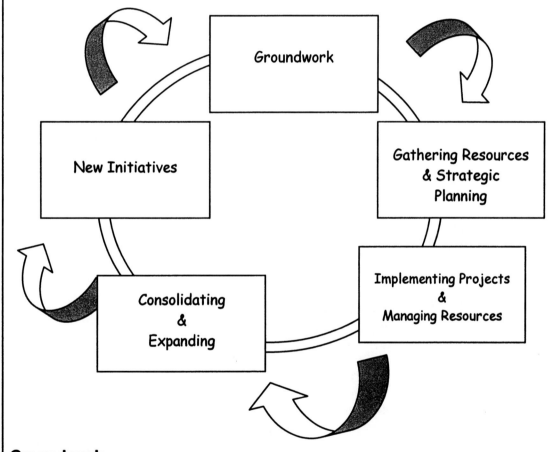

Groundwork

- Undertaking community development work
- Building relationships of trust with communities/target groups
- Encouraging people to become involved and gain new skills
- Assessment of needs, and issues emerging from these communities
- Developing the philosophy, aims, objectives and focus of the (new) organisation
- Creating a solid foundation for the growth of the organisation

Gathering Resources and Strategic Planning
- Strategic planning of initiatives
- Identifying resources (including volunteers, funding, partners, premises, equipment, etc.)
- Shaping the vision of the organisation
- Gaining `political` support for the organisation and its aims

Implementing Projects and Managing Resources
- Implementing innovative new projects, and maintaining them over a period of time
- Developing a policy framework for the organisation (e.g. equal opportunities, health and safety, staff development, etc.)
- Dealing with crises
- Managing staff and volunteers
- Supporting and expanding the management committee
- Developing the administrative infrastructure of the organisation
- Maintaining a public relations profile with key funders, community, etc.
- Responding to funding, or partnership, opportunities

Evaluation
- Meeting evaluation needs of funders
- Learning from own evaluation, and feeding the results into the work of the organisation
- Publicising the impact of the work

Consolidating and Expanding
- Finding ways of consolidating and expanding the work, e.g.
  - new partners and new funding sources
  - better premises
  - clearer aims and objectives
  - finding more volunteers
  - training staff, volunteers and management committee
  - finding more members, or enhancing the quality of the management committee.

Developing New Initiatives
- At this point the organisation can think about developing new initiatives.

HANDLING INFORMATION

Updated by
Val Harris

INTRODUCTION

There is a lot of printed material being targeted at the community sector and it is not always easy to decide if it is worth acquiring or following up.

The purpose of this technique is to assist an individual or groups to evaluate a piece of written information, and to assess whether a reference is worth pursuing.

CHECKLIST OF QUESTIONS TO ASK

- What is the document's relevance to your present interests?
- Does it say anything new? Will it add to what you already know?
- Is the document purely descriptive or "factual"?
    - If it includes analysis, is the analysis useful, sound or merely opinion masquerading as facts?
    - Are the facts relevant or important?
- What authority does the document claim? Is it entitled to its claim?
- What is the author's bias? Do you share this bias or perspective? Is the perspective or bias relevant to your context?
- What is the source/publisher of the document, and who is the author? What is your relationship to the source? Do you need to monitor the activities of the source?
- Does the document claim to be objective? (BEWARE)
- What is the physical form of the document? Can you handle the form if you wish to store the document?
- What limits does the document admit to? Can you identify any further limitations? Are the limitations important?
- Is the document clearly written, or is it full of jargon?
- Is the document dated? Is it up-to-date? Will it be updated; if so, when? Does the date matter anyway?
- Will the document be useful to others?
- What is the future availability of the document likely to be? Where is it available from?
- Why was the document produced?
- Does the document include any references or further reading?
- If you want to obtain a copy of the document you should record the following information where appropriate:
    - Title:
    - Author: (organisations and groups can be authors)

- Publisher: (address if given)
- Date published:
- Cost: (+ any postage and packing charges)

A document does not have to justify itself against all the questions in the list for there to be sufficient grounds for obtaining and reading it.

POINTS TO NOTE

The technique implies a rational approach to the use of information. While this will allow a more efficient and probably effective use of information there are occasions when it is necessary to speculate and trust your intuition.

Care should, however, be taken when speculating if you do not wish to turn your filing cabinet into a wastepaper bin. If your speculation fails, or your intuition is wrong, throw the document *out.*

PROJECT JOURNAL

Updated by
Val Harris

INTRODUCTION

Many projects are run with part-time staff and volunteers who need to find a way of keeping in touch with each other and knowing what is happening in the project.

The purpose of this technique is to establish a means of communication between the users/workers of a project, centre or office. The Journal should become a central reference point to which any person can refer, and should also provide a record of the project/ organisation's development.

Organisations are dependent on the flow of information; the power of individuals within organisations is linked to the information available to them. If individuals are not prepared to share information the organisation will suffer and members unable to participate in the decision making process.

This technique provides a method of seeking to ensure that all members of an organisation have the opportunity to communicate information and also receive/ obtain it without numerous pieces of paper flying round the office.

HOW TO USE A PROJECT JOURNAL

Obtain the agreement of all those using the office and or likely to make entries in the proposed Journal. Without the agreement of all concerned, forget it.

Agree the type of information to be recorded in the Journal. The essential information for each entry is

- ◆ the name of the person making the entry
- ◆ date of entry (time optional)
- ◆ the entry: possible types of entry include
  - telephone messages,
  - signing in and out,
  - when next in,
  - people expected to be coming in,
  - meetings,
  - conclusions and minutes of meetings,
  - notices,
  - reports of events that are likely to affect the organisations,
  - relevant press cuttings etc.

Do not swamp the Journal; be selective. Someone answering the phone won't want to wade through press cuttings and reports of meetings to find out if someone is in the building.

Select the most convenient place for the Journal to be located. Hanging it on a wall in a passage is unlikely to encourage people to make entries.

Equipment

- ◆ Notebook of some sort - preferably with attached marker, pen/pencil - and a table/ ledge at a convenient height and place for writing.

- ◆ If a loose-leaf form is used the Journal may be used as a day file as well.

Do not throw the Journal away. Its purpose is not just an immediate one. It can be used for evaluation and monitoring purposes.

CONDITIONS FOR THE TECHNIQUE TO WORK

In principle, the Journal is of value to any organisation, but there are a number of contexts in which it will be of more use than others; these include:

- ◆ direct action campaigns
- ◆ campaigns in general
- ◆ large buildings with no collecting points
- ◆ common areas or congregating area
- ◆ offices used by a number of people at different times.

There must be a need to share information; otherwise the Journal will become conversation by proxy.

People must be prepared to co-operate and place a high priority on maintaining the Journal. This is only likely if the benefits from the Journal accrue to many and people don't merely seek to use it as a management tool i.e. for control purposes.

Report Writing   Val Harris

Introduction

Report writing is quite hard to get right because, although there are some basic rules to follow, there are many variables to think about. There are so many different reasons and purposes for writing reports, and the people for whom you are writing may be expecting a particular style; and then, of course, we all have our own styles of writing.

In this section I will give some general guidance on the approach to take, followed by more specific guidelines for writing 4 different types of reports

- for funders
- for management committees
- for monitoring purposes
- for presenting research findings/ feasibility studies

General Comments

- When writing anything it is always useful to start by thinking about the purpose of the report and who might be reading it.
- Check if there is an established way of presenting the information or laying it out.
- Think about the main section headings; people can take in information better in small sized pieces - whole pages of text make us fall asleep, so use headings to break it up.
- Check that these headings follow a reasonably logical pattern; would someone who didn't know much about you be able to follow your train of thought?
- How much information do they have already? Or prior knowledge of your organisation/ project/ work? Your regular management group may just need an update, not all the background funders or new people might require.
- What sort of introduction do you need?
- What style is appropriate; can you use bullet points, diagrams, pictures, or do you need to write in detail? Think about the readers - what will get the information across best to them?
- Think about a summary or conclusion, or an action plan to move forward; don't just fade out as if you hadn't had time to finish the report.

Reports for Funders

In order to apply for funds through a letter or a report (rather than by completing a form) you need to work through headings such as

- who are you? What is your organisation all about
- why they might be interested in your project
- what is the need/ problems that you are trying to resolve/ solve
- how you will tackle the problems/ meet the needs – this means explaining quite clearly what you intend to do, how you will

approach it, within what time scales
- how much you require

If you are reporting back to a funder on money you have had (and again there is no form) you could use such headings as
- what you are doing, and how it fits with the original plan
- what you are doing that might be different, and why this approach is better or a response to changing circumstances
- what has changed as a result of the activities listed on the funding application
- your plans for the future

REPORTS FOR MANAGEMENT COMMITTEES / MANAGERS

When you have to give regular reports to a group or an individual then you may use these headings:
- activities you have undertaken since the last report – broken down into sub headings, such as meetings attended; groups worked with; funding applications made; people supervised and supported, research carried out etc.
- What were the results of all these activities? What outcomes/outputs would you want to record?
- Changes which have happened since the last report – within your project, within the area, with the local political set up, with national polices; anything that has impacted on your work, or will affect it now or in the future
- What are the issues they and you need to address ?
- What you are going to do next; your targets; areas of work . . .

REPORTS FOR MONITORING PURPOSES

Usually there is a (complicated) form for monitoring particular pieces of work, especially if the work is funded through various regeneration schemes, but just occasionally you will have the luxury of writing a summary account of your progress. So here you can include;-
- What milestones/ targets did you set, or agree to, in the relevant period of time?
- Are you meeting them? If yes, how do you know that you are meeting them? What ways have you for gathering information?
- If not, why not? What other factors have arisen which affects the figures?
- What are your next set of milestones/ targets? Why do you think they are realistic?

REPORTS FOR RESEARCH / FEASIBILITY STUDIES

There are many different ways of presenting this work, but if you assume that most people only want a summary of what it means for them, and a few will want to see all the details in order to check the validity of the piece of work, then this will give you an idea about the order in which to present it. I often use the following format:

♦ Introduction ; what the research/ study was all about, and its aims; a scene setting short piece

♦ An executive summary of the main points arising from the research/ study

♦ A list of all the recommendations you are making

♦ The methodology – what did you do? How? This is where you show how many people were involved, and how the information was gathered; how the questions were set etc. This is important in showing that the research is valid and that your findings and recommendations should be taken seriously

♦ A summary of any issues or factors which may have influenced the actual findings

♦ What you found out - split this into sections with headings and a summary

♦ What actions you think should follow from this report

♦ An appendix with additional information, questionnaires, interview schedules, lists of organisations who contributed etc

COMMON FAULTS

You will have seen a pattern emerging in my suggestions which reflect my approach. You will obviously have your own style and approach but, whatever that it develops into, it is worth trying to avoid some common problems, e.g.

✖ It doesn't have a date on it, so you have no idea if it's still useful

✖ It's not page numbered, and if you drop the bundle you can't make sense of it

✖ You haven't thought about the readers and what they want to know and how they want to see the information presented, so they don't bother with it

✖ You didn't start at the beginning, so the reader couldn't clue into what you were talking about

✖ You assumed people have more knowledge than they do, so its doesn't make too much sense

✖ You jump around all over the place, so its hard to follow your thoughts or see where it is going

✖ It's too descriptive and not sufficiently analytical - what does it all mean? Why are you making these recommendations? Why will more money solve the problem?

✖ It's too brief - the readers cannot see how you have jumped to such conclusions, or why you are asking for a particular decision, e.g. why do you need to recruit more volunteers?

✖ There is no obvious link between the findings, the title and the summary

✖ You have used jargon and abbreviations which are not explained.

LEGAL STRUCTURES AND CONSTITUTIONS Chris Murdoch

INTRODUCTION

Most organisations other than very informal groups need a framework to operate within and a written document to set out the rules for running the organisation. These are called your **Legal Structure** and your **Constitution**.

LEGAL STRUCTURES

In English and Welsh law there are 2 categories of legal structure. These are called:

INCORPORATED and UNINCORPORATED

UNINCORPORATED means that the organisation does not have a legal identity which is separate from the people that run it. The management committee members are personally responsible for all the activities, contracts, finance and debts. Most voluntary sector and community organisations start out as unincorporated, and many small ones stay that way.

INCORPORATED means that the organisation becomes a Limited Company which is a legal entity in it's own right. The company can therefore take on contracts and leases, buy property and owe money without the individual directors NECESSARILY being liable. The larger an organisation gets the more likely it is to consider becoming a Limited Company.

CONSTITUTION

Whether your organisation is incorporated or unincorporated it will need a constitution. This is a document which sets out the rules for governing the organisation.

The main points to include in a constitution are:
  ➢ The aims of the organisation
  ➢ The rules for running meetings and making decisions
  ➢ The procedure for changing or closing down the organisation

Most funders now ask to see copies of an organisation's constitution.

USEFUL CONTACTS & FURTHER READING

Local Councils for Voluntary Service can often advise on Legal Structures and Constitutions.

The Directory of Social Change, 24 Stephenson Way, London NW1 2PD
Tel 020 7209 5151 e-mail info@d-s-c.demon.co.uk has an excellent book list and runs courses on all aspects of running a voluntary sector organisation.

UNINCORPORATED ASSOCIATIONS   Chris Murdoch

INTRODUCTION

An unincorporated association is the legal term for a group or organisation which does not have a legal identity which is separate from the people that run it.

A group is not required by law to seek approval of any kind before setting up as an unincorporated association. It doesn't have to register anywhere or send information to anybody except it's own members.

This structure is most appropriate for groups with a low income which don't need to employ staff or acquire property.

PROS AND CONS

Advantages
- ➢ Quick and cheap to set up
- ➢ No outside agency needs to be involved
- ➢ Independent – accounts and annual reports only have to be sent to members and funders
- ➢ Simple constitution
- ➢ Can be easily wound up

Disadvantages
- ➢ No separate legal identity so that any property must be held by individuals acting on behalf of the group
- ➢ Individual members of the management committee can be held personally liable for the obligations and debts of the group

MODEL CONSTITUTION

1. NAME

The name of the Association shall be

2. OBJECTS

The objects of the Association shall be:

3. MEMBERSHIP

Membership is open to

4 OFFICERS AND COMMITTEE

4.1   The business of the Association shall be conducted by a Chairperson, Secretary and Treasurer plus other members of committee elected annually at a meeting convened for this purpose.

4.2   The minimum number of committee members shall be

4.3   The committee will have power to set up sub-committees to deal with specific interests. Such subcommittees will be made up of members of the association, but the committee will have power to enlist the services of any person who will be or benefit to the association for any specific purpose. Such persons will not thereby become members of the association.

4.4   % of committee members shall constitute a quorum.

5   FINANCE

5.1   The funds of the association shall be obtained by means of any fund-raising activities as the committee may deem acceptable or necessary.

5.2   The funds shall be lodged in a bank approved by the committee. The treasurer will be responsible for managing the financial affairs of the association.

5.3   An annual statement of accounts must be produced at the Annual General Meeting, properly audited, by a suitably qualified person elected at the AGM, and who shall not be members of the committee.

GENERAL MEETING

The **Annual General Meeting** will be held at such time and date as the Management Committee shall determine, provided that the interval between one AGM and the next shall not exceed 15 calendar months, and that 21 clear days notice in writing of the meeting shall have been sent to all members of the Association.

The Annual General Meeting will transact the following business:-

(1) Minutes of the previous AGM

(2) Consideration of the Annual Report prepared by the Committee

(3) Consideration of the Annual Accounts

(4) Election of the Management Committee

(5) Any other relevant business.

The Chairperson of the Committee may at anytime at his/her discretion, and shall within 21 days of receiving a written request signed by not less than twenty members having the power to vote and giving reasons for the request, call a **Special General Meeting** of the association for the purpose of altering the Constitution or of considering any matter which may be referred to him/her by the Committee or for any other purpose.

7.   AMENDMENTS TO THE CONSTITUTION

Amendments to the Constitution may be proposed at the Annual General Meeting. Any such proposals to alter this Constitution must be delivered to the Secretary of the Association not less than 14 days before the date of the meeting at which they are first to be considered.

An alteration will require the approval of a two thirds majority of those present and voting.

8.   DISSOLUTION

The Association may be dissolved at anytime by a resolution passed by a two thirds majority of those present and voting at a Special General Meeting of the Association of which at least 21 clear days notice shall have been sent to all members of the Committee.

Such resolution may give instructions for the disposal of any assets held by or in the name of the Association, provided that if any property remains after the satisfaction of all debts and liabilities, such property shall be given or transferred to such other institutions or institution (having objects similar to some or all of the objects of the Association) as the Association may, with such approvals as are necessary determine.

USEFUL CONTACTS

Try your local Council for Voluntary Services for sample constitutions and advice about running your group. The Charity Commission has as model constitution for Charitable Unincorporated Organisations (see paper on Charities in this section for the address)

LIMITED COMPANIES
Chris Murdoch

INTRODUCTION

When a voluntary sector organisation or community group reaches a stage in it's development where the Management Committee feel uncomfortable with the level of personal responsibility they have they may consider registering the group as a limited company.

INCORPORATED LIMITED COMPANIES

A voluntary sector organisation can register with Companies House as a Limited Company. The company then becomes a legal entity in its own right, quite separate from its members. The members' personal liability for the obligations and debts of the company is limited.

There are 2 types of limited company.

A **company limited by shares** is owned by the shareholders who invest money in the company with the intention of making a profit. Their liability is limited to the extent of their shareholding. This structure is generally found in businesses.

A **company limited by guarantee** is a more appropriate structure for a voluntary sector or community group, which wants to incorporate. There are no shareholders. Instead any profits that the company makes must be reinvested in the company. The members' personal liability is limited to an amount that they have previously guaranteed (usually £1).

Advantages

> The company can own or lease property in its own name

> Individual members are protected from personal liability unless they have acted fraudulently or continued to operate when they know the company can't meet it's debts.

> Directors can earn money from the company

Disadvantages

> Increased bureaucracy. Companies have to comply with Companies House regulations

> Annual returns and accounts must be sent to Companies House

> Documents, including the register of members and directors and the annual accounts are available to the public.

> May be harder to get charitable status

CONSTITUTION

A Company Limited by Guarantee has to use a constitution called a Memorandum and Articles of Association. The Memorandum sets out what the company is set up to do (it's objects) and the Articles explain the rules for operating.

FURTHER READING

The Directory of Social Change, 24 Stephenson Way, London NW1 2DP Tel 0171 209 5151 e-mail info@d-s-c.demon.co.uk have some very good books on legal structures.

Workers Co-operatives and Community Businesses

Chris Murdoch

Introduction

There is no legal definition of a workers co-operative or a community business. However it is generally accepted that they are both forms of business which have social as well as business aims. Most co-ops and community businesses are registered as Companies Limited by Guarantee.

Co-operatives

A workers co-operative is a business that is run by the workforce. There are no shareholders in the business who take a share of the profits in return for their investment. Instead any profits the business makes are generally re-invested in the business or paid out to the workers as a wage rise.

The rules (Memorandum and Articles of Association) of most workers co-ops state that only workers can be members of the organisation.

Community Businesses

A community business is one which aims to both create jobs and provide products or services. While the products and services may be sold both inside and outside the community that the business serves the workforce would generally come from within the community.

The rules of a community business may allow for members who are not workers. These can be people who bring additional skills to the Management Committee such as financial advice or marketing experience.

Because there is no strict legal definition of co-ops or community businesses you can chose what to call yourselves and adapt model Memorandums and Articles of Associations to suit your group.

If you are thinking about starting a co-op or a community business you will need to think carefully about the business side as well as the community side of the organisation. Get as much help and advice as you can.

Case Study

BB Cleaning Services is a Community Business in Keighley in West Yorkshire. It was set up in December 1993 and it's aims are:

➢ To create satisfying jobs in the local community that offer workers the opportunity to arrange their work around their family commitments.

➢ To provide a reliable, efficient and affordable cleaning service for clients, especially the older people who now no longer have home helps who clean.

> ➤ To train and support the staff in moving on to higher skilled jobs if they want to.

> ➤ To advise other local groups who want to do something similar.

In 2000 the company now employs 22 staff. Everyone decides for themselves how many hours they want to work and as most staff are mothers hours generally fit in with school times.

The company is registered as a company limited by guarantee. Decisions are made by the Management Committee which consists of workers, supervisors, clients and members of the community who support the project. Keighley Local Enterprise Agency provides business advice and support.

The company does not receive any funding or grants. All the income is earned by charging for cleaning and over 80% is returned to the cleaners in wages. One of the hardest things about running the company is maintaining the balance between charging a price for cleaning that everyone in the community can afford and earning enough to pay decent wages.

USEFUL ADDRESSES

For further information about co-ops and community businesses in West Yorkshire contact:
Keighley Local Enterprise Agency, Acorn House, Airedale Business Centre, Alice Street, Keighley BD21.
Tel 01535 607775 e-mail klea@legend.co.uk

Nationally, contact :
ICOM, 74 Kirkgate, Leeds LS2 7DJ   Tel 0113 246 1737

CHARITIES   Chris Murdoch

INTRODUCTION

A charity is an organisation established for charitable purposes and will generally be registered with the Charities Commission under the Charities Act 1993.

PROS AND CONS

Both unincorporated associations and companies limited by guarantee can become charities.

An organisation is charitable if the aims and objectives stated in its constitution are charitable. There are four recognised categories of charitable objects – these are called the four heads of charity which are set in charity law and interpreted by the Charity Commission.

They are:
- the relief of poverty
- the advancement of religion
- the advancement of education
- other purposes beneficial to the community

Advantages

- Tax relief. Charities can apply for a number of tax advantages including: not paying income or corporation tax on their income or stamp duty when buying property, not charging VAT on donated goods which are sold in a charity shop and not paying inheritance tax on money left to the charity in a will.

- Rates relief. Charities only pay 20% of the rates on buildings they use for charitable purposes. Local authorities also have the discretion to waive the 20% so that the charity pays no rates at all.

- Fundraising. Some trusts only fund registered charities.

Disadvantages

- The activities of a charity are tightly controlled by the Charities Commission

- A charity has to prepare its accounts in line with Charities Commission guidelines

- Committee members must not benefit financially from the charity. This means that employees cannot be committee members and effectively rules out workers co-ops from being charities

> ➤ Members should not benefit from the work of a charity, so community development activities, tenants and residents associations cannot become charities (although this is currently under review)

> ➤ It also means that committee members cannot be paid for their work although the Charities Commissioners are willing to discuss exceptions to this, particularly one-off payments to committee members in exceptional circumstances

> ➤ Charities have to conform to a model constitution as laid out by the charity commission.

USEFUL ADDRESSES

Contact the **Charities Commission** for advice about registering as a charity.

St Alban's House, 57–60 Haymarket, London SW1Y 4QX
Tel: 020 7210 4477 / 020 4432 4548

OR

2nd floor, 20 Kings Parade, Queens Dock, Liverpool L3 4DQ
Tel: 0151 703 1500/1653/1654

OR

Woodfield House, Tangier, Taunton Somerset TA1 4BL
Tel: 01823 345000 345190

Appendix

ACCESS CHECKLIST   Ruth Malkin

INTRODUCTION

Before organising a community event, make sure you know how accessible the venue is for disabled people. It is no longer acceptable for events organisers' to think 'The venue's got a ramp to the front door, it'll do'. To get a better picture of how accessible a venue is, use the checklist provided below, and go round the building you want to hire with a tape measure and check it out. You may be surprised. Some buildings which look accessible aren't very user-friendly.

The checklist will serve two purposes. It can help you, the event organiser, to decide which venue to hire. Or, if you are stuck with that venue, it will enable you to give out accurate information to disabled people who make enquiries about access.

A final word of advice: never use the phrase 'fully accessible' on your publicity. No one will believe you, even if access to the venue IS good. Always list access features: for example, 'The building has level access and a large adapted toilet. There is a small car park next to the building. There is an induction loop available in the meeting room'.

CHECKLIST: please tick boxes as applicable

APPROACH

The direct route from the nearest parking bays to the venue's accessible entrance is:
- ☐ level
- ☐ dropped kerb
- ☐ other (describe)

Are access routes into the venue clear of any hazard (e.g. outward opening doors, windows, parking bollards) ?
If no, describe hazards:

The surface in the parking drop-off area is:
- ☐ smooth & firm (e.g. tarmac or concrete)
- ☐ level
- ☐ other: describe the surface - gravel, grass, mud etc.

The surface of the route to the venue is:
- ☐ smooth and level
- ☐ other: describe surface of route to venue (e.g. sloping, gravel, grass, mud, wood chippings)

☐ There is a car park on site with designated orange badge spaces
☐ There are orange badge spaces, or accessible kerbside spaces, adjacent to the site

☐   The designated orange badge spaces are at least 5000mm long and 3600mm wide (including a wide transfer zone)

No of designated spaces:

How far are the designated spaces from the accessible entrance?

Other information about the approach to the building

How far is the building from the railway station?

How far is the building from the bus station?

☐   The route to the venue from the main public transport drop off point is fully fitted with dropped kerbs

ENTRANCES

E1.   Is the main entrance the most accessible one for disabled people?

Yes ☐ Go to E3   No ☐ Go to E2

E2.   Is there an alternative accessible entrance available?   Yes/No

Please tick all that apply:

☐   The accessible entrance is at the side/back of the building

☐   The accessible entrance is unlocked at all times when the public can access the building

☐   The accessible entrance is locked

☐   The bell for the accessible entrance is no more than 1200 mm from ground level

☐   The accessible entrance is clearly labelled from the front of the building/car park

☐   The route from the front of the building/car park to the accessible entrance is well lit and level

☐   Other: please describe

E3.   The main or most accessible entrance is

☐   level

☐   ramped: gradient of ramp

☐   stepped: number of steps

☐   All steps and stair nosings are edged in contrasting colours

☐   Tactile warnings are given for changes of level

☐   There is a handrail: height of hand rail from the surface of the ramp/steps

☐   All pedestrian approaches have an unobstructed width of 1000mm

EXTERNAL DOORS AND LOBBIES

☐ The main external doors, when fully opened, have a minimum width of 800 mm

☐ The most accessible entrance door, when fully opened, has a minimum width of 800 mm

The most accessible external door is

    ☐ automated: width

    ☐ manual: width: outward/inward opening

    ☐ revolving: is there an adjacent door with a minimum width of 800mm ?

☐ There is a glazed panel in the accessible external door giving a zone of visibility between 900mm and 1500mm above ground level

☐ There is an entrance lobby. If Yes, is there sufficient manoeuvring space for wheelchair users? (At least 1500mm by 2001mm)

WITHIN THE BUILDING

W1 Information

☐ Information signs within the building are clear, and positioned to be easy to read

☐ All signs giving directions within the building incorporate symbols

☐ Some, or all, of the written information relevant to the users of the premises is available in Braille or on tape

W2 Routes and Corridors

Tick all that apply. If there are no internal doors go to W3

☐ All doors throughout the building have an opened width of at least 800mm

☐ All doors opening into a corridor or passageway have a glazed panel providing a zone of visibility between 900mm and 1500mm above floor level

☐ Glass walls and doors clearly marked between 900 and 1500mm

☐ Doors within through-access routes are fitted with see-through panels

☐ All internal doors are fitted with lever type handles at between 700 and 1200mm

☐ All internal doors have a leading edge of at least 300mm

☐ All internal doors light enough to be suitable for use by wheelchair users

☐ Corridors or internal passageways have an unobstructed width of at least 1200mm

W3   Describe the floor covering throughout the building - e.g. slippery, carpeted, stone, wood:

W4 Smoking

☐   There are designated smoking and non-smoking areas

☐   The whole building is non-smoking

W5 Lifts

Is there a lift installed? If No, go to W6 If not applicable, go to T1

What sort of lift is it?

☐   a platform lift

☐   a stair lift

☐   a passenger lift: size: _____ by _____

☐   a goods lift

Tick as many as apply:

☐   Lift buttons/controls are tactile

☐   Visual floor indicator

☐   Audible floor indicator

☐   Visual flashing fire alarm within the lift

☐   Independent power supply to the lift for emergency evacuation

How far from the floor is the highest control button?

Describe the lift and the fire evacuation procedures, including any safety refuges for people with mobility impairments; and note whether there are visual flashing alarms throughout the building (as explained by building manager)

W6 Steps and Stairs

☐   There are steps within the relevant parts of the building

☐   There are flights of stairs within the building. If No, then go to T1

☐   All stairs and step nosings are edged in contrasting colour / texture / brightness

☐   The unobstructed width of the step landings is at least one metre: if not, give dimension

☐   The tread of each step is at least 250mm; if not then give dimension

☐   The risers are solid

No. of steps there are per flight

No. of flights of steps

Handrails extend alongside steps and stairs on:

☐   Both sides

☐   One side: height of handrails from surface of steps:

☐   No handrail

☐   All stair handrails extend, or turn down, to indicate the beginning and end of the flight

Describe the steps/stairs - including surfaces, e.g. carpet, wood, slippery

TOILETS

☐ There are toilets adapted for wheelchair users available for public use on the premises. If No, then go to public areas

　　　The cubicle is　　　　　　wide x　　　　long

　　　The toilet is　　　　　　　　mm from the floor

The toilet is left/right hand transfer/pedestal

☐ There are hand rails on both sides of the pan; if Yes, describe the hand rails

☐ There is an emergency alarm cord, or button, which is reachable from the toilet

☐ The door opens outwards

☐ There are appropriately sited fixtures and fittings in the adapted toilet

☐ The adapted toilet incorporates baby changing facilities

☐ There is a visual flashing fire alarm within the toilet

☐ The door to the adapted toilet is kept unlocked at all times

(You may find it useful to draw a rough sketch showing the position of the toilet bowl in relation to the door.)

PUBLIC AREAS – COMMUNICATION - SAFETY

☐ Counters in the reception/cafe/other public areas are no higher than 800mm from floor

☐ There is a glazed screen separating the receptionist from the public

☐ There are induction loops or other hearing aids in the reception area

☐ Induction loops have been provided for people with impaired hearing in the training room/s

☐ In areas of the building where a hearing impaired person may find him/herself alone, there are visual flashing fire alarms

☐ There is a dedicated minicom enquiry line available for public use

☐ Some of the staff have had Deaf Awareness training, or have sign language skills

☐ Payphones with induction loops and/or volume controls are installed on the premises for public use

How many payphone are there ?

Are the payphones

　　☐ all on one level? Height(floor to handset)
　　☐ at a variety of levels? Heights(floor to handset)

Note any obstacles that may prevent disabled people using the pay phone

GLOSSARY

Compiled by
Joy Leach

ACTIVE CITIZEN
♦ Used by central government to encourage people to provide services themselves rather than expecting the state to do so. It has an emphasis on people's responsibilities rather than their rights – encouraging people to become charitable.

ADVOCACY
♦ Ideas around the concept of advocacy were borrowed in this country largely from the Netherlands and the USA, and began as ways in which people with learning difficulties might benefit from representing themselves. The ideas have now spread into work with people who have emotional problems and physical difficulties: SELF, CITIZEN, and PATIENT or LEGAL ADVOCACY are all ways in which power relationships can be shared and rigid systems challenged.

- **Citizen Advocacy** is about working with and helping people who often have considerable personal physical and intellectual difficulties, to better represent themselves. The skill here is to create confidence in people who are often unpracticed and unknowing about how complex systems work - i.e. being prepared to explain, deliberately slow down routines and work at their pace so that they can order to clearly understand what is happening.

- **Self-Advocacy** means learning how, for oneself, to take on organisations which prevent everyone's right to participate. It is about learning how to be prepared and confident when you are in someone else's territory - learning the rules, which are too often made by others, and turning them to your advantage. It's also about making it clear to the people who seem to be holding all the resources that good practice and equality are legitimate tools we should all be using. It's important to insist on knowing WHAT people with authority in organisations are doing, as well as how and when.

  Both self and citizen advocacy are about consciously transferring and developing power in a sharp, intelligent way in order that everyone can function more effectively.

- **Patient Advocacy,** sometimes known as **Legal Advocacy,** focuses on welfare rights, legal and other advice on one's status in relation to the 1983 Mental Health Act and other pieces of legislation. The aim is to offer independent support and advocacy to the user on any issue relating to her/his experience of the mental health system.

ALLIANCES
♦ Alliances usually have a common purpose, and particular objectives. They bring allies together, but have little in the way of formal or informal contractual arrangements between participants.

BUSINESS PLAN
♦ A costed development plan, which will usually cover a period of 3 or more years. The items to be included depend on the purpose for which the plan is to be used. Business Plans are frequently required by funding bodies.

CAPACITY BUILDING
♦ Helping people to develop the skills and confidence to become involved in community activities.

'Assisting this process, without pushing people to go in directions they do not want to; i.e. growing projects rather than designing and building them'.
(Brian Davey *ACW Talking Point No 175)*

Brian Davey also points out that:

'Capacity Building should not be seen as an attempt to set things up in the professional manner of large organisations and the business sector. In neighbourhood development this is not only unnecessary – it misses the point'.

COLLECTIVE ACTION
♦ Working together with others to achieve a common aim.

COMMUNITY
♦ The web of personal relationships, group networks, traditions and patterns of behaviour that develops among those who share either the same physical neighbourhood and its socio-economic situation, or common understandings and goals around a shared interest.

COMMUNITY ACTION
♦ Community based campaigns and networks concentrating on issues of concern to that community. Methods can range from the presentation of a petition to a local councillor to non-violent protests, such as those held by some Community Development Projects of the 1970's, the public demonstrations against deportations or in support of the miners, and the camps set up in 1993 to save the pits.

COMMUNITY DEVELOPMENT
♦ is the work done to help people develop both the individual and the collective self-confidence that enables them to contribute in a beneficial way to the growth of their communities.

♦ aims to enrich the web described in "Community" above and makes its threads stronger in order to develop self-confidence and skills, so the community (the people) can begin to make significant improvements to their neighbourhood (the place and its material environment) or its cause.
(Adapted from McLellan and Flecknoe)

This leads to community development being a method of working which
- focuses on collective action, rather than individual change
- actively works to counter discrimination and prejudice
- gives disadvantaged and oppressed groups a priority

♦ recognises the importance of formal and informal support networks in bringing about change

♦ is about opening up access to resources, services and information to assist people in making informed decisions.
(Taken from the paper: Community Participation for Health for All)

COMMUNITY GROUP / VOLUNTARY ORGANISATION
Over the past ten years, there have been attempts to define the distinctions between the two more clearly.

♦ **Community groups** are local groups or organisations run by people who get together on a voluntary basis to pursue common interests or tackle joint problems. They are, therefore, a type of voluntary organisation - in fact, the most common. It is the fact that they are engaged in meeting their own needs, under their own control, that distinguishes them from other voluntary organisations

COMMUNITY ORGANISING
♦ An American term used to describe the way groups organise to defend/ promote the interests of their neighbourhood.

COMMUNITY INVOLVEMENT (A statutory authority view):
♦ Communities organising themselves to actively tackle problems and become involved in local decision making, ensuring the fair and equitable representation of the community's views.
Draft policy 'Health Action Zone and Community Involvement' – *Healthy Bradford Programme Team 1998.*

COMMUNITY REGENERATION
♦ Renewing communities by responding to the needs expressed by their members, and by ensuring they are involved as equal partners in any funding or improvement initiatives. Community regeneration recognises that, as stakeholders in regeneration, communities have the strongest interest and commitment to the long-term future.

COMMUNITY SECTOR
♦ Mainly unpaid activity. It is most visibly expressed in, and often spearheaded by, local community groups and community-based organisations. At the level of these groups and organisations it overlaps with the **voluntary sector**, and generally forms the largest and most voluntary and independent part of that sector.
'Local Authorities and Community Development – a Strategic Opportunity for the 90's' *Association of Metropolitan Authorities 1993.*

COMMUNITY SOCIAL WORK
♦ An approach to working which:
- embraces the functions of a whole social work agency. It is based on collaboration between team members, and between social workers and the formal and informal carers
- involves taking into account parents, relatives, neighbours, other informal carers and staff in other agencies when planning priorities and methods of working
- is concerned with helping those who are disadvantaged by their social networks to achieve new, more advantageous relationships

- makes services more accessible, and appropriate, through involving users in decision making and delivery of services
- emphasises the strengths and abilities of people to engage in their own problem solving.

(Adapted from introductory chapter of Partners in Empowerment)

COMMUNITY WORK
♦ A process whereby oppressed people gain the skills, knowledge and the confidence to tackle the sources of their problems and bring about desired changes. (A fuller definition can be found in section 1).

COMMUNITY WORKER
♦ A paid or unpaid person who works as a partner with others in a co-operative venture. A community worker must be skilled in acting as an enabler, a facilitator, a catalyst for action, an energiser. She/he must be able to bring information, support and advice to people so that they can make their choices about what they want to do.

(McLellan and Flecknoe)

CONSULTATION
♦ Seeking the views of individuals and organisations in order to gauge opinion, and, in some instances, involvement with, a particular issue. An agency commissioning the consultation may seek to involve the parties more or less actively, depending on the intended purpose.

In recent years a ladder of 'citizen' participation has been described, moving from
- the passive (completing and returning of questionnaires) to
- the active (active involvement of participants in the designing and implementation of a project) etc.

For further reading:
Draft policy 'Health Action Zone and Community Involvement' – *Healthy Bradford Programme Team 1998.*
'Contested Communities' Ed. Paul Hoggett. Section R. Atkinson & Stephen Cope p 205. *The Policy Press 1997.*

CONTRACT
♦ A contract is a legally enforceable agreement between two or more parties, e.g. a local authority (service purchaser) and a community organisation (service provider). There is a contractual agreement in which the "service provider" promises to fulfill the contract. Service purchasers tend to closely monitor contracts to ensure the service provider is delivering a good service - what is called "value for money". Under this arrangement the community organisation has to cost the service it is to provide (e.g. staffing, running costs, premises, transport etc.), before it agrees to take on the contract. Monitoring the service they provide once it has started is important as it can provide evidence to demonstrate to the service purchaser that the contract should be renewed, perhaps with changes, given the experience so far.

EMPOWERMENT
♦ Ways in which knowledge, skills, resources, and power can be transferred to people previously on the margin of an organisation.

EXIT STRATEGY
♦ What will your organisation do next, after the funding for the project has run out? Will you seek funding from another source? If so, when will you begin the process? Funders often ask for an exit strategy as a condition of grant aid.

MENTOR
♦ Experienced and trusted advisor.
Pocket Oxford Dictionary Clarendon Press 1984.

MILESTONE
♦ A stage of achievement within a funding programme. Funders will often ask for an indication of milestones as a condition of grant aid. e.g. Barchester Play Organisation indicate that six months into their grant programme they will have employed a part-time worker and publicised their new library project in a number of community languages.

MONITORING
♦ The systematic collection and recording of information to help an organisation know how it is doing; it helps to account for the work of the organisation.

NEIGHBOURHOOD WORK
♦ Using a community development approach to work with neighbourhood organisations, or groups of local people who meet together as peers, to try and solve their own problems or those of the locality (particularly those of a social, environmental or economic nature).   Twlevetrees

NETWORK
♦ A loose semi informal collection of individuals or groups who are in direct or indirect communication with each other. They operate as horizontal channels of communication within communities.   A. Gilchrist

NETWORKING
♦ '..is the process by which relationships and contacts between people or organisations are established, nurtured and utilised for mutual benefit'.
Alison Gilchrist, 'Community Development and Networking' *CDF and SCCD Briefing Paper No7 1995.*

NOT-FOR-PROFIT ORGANISATIONS
♦ An organisation either run by a voluntary management committee as a co-operative/collective employing workers or a company to providing a service and whose excess funds are ploughed back into the provision of services.

OUTCOME FUNDING
♦ Funding which looks to provide grant-aid to an organisation in return for previously agreed benefits for a target group. e.g. Barchester Employment Advice Group will agree to assist 20 people find full time work of longer than 6 months duration in return for 12 months funding of a full-time post.

The model will be familiar to community workers who have been/are involved with funding from regeneration programmes such as the Single Regeneration Budget.

For definitions of related terms, see Jargon Buster, Jackie Drysdale & Rod Purcell in Section 10 of this Manual.

PARTICIPATION
- The process by which users become partners in contributing to, and sharing in, decisions affecting the lives of the users' groups they represent. There is a distinction between user and community participation.
  - **User Participation** involves working with individuals to enable them to make their own decisions.
  - **Community Participation** involves groups of people representing the community having a voice in the decision making processes that affect them.

PARTNERSHIP
- Joint business   (*Pocket Oxford Dictionary Clarendon Press 1984*).

- Within urban regeneration: groups of organisations jointly undertaking particular pieces of work. The organisations may include statutory agencies, voluntary and community organisations, the private sector and individuals.

- The structure of partnership arrangements ranges along a continuum from highly formalised partnerships to looser arrangements. There are many models of how partnerships operate in practice, and no single blueprint fits all circumstances. e.g. Ferguslie Park in Scotland – principles agreed for the Partnership included:
  - 'ensuring the active involvement, including appointment to the Board of (statutory agencies) private sector and community representatives'.

  'Partnership in the Urban Regeneration of Scotland', HMSO 1996.

For details, see *Meryll & Jones in Section 11 of this Manual*

PARTNERSHIP WORKING
- This usually involves some kind of contractual arrangement between participants operating within a formal, or semi-formal, framework in which roles and responsibilities are identified and agreed.

See Meryll & Jones in Section 11 of this Manual.

REGENERATION
- Bring into renewed existence - *Pocket Oxford Dictionary. Clarendon Press 1984.*

SERVICE <u>LEVEL</u> AGREEMENT
- Service level agreements have been in existence for some years. They are somewhere in between contract and grants. For example, a local authority will set out in detail the service it requires and a voluntary sector community organisation/ project will agree to provide the service.
  - The local authority will usually provide a "service specification" for the level and quality of the service to be provided, and how the arrangement will be monitored to ensure "value for money".

- ▪ The funding agency (the service purchaser) and the community organisation (the service provider) will usually exchange letters formalising the agreement.

- ▪ The agreements are usually reviewed annually and tend to last for a period of three years. This gives the community organisation a sufficient period of time to recruit staff, give them job security, develop the service and monitor its effectiveness.

SINGLE REGENERATION BUDGET

♦ Government Programme to provide support for local initiatives towards the regeneration of their areas. It acts as a catalyst to complement, or attract, other resources, private, public or voluntary to help improve the quality of life in local areas.

Information provided to the Policy Action Team 10 on the Arts and Sport by the
DETR.
July 1999.

SOCIAL CAPITAL

♦ 'The trust, or community spirit, that is the foundation of communities.'.(National Strategy for Neigbourhood Renewal   *Social Exclusion Unit April 2001*)

SOCIAL ENTREPRENEUR

♦ A term that, at the time of writing, is being bandied about in a number of government documents. However, there seems to be little clarity about the meaning intended. Assumptions range from

- ▪ 'Charismatic, articulate individual who has an ability to enthuse others' to

- ▪ 'Individual with business acumen whose skills, if tapped and assisted, may 'grow' local companies out of a deprived, run down estate'.
Quotes from Mike Waite

♦ Tony Gibson of Neighbourhood Initiatives Foundation proposes:
- ▪ 'A moving spirit, operating in the social, not-for-profit sector and seeking new and innovative solutions to social problems'.

For further reading *–ACW Talking Point No 188 – (Mike Waite)* is advised.

STAKEHOLDER

♦ A person or organisation with some influence over another group – this may include funders or key individuals.

STATUTORY SECTOR

♦ The group of agencies which includes government departments, local authorities and quangos set up by statute to provide a particular service.

SUSTAINABILITY

♦ Setting up and maintaining a service on a long-term basis.

SYNERGY
- The extra effect of working together'.

        'Partnership in the Urban Regeneration of Scotland' HMSO 1996.

VALUE BASE OF COMMUNITY WORK
- The principles/ ethics informing community work and practice.

VOLUNTARY SECTOR
- The collective name for organisations which carry out beneficial public services, non- profit making, and not public or local authorities.

    - ...'the organisations are not usually controlled by their users and are more likely to be formally registered as charities, to have paid staff and to be running service to meet specialised needs.'

                      Gabriel Chanan *Community Development Foundation.*

See also **Community Groups** and **Community Sector** above.

RESOURCE AND CONTACT LIST

ACRE (Action with Communities in Rural England)
Aims to improve the quality of life of communities and disadvantaged people in rural England, particularly through the support and promotion of its members, the Rural Community Councils.

Somerfield Court, Somerfield Road, Cirencester, Glos GL7 1TW
01285 653477

ACTAC (The Technical Aid Network)
National network of architects, landscape architects, surveyors, planners and community artists all committed to providing technical support to community based initiatives concerned with the design and development of neighbourhoods.

64 Mount Pleasant, Liverpool LS 5SD
0151 708 7607

Action for Sustainable Rural Communities
Aims to generate sustainable rural communities through community-led partnership development based upon ecological principles.

c/o Nicole Armstrong Lowe, 3 Crowns Yard, Penrith, Cumbria CA11 7PH
01768 863812

Advisory Service for Squatters
2 Saint Paul's Road
London N1 2QN
020 7359 8814
advice@squat.freeserve.co.uk

ALARM UK (The National Alliance Against Roadbuilding)
The umbrella body for local anti-road groups; campaigns for a sustainable transport policy.

9-10 College Terrace, London E3 5AN
0208 983 3572

ARVAC
For research in the voluntary and community sectors.

60 Highbury Grove, London, N5 2AG.
Tel: 020 7704 2315. Fax: 020 7704 2336
arvac@arvac.freeserve.co.uk
www.arvac.org

ASEED Europe
Action for Solidarity, Equality, Environment & Development, working especially on European government issues

PO Box 92066, 1090 AB Amsterdam, Netherlands
0031 20 668 2236
aseedeur@antenna.nl
www.antenna.nl/aseed/ -.

Association of British Credit Unions Ltd
Tel 020 7582 2626

Autonomous Centre of Edinburgh
17 West Montgomery Place
Edinburgh, EH7 5HA
0131 557 6242
ace@punk.org.uk

A-spire, Leeds
0113 262 9365
a-spire@geocities.com

Citizen Smith
Old Community Centre, 161 College Road, Kensal Green, London NW10 3PH
citizensmithuk@hotmail.com

BASSAC – British Association of Settlements and Social Action Courses.
Winchester House, 11 Cranmer Road, London SW9 6EJ

Black Environment Network
Promotes equality of opportunity within the ethnic community in the preservation, protection and development of the environment; maintains a network of individuals and organisations working for change.
UK Office, No.9 Llainwen Uchaf, Llanberis, Gwynedd, Wales LL55 4LL
Tel: 01286 870 715

The Black European Community Development Federation
Springside House, 84 North End Road, London W14 9ES.
Tel: 020 7610 5444. Fax: 020 7603 9918.
cmass@ubol.com

Blatant Incitement Project
Outreach and small group support for ecological direct action. Facilitates sharing of skills and resources mainly through website
c/o Dept 29, 255 Wilmslow Road, Manchester M!4 5LW
0161 226 6814
doinit@nematode.freeserve.co.uk
www.eco-action.org/blinc

BCODP – British Council of Disabled People.
Litchurch Plaza, Litchurch Lane, Derby DE24 8AA
Tel: 01332 295551. Fax: 01332 295580

British Trust for Conservation Volunteers
Works to involve people in conservation activity in both urban and countryside areas; activities include practical projects, holidays, publications and training; network of local groups.
Tel: 01491 839766

Camcorder Action Network
See Undercurrents

Campaign Against the Arms Trade
Campaigns against arms exports. Network of regional and local groups.
11 Goodwin Street, Finsbury Park, London N4 3HQ.
Tel: 020 7281 0297

Centre for Alternative Technology
Aims to inspire, inform and enable society to make the changes necessary to move forward to a sustainable future, via a seven acre site in mid-Wales, publications, courses and school visits. Mail order service.
The Quarry, Machynlleth, Powys, Wales, SY20 9AZ Tel: 01654 702400

The Children's Society
East Midlands Regional Office, Mayfair Court, North Gate, New Basford, Nottingham. NG7 7GR.
Tel: 0115 942 2974. Fax: 0115 942 3010.
bill-badham@the-children-society.org.uk

C.D.F. (Community Development Foundation)
60 Highbury Grove, London, N5 2AG.
Tel: 020 7226 5375. Fax: 020 7704 0313
info@cdf.org.uk

Chiapas Link
British link with Zapatista movement in southern Mexican region of Chiapas. Lots of information about background to and practices of the Zapatistas. Worth investigating their community decision-making processes, which led to the removal of alcohol from the Zapatista autonomous zones, a major blockage to women's development.
Box 79, 82 Colston Street, Bristol
chiapaslink@yahoo.com

Climate Action Network UK
31 Pitfield Street, London N1 6HB
020 7251 9199
canuk@gn.acp,org
www.climatenet.org

Common Ground
Campaigns for greater awareness of locality and local distinctiveness
Seven Dials Warehouse, 44 Earlham Street, London, WC2H 9LA
Tel: 020 7379 3109

Communities Against Toxics
PO Box 29, Ellesmere Port, Cheshire CH66, 3TX
0151 339 5473
ralph@tcpublications.freeserve.co.uk

Community Foundation Network
>   2 Plough Yard, Shoreditch High Street, London, EC2A 3LP.
>   Tel: 020 7422 8611. Fax: 020 7422 8616
>   network@communityfoundations.org.uk

Community Health UK
>   4-5 Bridge Street, Bath, BA2 4AS.
>   Tel: 01225 462680. Fax: 01225 480646.
>   Mail@chuk.org
>   www.chuk.org

Community Links
>   105 Barking Road, London, E16 4HQ.
>   Tel: 0207 4732270. Fax: 020 473 6671.

Community Matters
>   Supporting democratically elected community organisations and linking up with local authorities.
>
>   8/9 Upper Street, London N1 0PQ.
>   Tel: 020 7226 0189 Fax: 020 7354 9570.
>   Communitymatters@communitymatters.org.uk

Corporate Watch
>   Provides valuable information on multinationals for local campaigning groups.
>
>   16b Cherwell Street, Oxford OX4 1BG
>   01865 791391
>   mail@corporatewatch.org

Council for the Protection of Rural England
>   Campaigns for the countryside through well-informed research and briefing of national and local government; network of active local groups
>
>   Warwick House, 25 Buckingham Palace Road, London SW1W 0PP.
>   Tel: 020 7976 6433

Development Trusts Association
>   20 Conduit Place, London, W2 1HS.
>   Tel: 020 7706 4951. Fax: 020 7706 8447
>   www.dta.org.uk

Disabled Action Network
>   3 Crawley Road, Wood Green, London N22 6AN
>   020 8889 1361

D.S.C – Directory of Social Change
>   24 Stephenson Way, London, NW1 2PD.
>   Tel: 020 7209 515.
>   Info@d-s-c.demon.co.uk

Earth First! Action Update

Monthly round up of ecological, and other, direct action from around Britain. Good contacts list, British and International.

Subscribe EF!AU, PO Box ITA, Newcastle, NE99 1TA

0797 4791841

actionupdate@gn.apc.org

www.eco-action.org/efau

Ellen Gee Foundation

A new organisation dedicated to researching the experiences of lesbians and gay men in relation to a range of social policy issues; highlighting where discrimination and disadvantage occur, identifying gaps in knowledge and provision, and promoting a social policy agenda that addresses these needs.

5th Floor c/o Comic relief, 89 Albert Embankment, London SE1 7TP

ellen.gee@talk21.com

Federation of Community Work Training Groups (FCWTG)

Can provide contacts for community work training in Britain. Membership (sliding scale) gives regular bulletins, focusing on particular community work skills, and access to FCWTG library.

4th Floor, Furnival House, 48 Furnival Gate, Sheffield S1 4QP

Tel: 0114 273 9391. Fax: 0114 276 2377

Info@fcwtg.co.uk

Freedom to Care

support for whistle blowers

PO Box 125, West Molesey, Surrey KT8 1YE; 0208224 1022

info@freedomtocare.org

www.freedomtocare.org

Greenet

Web-based information, news and resources for a wide variety of environment and social change groups.

www.gn.apc.org

Health for All Network (UK)

PO Box 101, Liverpool, L69 5BE

Tel: 0151 231 4283. Fax: 0151 231 4209

UKHFAN@livjm.ac.uk

I-Contact video network

76 Mina Road, Bristol BS2 9TX

0117 914 0188

i-contact@videonetwork.org

Initiative Factory

Community centre established by sacked Liverpool dockers.

0151 207 9111

LAGER

An independent advice centre offering experienced and free legal advice on any employment-related problem including discrimination. Two lesbian caseworkers, (one black), and two gay male caseworkers. Initial contact is by telephone, fax, letter or minicom. Provides training and publications for organisations and individuals.

1G Leroy House, 436 Essex Road, London, N1 3QP
Women's Helpline:020 7704 8066   **Men's Helpline:**020 7704 6066
Admin: 020 7704 2205   **Fax**: 020 7704 6067
lager@dircon.co.uk

Lets Link UK

Support for local currencies

2 Kent St, Portsmouth, Hants PO1 3BS
01705 730 693
www.letslinkuk.demon.co.uk

Local Government Association

Local Government House, Smith Square, London, SWIP 3HZ
Tel: 020 7664 3000. Fax: 020 7664 3030
Info helpline: 020 7664 3131
www.lga.fov.uk

London Lesbian & Gay Switchboard

24-hour telephone line, providing high quality information, support and referral for the empowerment of all lesbians & gay men, and anyone considering these issues.

PO Box 7324 London N1 9QS
Helpline: 020 7837 7324

Low Level Radiation Campaign

Campaigns and publishes Radioactive Times

Ammondale, Spa Road, Llandrindod Wells, Powys LD1 5EY
01597 824 771
bramhall@llrc.org
www.llrc.org

Minority Rights Group

379 Brixton Road, London, SW9 7DE.
Tel: 020 7978 9498

NACVS – National Association of Councils for Voluntary Service

3rd Floor, Arundel Court, 177 Arundel Street, Sheffield, S1 2NU
Tel: 0114 278 6636.   Fax: 0114 278 7004.
nacvs@nacvs.org.uk
www.nacvs.org.uk

National Association of Credit Union Workers

7 Mansfield Road, Nottingham. NG1 3FB

National Association of Volunteer Bureaux
New Oxford House, 16 Waterloo Street, Birmingham, B2 5UG.
Tel: 0121 633 4555.
www.navb.org.uk

National Centre for Black Volunteers
4th Floor, 35-37 William Road, London, NW1 3ER.
Tel: 020 7387 1681

National Centre for Volunteering
Regents Wharf, 8 All Saints Street, London, N1 9RL.
Tel: 020 7520 8900. Fax: 020 7520 8910.
www.volunteering.org.uk

National Council for Volunteer Organisations
Regents Wharf, 8 All Saints Street, London N1 9RL.
Tel: 020 7713 6161

National Federation of City Farms
The Green House Hereford Street, Bedminster, Bristol, BS3 4NA.
Tel: 0117 923 1800

National Playbus Association
93 Whitby Road, Bristol, BS4 3QF.
Tel: 0117 977 5775. Fax: 0117 972 1838.
ericwilson@playbus.org.uk

Neighbourhood Initiatives Foundation
The Poplars, Lightmoor, Telford, TF4 3QN.
Tel: 01952 590777. Fax: 01952 591771.
nif@cablenet.co.uk

OTDOGS – Opposition to Destruction of Green Spaces
especially against supermarket developments

c/o John Beasly, 6 Everthorpe Road, London, SE15 4 DA;
020 8693 9412

People's Global Action
Global network of activists working against neoliberalism and it's effect on their communities. Originating from the South countries. Useful for groups interested in pairing with a group abroad working on a similar issue.
+4122 344 4731
info@agp.org

Refugee Council
3/9 Bondway House, London, SW8 1SJ.
Tel: 020 7582 6922

Refugee Support Centre
47 South Lambeth Road, London, SW8 1RH.
Tel: 020 7820 3606

Refugee Action

The Old Fire Station, 150 Waterloo Road, London SE1 8SB.
Tel: 020 7654 7700

S.C.A.D.U

Oxford House, Derbyshire Street, London, E2 6HG.
Tel: 020 7739 0918

Schnews

The news you don't hear, produced weekly from Brighton. Send SAE for free paper version, or on web:

PO Box 2600, Brighton BN2 2DX
01273 685913

Shell Better Britain Campaign

King Edward House, 135a New Street, Birmingham B2 4QJ.
Tel: 0121 248 5900.
info@sbbc.co.uk
www.sbbc.co.uk

Standing Conference on Community Development (SCCD)

An umbrella organisation providing information, networking support and an effective voice for grass roots community development practice.

Floor 4, Furnival House, 48 Furnival Gate, Sheffield S1 4QP
Tel: 0114 270 1718   Fax: 0114 276 7496
Admin@sccd.solis.co.uk

Undercurrents

Can provide video training with groups, helping them publicise their campaigns. Produce regular video round-up of direct action globally.

16b Cherwell Street, Oxford OX4 1BG
01865 203662
underc@gn.apc.org

Urban Forum

4 Deans Court, St Paul's Churchyard, London, EC4V 2AA.
Tel: 020 7248 3111. Fax: 020 7248 3222.
info@urbanforum.og.uk

URGENT

National network of groups working against greenfield housing developments.

Box HN, 111 Magdalen Road, Oxford OX4 1RG
01865 794 800
info@urgent.org.uk

Wales Council for Voluntary Action

Baltic House, Mount Stuart Square, Cardiff Bay, Cardiff, CF10 5FH.
Tel: 029 2043 1700. Fax: 029 2043 1701
enquires@wcva.ork.uk

CONTRIBUTORS TO THE MANUAL

Barbara Booton is a freelance trainer and consultant in community work following several years as a community worker for both voluntary and statutory organisations. She has over 12 years experience of designing and delivering training on Community work skills, training skills, Disability Equality, and team building. Consultancy work has included: a community evaluation project, mapping exercises, feasibility studies, business planning with community groups, community consultation.
E-mail: barbara-booton@communitrain2.demon.co.uk

Helen Bovey has been working in community development for over 10 years, with a particular focus on rural areas. For the last 7 years she has combined a specialism in training and development with her work on community participation. She works with a wide range of organisations, from national charities to local government and small local community groups.
E-mail: HBovey@aol.com

Vipin Chauhan is the Principal Partner of Lotus Management Consultancy, an independent practice that works in the voluntary, independent and public sectors, providing training, research and consultancy services nationally. Vipin has produced many reports, including a national evaluation of the quality of alcohol services provided to Black communities, and action research on the quality of the relationship between Government and the Black voluntary sector. Vipin is a half-time Senior Lecturer on the Community and Youth Work programme at the University of Derby.
Contact him on e-mail: lotus@vipin.freeserve.co.uk

Ros Chiosso I currently teach on a community and youth studies degree programme and I am also an active member of a local community regeneration group. I am a local and national executive member of Child Poverty Action Group. My background is in welfare rights and community education.

Sue Dodsworth : I have been an active member of Mind in Bradford for over five years now, and Chair for the last three years. I was originally trained as a social worker, but always felt drawn to community work. Through ending up in the mental health system myself I have learnt first-hand about the effect mental health problems have on your life and have in a roundabout way ended up doing the sort of work I've always wanted to!

Jacky Drysdale teaches social work at the University of Wales, Bangor. She has considerable experience in working with communities of interest, especially disabled people, as a social worker, manager, trainer and planner. She has several joint publications on community development and community care.
Jacky can be contacted at j.drysdale@bangor.ac.uk

Alison Gilchrist has been involved in community development for nearly 20 years, as local activist, paid worker, trainer, researcher and policy advisor. She worked as a neighbourhood worker in inner-city Bristol in the 1980s and early 1990s, taught on the Community and Youth Work course at the University of the West of England, and currently works for the Community Development Foundation as their Regional Links Manager (England).
Contact: 0117 935 5483 (Tel/fax) e-mail: regions@cdf.org.uk

Val Harris - well... I seem to have been involved in the community and voluntary sectors for most of my life. I've been paid to be a community worker, run lots of campaigns as an activist, have been a volunteer, and sat on many management committees. I am an independent trainer and consultant for the community and voluntary sector, working in the UK and eastern Europe. I am still involved with the production of ACW's regular newsletter and Talking Point, and on the management group of the Federation of Community Work Training Groups.

Murray Hawtin is a Senior Policy Analyst at the Policy Research Institute, Leeds Metropolitan University. Before joining the PRI in 1992, Murray was a social worker and a community worker. His main areas of interest are within social housing and community development. He has written extensively on tenant participation, social needs auditing and about the links between housing, health and social care.

Martin F. Jenkins spent 11 years as a social worker, then realised that what he really wanted to do was to help people so he became a community worker. Since 1988 he has supported communities and annoyed local authorities in seven London boroughs and one Yorkshire parish. He currently leads a development team in an outer London Council for Voluntary Service. His specialist interests are employment law and constitutions.
Contact: 020 8854 4899 (phone/fax)

Paul A. Jones   Paul's started as a youth worker within the voluntary, church-based sector, followed by 13 years as a neighbourhood worker, moving onto a youth and community team leader within the local authority. Since January 1998, he has been a senior lecturer - youth and community work - at Liverpool John Moores University teaching management, community development and urban regeneration. He has a particular research interest in community enterprise and community credit union development.

Joy Leach has been a Community Development worker since 1982, first working as Neighbourhood Warden for a residents association in Hackney, then for Islington Council at the start of its 80's decentralisation. Her experience includes 'doing' partnerships, community safety, urban regeneration, fund raising, youth work and a street drinkers' project. Now a coach-card carrying 50+ year old, she is taking time to write up her community work experiences as training materials.

Leeds Earth First! is a convenient banner under which people organise to confront those responsible for the destruction of the planet. We use direct action to achieve this, and encourage people to take responsibility themselves rather than rely on governments and business to solve the problems we face.
You can contact us at leedsef@ukf.net and c/o CRC, 16 Sholebroke Avenue, Leeds, LS7 3HB. See also <www.geocities.com/a-spire> and <www.eco-action.org>

Angus McCabe is currently a part-time Research Fellow in the Department of Social Policy and Social Work, University of Birmingham, and an independent trainer. His background is in community development in both rural and urban settings. Recent publications include 'Community Networks in Urban Regeneration' (Policy Press, 1996), 'Partnerships and Networks' (York Press, 1997) and History, Strategy or Lottery' (IdeA, 1999) – on voluntary sector relations with local Government.

Ruth Malkin has been involved in disability rights issues for over 10 years, variously as a volunteer organiser, disability arts worker, access consultant and equality trainer. She runs her own business, aScribe, and writes poetry and short stories in her spare time.
You can contact her at: aScribe, 4 HIllside Terrace, Bradford, BD3 0BD.   Tel:01274 725541.

Rob Martin is an outreach worker for the Community Work Training Company and a freelance tutor. For many years he has been a "community activist", the last ten with some pay! He previously worked at Bradford Community Broadcasting where he invited you "Into the Buttercup" for Blues, Comment and Poetry.

Joe Micheli   I have been involved in community work in Yorkshire for 13 years. I am currently working with the City of York Council as a Senior Neighbourhood Co-ordinator, with specific responsibility for community development. I also carry out freelance work for the Community Work Training Company and for Community Matters as one of their licensed community consultants.

Chris Murdoch is a business advisor and trainer specialising in work in the community, with community groups, co-ops and not for profit businesses. She is particularly interested in the areas where community groups and voluntary sector organisations need to get to grips with traditional business skills like financial planning, employment law and legal structures.

Julie Pryke has been involved in Community Work as an activist for over 20 years, returning to college as a mature student to complete a Community Studies Degree, followed by an MA. She was a neighbourhood community worker full-time for 10 years on an inner-city estate in Bradford. Her special interests are in Poverty issues, Violence against Women, Community Campaigns, 'Race', and the use of IT within Community Work. She currently teaches Community Practice at Bradford College.

Rod Purcell co-ordinates the Community Education and Community Development programmes in the Department of Adult and Continuing Education at the University of Glasgow. He has wide experience of community development as a fieldworker, trainer, consultant and researcher. He has several joint publication related to community development, evaluation and community education.
Rod can be contacted on: r.purcell@educ.gla.ac.uk

Refugee Action is a prominent national charity working with refugees to build new lives. We deliver direct services to asylum seekers, refugees and their communities; respond to emergencies; and influence local and national policy.

Alan Robinson is a solicitor and trainer working largely with the voluntary sector. As a solicitor he works with management committees covering issues such as company organisation, charity formation and employment. As a trainer he undertakes training on all aspects of the voluntary sector and the law. He can provide a fixed-fee package covering both training and legal support.
Contact: telephone and fax 01724 710819. e-mail alan@lwrt.co.uk

John Street lives and works in inner city Birmingham. He is an independent youth and community worker who is funded by several different statutory and voluntary organisations. He also runs a charity called free@last which aims to release people

from whatever holds them. John follows the CCDA's 3 R's of community development - relocation, redistribution and reconciliation.
E-mail: free@last1.org.uk

Gersh Subhra has experience of Community and Youth work in a variety of settings. He is currently a Senior Lecturer on the Community & Youth Studies degree at the University of Derby. He has worked on a number of community action research projects and evaluations, including a national evaluation of Black alcohol projects for the Dept. of Health and Alcohol Concern and a mapping of the Black & Minority voluntary sector in Derby. Additional experience has been gained through his role on various management committees.

Tom Taylor is a part-time community development worker in Bradford and a freelance trainer. He delivers Community Work Skills courses, facilitates team development sessions, designs 'Taylor Made Training' sessions for a range of not-for-profit organisations, and undertakes research and development of resources. He is an NVQ assessor, and has developed the 'People and Places' board game which introduces community work principles. Tom is also involved in campaigning on ecology issues.

Nick Waterfield has over eighteen years experience as a paid worker, volunteer, management committee member and trustee in a variety of voluntary and community organisations. His background includes youth work, welfare rights, community arts and neighbourhood community work. Nick has worked at both local and national level, as a development worker and also at a policy level. He has been working freelance as a consultant and trainer since 1997.